D1125857

THE RIVER HOME

THE
RIVER
HOME

A Memoir

DOROTHY WEIL

OHIO UNIVERSITY PRESS
ATHENS

Ohio University Press, Athens, Ohio 45701
© 2002 by Ohio University Press
Printed in the United States of America
All rights reserved

Frontispiece: Island Queen photo courtesy of Paul Briol Collection, Cincinnati Historical Society Library. Copy by Public
Library of Cincinnati and Hamilton County.

09 08 07 06 05 04 03 02   5 4 3 2 1

Library of Congress Cataloging-in-Publication Data

Weil, Dorothy, 1929-
    The river home : a memoir / Dorothy Weil.
        p. cm.
    ISBN 0-8214-1405-4 (alk. paper)
    1. Weil, Dorothy, 1929- 2. Weil, Dorothy, 1929—-Family.
3. Authors, American—20th century—Biography. 4. Authors,
American—20th century—Family relationships. 5. River
travel—United States. I. Title.

PS3573.E3837 Z47 2002
818'.5409—dc21
[B]
                                                        2001036001

First time I seen Boll Weevil
He was standin' on the square.
Next time I seen Boll Weevil
He had his whole family there.
He's lookin' for a home.
He's lookin' for a home.

"Boll Weevil Song," Traditional

To my family with love

*I hope my granddaughters, Sonia, Frances, Julia, and Mei-Li,
will always appreciate the richness of their heritage.*

Contents

Preface

WHEN I think of my family, I always picture the river and hills of the Ohio Valley. They stand for the many places we lived, the rivers my father worked on as a steamboat captain and mate, the hills where my parents were born. These places, and all the meanings connected to them, formed my father and mother. The surfaces and textures of their worlds, the voices and sounds they heard, came through their hands and voices to my brother and myself, became our inner landscapes. Their stories are woven into ours.

The need to tell our stories began for me at my father's funeral in 1980. James Harvey Coomer died at eighty-six. He was laid out in his navy-blue mate's uniform from the steamboat *Delta Queen*. His beard, which had grown long and shaggy, was clipped and neat. His coffin lay in a funeral home in Burnside, Kentucky, the little hill town where he was born. He looked good, peaceful for the first time. In life, we never saw him at rest, this man from the hills who found the river early, kept leaving it, but always returned. Intelligent, unread, angry, half hillbilly, half man of the world, he would, said old Captain Lucas, "fight a buzz saw."

Family life was lived at the high-water mark—with houses floating by and things uprooted. My mother, Mildred Ethel Beamer, was a proper Cincinnatian from a stolid German family. She was an actress, an artist, a believer in women's rights. She was never prepared for living with a wild river man from the hills.

My brother and I were forever grappling with opposites, developing lives that combined action and the more contemplative path of art. Jim spent thirty years as a towboat captain, then became a sculptor and writer. I was wife and mother, then teacher, writer, and painter. Neither ever really settled down, for the only home we could find in our hearts was a watery one.

"Appalachian and German, a formidable combination," I once told a friend.

"But typical around here," he said.

He was right. The patterns of conflict in our family stretch over the Ohio Valley, a net with many varieties of thread, mended and remended, full of iridescent colors and destructive zebra mussels.

We buried my father in the veteran's cemetery near Burnside and the Cumberland River that had been his way out of town. An old man on crutches, whom I didn't know, watched the coffin being lowered into the earth. He waved one crutch and said, "I'll be seein' you soon, Harv!" That promise made me feel good. My father never aimed at Heaven. But it was nice to think he might not be going off among strangers.

My mother died eight years after my father. Her ashes are scattered on the Ohio River—the river that was the dividing line between her Ohio background and my father's Kentucky heritage, the place where they came together, the home in which my family was happiest, and to which each of us, in his way, returned.

After the death of my father, I embarked on a series of journeys during which I became dedicated to finding our family's past—trying to see where we fit into the character and life of the Ohio Valley. Traveling by towboat, steamboat, and even an old-time flatboat, I started with stories about other people who lived and worked on rivers. Until I finally came to our own.

For me, it began on a steamboat trapped for the winter in the iced-over Missouri. On one bank was Omaha and on the other was Council Bluffs. I thought of the water roiling beneath the ice as simply "the river." And I still think of the rivers that nourish the Midwest as one: all lead to the Ohio and her hills.

Acknowledgments

I AM grateful to the many river people who welcomed me back to the place I remember as home. In travels on towboats and steamboats in the nineteen eighties, I met veterans who recalled my father, and younger people who shared their knowledge. Steamboat old-timers who deserve special mention are purser Bob McCann, Captain Russell "Chick" Lucas, Captain Clark "Doc" Hawley, and Captain Fred Way. My brother, Captain James Harvey Coomer, Jr., provided help in arranging my river return and taught me about towboats. M'Lissa Herrman and Sylvia Metzinger, of the Public Library of Cincinnati and Hamilton County's rare book room, provided much help with steamboat facts. The Sons and Daughters of Pioneer River Men helped fund a video documentary that had a strong influence on the writing of this memoir. John Knoefle, an Illinois poet, taped the reminiscences of my father, among those of a number of old-time steamboat men.

Memories and pictures were provided by family members. My mother saved everything. I have the old scrapbooks she carried all over the Midwest. They contain photographs of her relatives along with her children's report cards, our childhood scribblings and drawings, any later bits of recognition, and a sketch of her early married life. Long-lost cousins who provided recollections are James Fitzgerald, Joanne Canada, Sherri MacDonald, Thelma Jones, William Silver, William Coomer, and Rita Niman. My own store of recollections was my central reference, along with some notes made earlier in my life when family conversations were still ringing clearly in my ears.

THE RIVER HOME

Prologue

THE VALLEY QUEEN

1934

ICE. WHITE, ENDLESS. A river iced solid from bank to bank as far as the eye could see upriver and down. The boat, a three-tiered steamboat, was stuck there, frozen stiff.

Her decks were jagged with crystal stalagmites. The spar that held the boat to land, an old telephone pole, was covered with rime. My brother Jim was five and I was four, and we ran over it to play on the bank as gracefully and fearlessly as mountain goats. Daddy, the captain of the *Valley Queen*, spent many days chopping a kind of moat around her so the ice wouldn't crush her wooden frame. We played to the sound of his axe, chipping and chopping.

Our home was a tiny stateroom on the texas deck, with leaky skylights and only a small pot-bellied stove, glowing red, for heat. Daddy brought wood from the shore and kept the fire going throughout the day. At night the cabin was so cold, we used layers and layers of blankets: it made our sides ache to turn over in bed. Mom read to us while outside the wind clawed at the skylights and the flag flapped madly. We loved *Black Beauty*—any story about wild animals, creatures that were free and could gallop without reins or rules as we did when let loose on the banks to run in the snow. Our whole world was white, and happy.

Daddy was tall and had a black mustache and thin, slicked-back hair. His voice was loud. Mom was tiny, with huge green eyes, thick bristly hair, and a soft voice.

There was barely an "I" apart from Jim. We were almost the same size, though he was stronger. We played together, for there were no other children in our iced-in world. We slept together in the cozy upper bunk of our cabin, listening to the boat groaning beneath us, in seeming agony as the ice squeezed her fragile ribs.

When we'd awake in the morning, I'd say to him, recalling some exciting adventure during the night, "Remember we were in a department store and Tarzan saved us from a bear?" And he, the older and wiser, would say, "That was just a dream. You dreamed that." I couldn't believe I could go anywhere without him. But I gradually began to have a memory and a life apart from his.

Slowly my world came into focus, became clear and definite, a matter of contrast and separation. There was man and woman, boy and girl, dog and cat, land and water. Jim and me.

Memories drifted into my mind like dreams, but I knew they were not dreams. We were on a farm. Our Auntie, fat and dressed in soft cotton, hovered over everything. A bright green parrot with a vicious beak squawked and flapped his wings when we reached into his cage to steal his sunflower seeds. There were big St. Bernard dogs we rode like horses. Trees. Pies. A black man named Press. Mother and Auntie told us what to do. Daddy was somewhere else

Jim and I talked about the parrot. We talked about Auntie and her pies. But we never talked about going to see Daddy in a strange room. About how white and hurt he looked, his shoulders scarred like chipped marble.

On the *Valley Queen* we saw his scars when he washed. All he said was, "You have to be tough on the river." This was all we knew of him: that he came from the Kentucky mountains, that there had been a shooting. Our grandfather was dead.

Mom's father had been rich, but lost all his money in the Depression. Her mother died when she was born. Mom loved to talk about her family and show us their pictures in her big photo album. When one of her aunts threatened to come and visit us on the boat, Daddy joked that Jim and I had better be sure to wash our ears clean because Aunt Ninnie would be checking them and if she had to do them over, we would feel it. She never arrived, and our family, all but Daddy and Mom, remained distant memories or pictures in a book.

ON THE *Valley Queen* Jim and I ran from top deck to bottom. The boat had so many nooks and crannies, little covered porches, railings to sit on, steps and ladders to climb. We were never cautioned to be careful and were never afraid. We walked on the ice.

I watched while Jim helped Daddy chop it away from the *Queen's* hull. As the ice gradually began to break up and slide into the current, they chipped all around the johnboat, which had been frozen in place. Jim was working with his hatchet, making an island of ice. Suddenly, the boat and its brittle edges, with my brother on it, broke loose and started down the river. I saw him disappearing into a white world: white river, white sky. I'd never see him again.

Jim-Boy, towheaded, round-faced, with a big smile: he was my model in everything. I even wanted to dress like him, in a leather jacket and aviator goggles. Now he was gone.

His long, drawn-out "Hey-y-y" came ghostly over the crashing ice. My father turned from his work, dropped his own axe, and went leaping from one block of ice to the other, Jim going faster as his ice-boat swept out into the warming current. I stuffed my fingers in my mouth, never dreaming they could outwit the ice and water. But Daddy got closer, grabbed Jim out of the skiff, and started back over the chunks of white. The skiff went on down the river and disappeared. Daddy laughed at Jim for chopping himself into danger. "Like paintin' yourself into a corner," he said. I was glad to see Jim and didn't fight with him all day.

I learned that women could be heroes, too. It was night, the stars cold pinpoints in the black sky. Our dog Jerry, a mop-like Spitz, chased our cat Skipper overboard. Jim and I stood shivering at the railing as Mom was lowered onto the ice on a rope to rescue her. Mom was light, and Daddy figured she would not break the fragile surface. We could see our breath and taste the fear coming up like sour food as our tiny mother crept across the thinning ice toward the black cat. Skipper was arching her back and freezing in terror as Mom got closer to her.

At last, when Mom was close enough to grab her, the cat backed away on the slippery surface and the wind began to howl in concert with the cat's whine. We sobbed quietly until Mother finally grabbed Skipper by the scruff of the neck and jammed her—scared stiff, claws out, and fur spiked—into her jacket. Daddy began pulling them slowly across the ice. We held our breath as mother climbed back over the rail and Daddy lifted her gently onto the deck, the rigid cat beneath her almost-shredded coat. We climbed to our cabin, even the guilty party, Jerry. In our tiny room, Skipper was given a big saucer of milk and we petted her icy fur and took her to bed with us. We fell asleep as the glowing pot-bellied stove went from bright red to black.

We thought our white world would last forever. But as the sun came out more often, the great icicles dripped like slavering teeth, and slowly disappeared. The trapped water escaped and churned up in the wind. When Daddy took me along in the skiff to check the lines, he had to pull hard on the oars to stay on course. The river seemed even more vast to me as the boat rocked back and forth and whitecaps whipped up all around the small wooden vessel. I held tightly to the seat at the stern of the boat. Were we going to drown? My father laughed at the fear on my face. I watched his strong arms pull the oars and knew I was safe. He could out-row the waves.

Mom read us a poem: "Bye Baby Bunting / Daddy's gone a-hunting / He'll bring home a rabbit skin / to wrap his Baby Bunting in." She recited, "The year's at the spring / The day's at the morn / The morning's at seven / The hillside's dew pearled/ God's in his heaven / All's right with the world."

WHEN SUMMER came, we had to leave the *Valley Queen*. Now she belonged to the owners and the passengers who paid to go dancing and gambling on the evening excursions. Mr. Clarence Hanfeldt appeared once a week to pay Daddy. He carried a roll of dollar bills the size of a baseball. He always gave us children a stick of Juicy Fruit chewing gum. He was, we thought, a very nice man.

Our family moved to the Del Mar hotel, a small establishment in Omaha, five or six blocks from the river. There was a lobby with leather chairs, metal ashtrays on stands, potted palms. A registration desk was presided over by Joe, the hotel clerk. The front windows were full of scraggly overgrown plants and ads for events going on in town. The halls were dark, carpeted in a dingy red. Our apartment had two rooms and a small concrete porch wedged between two outside walls; the bath was one door down the hall. Jim and I were set up with cots in the kitchen and the parents slept in the adjoining room. We could hear the traffic of the busy little city: buses grunting, people walking by on the sidewalk below our windows.

We only got to see the *Valley Queen*, in her hot-time finery, from the bank. Daddy had forbidden us to go on board because of the gambling. We stood on the landing as she prepared to leave for an excursion, brilliant with lights. It was like seeing our mother dressed up to go out for the evening and leaving us behind. Music came to the cobbled landing where we stood, the shrill calliope from the open deck, the dance band from the salon. Daddy, dressed in a smart navy-blue uniform with gold buttons and his captain's hat with gold braid, looked like a king in one of our books.

While Daddy was busy on the boat, Mom and Jim and I spent our time at the hotel reading and crayoning in our coloring books and listening to the radio. We were in the apartment at the Del Mar one morning when Mom shook us awake. There was a picture of the *Valley Queen* in the paper, rolled over on her side. Mom read us the story: "River Pride Listing to Port on Sandbar: the good ship *Valley Queen*, which grounded on a sandbar off the foot of Hickory Street Thursday night, is breaking up on the bar this morning." She read about the government barge trying to get the *Queen* loose while "the band continued to play and the merrymakers continued to make merry." Then the dance floor buckled and began to break up and "the piano skidded into the ice scuppers."

The picture of the *Queen* looked like the one in "The Wreck of the Hesperus," our favorite poem. What was happening was just as unreal. Until the part about Daddy: "The crew, all but Captain James Harvey Coomer, who stuck with his ship like a veteran mariner, were returned to the Douglas Street bridge aboard the government boat. The ship has a drunken list to port and Captain Coomer is preparing to abandon the vessel. Timbers on the side of the ship are cracked. Captain Coomer estimated the ship could remain above water only a few hours."

Mom made us eat breakfast and get cleaned up before we could go down to the river. Then we went to the end of Hickory Street where the boat was sinking. The *Valley Queen* was crushed like a matchbox. A crew of men was busy taking off slot machines, bottles, ropes, fire extinguishers. One man carried a saxophone as though about to play it. A few shanty boaters were pitching beer, chairs, and tables over the side to their cohorts in johnboats.

Daddy stood on the landing, watching the *Queen* slowly sink. We stood beside him. I felt the way I did when I saw Jim disappearing into the whiteness of the winter river. I looked to my parents to see how they were feeling. Mom had tears in her eyes. When we saw the last of the *Valley Queen*, all Daddy said was, "Whew."

JIM AND I didn't cry or mourn, but even now a sunken steamboat is lodged in my imagination and dreams. I have always wanted to rescue the father and mother who lived on the *Valley Queen*. Parents had lives before we were born, names we never knew them by, dreams we weren't in—stories that began long before our own.

ΗΑRV AND MILDRED

1894–1934

1

THE CUMBERLAND

.

LIKE THE *Valley Queen*, the old town of Burnside, where my father was born, is under water. The Cumberland River was dammed to create Lake Cumberland, and the hilltops now are islands. Water skiers and houseboats glide over the surface, while down below, my father's old house, the town jail, and the steamboat landing sink deeper beneath the water and the years.

When my father was in a talking mood, he'd recall some of his past. All his memories were hard: the men spitting tobacco juice on the boys' legs at the saw mill in Burnside; a flock of angry geese taller than he that came at him, clacking their beaks and beating their big wings; he and the other kids racing past the cemetery at dark; long hours in the poultry house candling eggs—holding them up to the light to find the ones with blood spots.

He and his seven brothers and sisters were expected to work. Though the family often took in people stranded in Burnside by low water, John and Charity Coomer, his parents, were not wealthy. My father remembered lunch as "greens and a bit of grease wrapped in bread" and joked that the family meals were "dried apples for breakfast, hot water for lunch, and swell up for supper."

In Burnside, my father was always known as Harv, and that's the way I think of him as a boy and young man. I picture him with a mouth ready to demand his rights and his fists up to defend himself. He was small, the middle boy between his elder brother Stafford and his younger brother Joe. He always claimed "the bigger they are, the harder they fall," a creed he lived by, especially on the river where he became a legendary mate who would "fight a buzz saw."

Harv had only a few years of school, always combined with work at the lumberyard or in the poultry house. He drove a stage coach from Monticello to Burnside in his teens. He never saw the Daniel Boone National Forest that is very near his home town: "You can't eat scenery."

Burnside was a busy little place. Formerly a settlement called Point Isabel, it had become a town just four years after Harv was born in 1894. Steamboats lined the landing where the Cumberland and South Fork Rivers met. They were filled with timber, eggs, and poultry going to Tennessee, and they brought in goods like shoes and furniture from Cincinnati, New Orleans, and St. Louis. Besides the lumber mill, there was a grocery store called Matty's, Wagie Singleton's General Store, several drug stores, churches and saloons, and two hotels, including a big frame Victorian called The Seven Gables, where visiting dignitaries and wealthy guests stayed. With all this growth, and a population reaching two thousand, pigs and cows still roamed the streets freely, merely ear-marked by the owner to be protected from theft. Everyone knew everyone else.

Harv's father, the town marshal, supervised the upkeep of the town's wooden sidewalks and dirt roads, pressing his own boys into service, as well as any others he saw loafing. John Coomer saw that no stranger remained in town after sundown. He detained petty offenders a day or two in the tiny wooden jailhouse and escorted more serious criminals to the penitentiary in Cincinnati.

A man respected by everyone, Marshal Coomer was tall and slim and utterly fearless. He dressed in a black frockcoat and wore his black hat at a rakish angle and a silver star on his breast. He walked with a cocky air, ignoring the danger of his job, though gunfights were common: three U.S. marshals were shot to death in one year.

Harv, who idolized his father, was just six years old when John Coomer was shot in the stomach.

The marshal had been called to Tom Smith's barbershop, a little shingled establishment with the old-fashioned red-and-white pole. He found a man named John Satersfield standing over Smith with a gun and Smith on the floor bleeding onto the wisps of hair that he had just cut from a customer. Satersfield started to run, and when commanded to stop, turned and shot Harv's father, who, in turn, shot and killed Satersfield. John Coomer survived his own wounds, but after this incident, he temporarily left the police and worked on the steamboats that navigated the Cumberland River from Burnside to Nashville.

Harv began hanging around the river. His first experiences on the Cumberland were on log booms, great pens of lumber that had been cut in the hills and left in the river by country people and paid for via mason jars left along the banks with the names of the cutters. Harv walked across the river on these logs, some floating as high as four feet above the water's surface. The work of getting the corralling staves upriver to the sawmill for shipping on the trains was dangerous. The hand-cranked windlasses employed to pull staves from the water could cut a person in two. The water was cold—legend had it that the river where the South Fork and the Cumberland met had no bottom.

With his father on the steamboats, Harv begged to go along and work. John Coomer forbade it, but Harv would cut school and sneak on board the boat his father was on. When it pulled away from the landing, he would pop out from wherever he was hiding. "There I would be," he recalled of those days. "My father just had to put up with me. So finally he just said to me to quit school and go to night watchman."

Harv worked on the packets running between Burnside and Nashville, the *Burkesville*, the *Rowena*, the *Celina*, the *City of Burnside*, the *Patrol*, and the *Crescent* among them. They were typical steamboats of the day, shallow-bottomed, wooden, and prone to fire and holes knocked in their hulls. They navigated packed tight with freight—groceries, hardware, plows, rope, corn—to be discharged at Nashville. There, they would load up with fertilizer, salt, sugar, clothing, dry goods, fencing, and oil.

The Cumberland was a dangerous river. Smith's Shoals at Burnside was seven miles long, and so many coal barges sank there that coal shipping died out. There were Greasy Creek Shoals and Belnap Island where the water was so swift and the channel so narrow a boat coming upstream could not make it through; it would have to be pulled along with a rope.

At Wild Goose Shoals the current was so swift it would hit a boat bow and stern so hard it seemed as though the boat would go right over the wing dams built in the water. "Crazy thing. It would scare people to death to do it," Harv said.

Alma, Harv's older sister, was married to a steamboat man who died working on the Cumberland.

The river's shallow stretches made the work hard. Sometimes cargo would have to be pitched overboard to lighten the load. Wire fencing was thrown into the water and carried down by the swift current to a spot where the men could retrieve it with spike poles. Hogs and cattle were occasionally driven overboard to swim ashore, then picked up fifty or seventy-five feet farther along when the boat reached deep water again.

As night watchman, Harv had a lot of responsibility for a young man. He had to keep fires going in the pilothouse and engine room of the boat he was serving; each day he filled some forty lanterns with oil and assisted the mate in the loading and unloading of freight. While the mate stayed on the boat, Harv took over on the hill and supervised the roustabouts handling the big loads. There might be a thousand coops of chickens, eight hundred cases of eggs, three hundred hogs, five hundred head of cattle.

Harv was never content to stay in one place or one job (we found this out living with him). He convinced his father to give him the higher-ranking and more responsible job of second mate. No license was required, just some knowledge as night watchman, which Harv had. As second mate he stood watch by himself and oversaw the loading and unloading of cargo. The cargo had to be placed aboard correctly because the boats were of such light material that, as Harv said, "You can throw a leak in them very readily." He took his duties very seriously: "It is just the knack of a good mate knowing when there is any strain in the boat by just walking up the deck. He can feel it under his feet. It is just inner knowledge that when you walk up the deck if there is a little strain in the boat, you will feel it."

Harv was nineteen years old. His brother Stafford was also on the steamboats by now, and twelve-year-old Joe was agitating to go along. Harv's father had returned to his job as marshal.

Because of the shooting in Smith's barbershop, John Coomer decided not to carry a gun. The killing of another man, and his own wounds, made him very much against firearms—a hatred of guns that was passed down to his sons. Joe would have nothing to do with them, and Harv always said more people were killed by "unloaded" weapons than by loaded ones.

Every day Harv's father went to the Burnside depot and met the train from Cincinnati to see that there were no troublemakers on it. On August 13, 1913, a friend, Josh Tarter, staggered off the train, drunk. He had gone to Somerset, where there was an open saloon, to get whiskey. Marshal Coomer told Tarter he would have to go downtown for a while to sober up in the jail. Tarter was from a pugnacious clan, but Harv's father had no reason to think an order to "sleep it off" in the little wooden cell would cause Josh to turn vicious. He was taken completely off guard when, as he was led into the cell, Tarter pulled a pistol from his pocket and shot the Marshal in the neck.

Charity was at the jail, bringing lunch to the men, and John asked her to run home and bring him his pistol from his dresser drawer. Tarter was running toward the Cumberland River, and the marshal meant to catch him. When Charity came back with the gun, she found her husband could not stand. He was too injured.

At the river, Tarter asked Ben Brown, the ferry operator, to take him across to the Slab Town side and the road back to Somerset. Brown was unaware of what had happened and proceeded to take Tarter across the Cumberland. Meanwhile, Marshal Coomer, holding his own blood back with a towel, deputized a posse of Louis Ramsey, Lum Evans, Fred Perdue, Loge Hamm, and John Fitzgerald. The men ran to the river. Seeing Tarter on the other side, they called for Brown to return him to their side of the water, but Tarter pulled his weapon and held it on the ferry operator, saying, "I'm closer to you than they are." The posse opened fire, and Tarter was shot in the lower part of his right arm. Tarter shot and killed John Fitzgerald, who died there on the river bank.

John Coomer was brought home bleeding and weak but not dead. With the wound still festering, he even took a bank robber to the jail in Cincinnati. On returning home, he weakened further. He sat about the house, and would beat at his chest. For six weeks the family heard him coughing in his room.

Meanwhile, Tarter had gotten away. John asked that if found he not be prosecuted, for fear Harv and Stafford would get into a fight with the Tarters and get themselves killed. He worried that there would be no one to take care of his wife and young children. Edna, Ina, Sarah, and Jewel were still at home.

On October 1, 1913, at the age of fifty-two, Marshal John Coomer died. To follow his request, the doctor described the cause of death as "unknown."

Charity came to the children and told them their father was dead. She and the girls washed and dressed the body, and the three boys were sent down to Singleton's general store to buy a coffin. The boys were told to get cleaned up, polish their shoes with blacking from the stove, put on their Buckeye hats. They did as they were told and helped the men from the town carry the coffin to the cemetery. No one cried. The family stood stoically as the father was lowered into the Kentucky earth where he was born.

2

COCK OF THE WALK

HARV USED TO say, "I believe in one thing and one thing only: the Almighty Dollar!" Of course, this was during the Depression, when one of the biggest problems in life was where our next meal was coming from. But money was always important.

After Harv's father died, the Coomers had little. John left a widow with four daughters and an adolescent boy to raise. Charity and Sarah, the oldest daughter still at home, had to go to work at the Seven Gables hotel. They lit fires in the guest rooms and washed towels and sheets.

Harv was still working on the river and, along with his brother Stafford, was sending what money he could to the family. In order to make a better wage, he applied for a license to be a first mate on steamboats. There was a three-day test held in Louisville at the new Custom House, presided over by steamboat inspectors. Applicants were supposed to be twenty-one. Harv was nineteen, but by fibbing about his age, he managed to take the test. As he told the story, "I had very little schooling and I didn't know how to read and write very readily, so I took the book of rules and regulations and everything governing steamboats and I memorized all these big words at heart that I was going to have to spell out." He took the train, the first one he'd ever ridden, to Louisville. He was intimidated by the elaborateness of the Custom House: "Not knowing much about reading and writing, I was kind of lost. But I wrote out and answered every question they put at me." He got a very good rating on the test and a first mate's license.

Soon after this step up, Harv became more and more restless in Burnside. He heard wonderful tales of giant steamboats carrying freight and passengers all the way to New Orleans. A boy who had been to St. Louis and Cincinnati told him all about them. Dreaming of big cities and bigger money, Harv "got together a dollar and a half" and bought a round-trip ticket on the train to Cincinnati. He sold his return ticket and spent the seventy-five cents for a hotel room. "I had spent all of my wealth. So I looked up at the tall buildings in Cincinnati and I was a little bit scared of them. I could not see where they were going to stand up."

Some had ten and fifteen stories. The Central Trust tower, just completed, was thirty-four stories high, the tallest building in the world outside New York. It was all fabulous. The towers of the Roebling suspension bridge rose high above the river. The Tyler-Davidson fountain, a bright brass female figure surrounded by boys and dolphins, was at the center of town on Fountain Square. Several streets away was the gigantic, fancy music hall, a two-block-long pile of red brick. The steeples of brick and stone churches reared above the rows of houses. Streetcars buzzed about the streets and even crawled up the hills on inclines. Factories rang with the sounds of hammers and saws. The great breweries gave off a sour smell of hops that blended with the stench from the stockyards and made people hold their noses. There were parks, theaters with plays and music, lighted-up expensive restaurants, none of which Harv had ever seen before.

Standing on the cobblestone landing at the riverfront, Harv counted thirty steamboats, "great big, fine steamboats, tremendous large boats compared to what I had been seeing." Herds of pigs and sheep straight from the stockyard were guided toward the gangplanks, led by a frisky billy goat—the "judas goat"—who wore a little bell on a ribbon around his neck. Pretty women waited beside their suitcases for the pursers to get them on board, and families stood about just to watch all the activity.

The mates were lining up the cargo and yelling for the roustabouts—seventy-five or more, carrying kegs of pork and boxes of dry goods—to get a move on. The men were bent with the weight of the loads they carried. The mates were big men, with voices that carried and swear words new to Harv. He was a hundred-and-thirty-pounder from the hills. But he had to go down and get a job on one of the boats, or go back home. Burnside had become dull, and he could make better money here.

As Harv told it, "I finally got up courage and went in and asked a fellow named Walter Quiggin about a job as mate, and he looked me over and said 'You got to be tough around here. You are too small.' But I was pretty tough because you had to be tough in the Cumberland River, or on any water you have to be tough. Of course, I was a little scared because it looked pretty rough. I said, 'Well, just give me a job and I'll show you how tough I am.'"

Harv was hired on a boat that ran between Cincinnati and Madison, Indiana. As second mate, he was paid eight dollars and seventy-five cents a week and his room and board. The boats ran seven days a week. He was efficient and capable, and after a few months he got the job of first mate.

Over the next decade, he worked on some thirty packet boats, running from Pittsburgh to Cairo and Cairo to New Orleans. Some were grand, with luxurious passenger suites, gilded salons, and dining rooms with crystal chandeliers and imported carpets. Every kind of person rode the steamboats, from gamblers and prostitutes to presidents. Many boats stopped at every little town to pick up cargo, and the whole town would turn out to see the lucky passengers on board, listen to the music from the salon, and watch the excitement of loading and unloading. People knew when the boats were coming and sometimes which boat by the various distinctive whistles. A steamboat was a great sight, puffing along, almost breathing, smoke pouring from the great smokestacks, fancy woodwork painted a bright white.

The mate did not go to bed as long as the boat was in the landing and loading was taking place; he stayed on watch. Accidents on the fragile wooden boats were frequent: tales of exploding boilers and fires and busted hulls were common. The mate had to know a boat's moods, its every creak and groan; he had to place the freight "where it could be discharged, and always keep the boat on an even keel. If you don't get it that way, why, you would spring leaks which causes a tremendous lot of trouble." The mate was in charge of the entire boat when the captain was sleeping: "He feels that he can lay down and get a good rest. He has got a good mate. You have got a lot of people's lives at stake there. The boat hazards of fire and wind and hitting logs or in case of emergency, he has got a good mate."

Harv ran cattle all night sometimes. Or maybe he would have to get a hundred hogs on board a boat: "Once in a while, one of the roustabouts would be bored to death, but then they always are. He would go to sleeping and the hogs would get quick and then every damn hog goes out. Then you got to corral them up again." For that job, Harv would supervise the making of a "seine," a heavy canvas corral which would be dragged as far as a mile away to bring in the animals. Horses were a problem, too: "There's occasions where we have handled stud horses and that is really one of the tragedies of hauling stock aboard a steamboat with the wooden hull—you take a stud horse and put him aboard a boat and let him pass a field where there might be some mares—he gets a whiff of colt or something in the field and he'll go to stomping. And he will stomp and stomp and then nothing you can do, except just put one of your rousters back there in the pen with him to chew on his ears. It seemed to pacify him and he will quit stomping, otherwise he would stomp holes right through the deck."

Harv didn't like boat pilots. They got all the glory, but, in Harv's view, didn't have to work too hard, just sitting in the pilothouse and turning the wheel. He claimed the mate, fireman, clerk, and roustabouts did the real work.

The roustabouts were mostly black, except for a few who would do loading part-time for ready cash. In packet boat days, all were considered pretty much cogs in the machinery of steamboating and sometimes were worked around the clock. The weather didn't matter: the boats had to go. When rain or sleet would freeze on the bales of hay carried on the men's shoulders, the flesh would get very raw. The metal bindings on cotton bales would cut into the rousters' legs. Fertilizer would sometimes run onto the men's necks and make them bleed. To get men to carry fertilizer, the mate would have to promise "a dollar a day and a penny a sack"—give each roustabout one penny for each bag of fertilizer he got to the boat, along with his usual wage.

Naturally there were rebellions, which the mate was faced with. Tales went around the river of mates pushing roustabouts overboard. Harv himself had many fights (there were those scars on his shoulders). He told us, "I have been cut several times and shot once by rousters. I had to be pretty tough with them sometimes. Maybe they would just work until they were tired out, maybe go hide on you. They would go down in the hatches and lay back there and you just had to go down in there. The ones that would fight would kill you."

Much later in life Harv admitted the cruelties of the packet-boat system. At the time, he was trying to survive.

ON THE Ohio River Harv often felt that the veteran mates were trying to "dog it over" him, that they considered him inexperienced and small and the Cumberland River "a little pond." But he proved himself efficient, and thought the "old-timers that was born and raised on the Ohio River maybe were probably a little jealous."

Harv told of "Meet the Boat" trips, in which boats would come together and transfer passengers from one to the other: "The deckhands on the boats got to jiving with each other, and first thing you know the mate would take it up and if I caught him back in my deck room I would let him have it, and if he caught me over on his boat somewhere, why, he would let me have it, so first thing you know we had a little clash here and there."

In the midst of Harv's packet-boat career, more and more news reached the river about America being drawn into the war in Europe. In April of 1918, Harv joined the army and was sent overseas. Pictures show him looking handsome in his uniform. He was always proud of his good looks.

He was given the job of stoking mortar, that is, inserting the plunger into cannon. His character rating was "excellent," and he was honorably discharged in May 1919. "I was *patriotic*," he claimed in answer to our questions about his service. "I heard the Kaiser was killin' women and cuttin' babies' arms off, and I damn-fool went and enlisted!"

He was not impressed with Italy, France, or Germany—they were dirty and old, and Harv always bragged that America was the greatest and most beautiful country in the world. He became bitter about the army; we spent many hours during the Depression waiting around courthouses to collect a pension which never seemed to come.

When Harv returned from the army, he went back on the river. When he would recite the names of the packet boats he worked on to us children, we wanted to be on those old boats. We could see them in dim outline: the *Bowling Green*, the *Liberty*, and especially the *Jo Horton Fall*, a packet that carried hogs and cattle like the rest until she was tricked out as a pleasure boat and renamed the *Valley Queen*.

The *Idlewild*, on which Harv worked with his brother Joe, was one of the boats he loved best; she was built in 1914, a "Mark Twain" type of vessel with staterooms and a fancy steel hull. She would come back into his life, first as the *Avalon*, and then in his later years as the *Belle of Louisville*. In his travels Harv acquired a taste for elegance, for exotic food and certain luxuries: he liked silk sheets and good clothes.

Harv got the job of first mate on the new and sparkling second *Island Queen*, built by the Coney Island Company in 1925. The job was a plum. Harv headed the deck crew on her maiden voyage from Cincinnati to Fernbank, then on daily trips from Cincinnati to the Coney Island amusement park several miles upriver. On this glamorous new excursion boat, there were no messy hogs, cattle, or horses to contend with, just a deck crew of ten or so and a herd of passengers—many of them pretty girls out for a good time.

Harv was cock of the walk. The girls swarmed all over this handsome fellow with the quaint accent and the army record. One girl jumped overboard because he shifted his attention to another. Then one evening he noticed a small girl linking arms with an older woman. She was adorable, and seemed to be sneaking looks in his direction.

3

CINCINNATI DUTCH

MILDRED BEAMER WAS a tiny woman, only four feet eleven inches tall. She was pretty, with wiry brown hair, big green eyes, and a slim figure. She was romantic and dreamy and loved to read, draw, and write poetry. She was also a good athlete, fond of tennis and acrobatics; energy came off her in waves, from her size four-and-a-half feet to her springy electric hair.

Born in 1904 (or thereabouts—she habitually fibbed about her age), Mildred had been a severely underweight baby who was not expected to survive. At the age most children walk, she had to be helped to stand up. Mildred's five brothers and sisters died at birth, and her mother died giving birth to her. Her father, Roy Beamer, remarried, had five children with his new wife, and left Mildred with his parents like something forgotten. Mildred visited him and her stepmother Lulu Neiderhelman and the children often—the little outsider looking in.

The grandparents' house on Windsor Street in Cincinnati was big and lively. A young uncle, Morris, called "Bud," was still at home. Sometimes another of Melissa and George's nine grown children moved in. Mildred's cousins Alice and Pearl, girls about her age, were also occasionally left with Melissa and George Beamer because of their father's marital difficulties.

The atmosphere at the Beamer household was fun, but strict: the family was German on both sides, "Cincinnati Dutch" who believed "Cleanliness is next to godliness" and "A penny saved is a penny earned." Mildred's classes at Windsor School, right across the street from her grandparents' house, were taught in German as well as English, until World War I created prejudice against the Germans. Street names that had been German were renamed (Bismark became Montreal). The bilingual approach in the public schools was dropped. The non-German kids teased and threw rocks at children who spoke anything but English.

Mildred adored her grandmother, a pretty woman who was born with a club foot. Melissa wore an ugly five-inch riser on the shoe of the shorter leg. But she never stopped doing the work of her large household and raising the children who came to her. Mildred always kept her grandmother's photograph in a place of honor and often spoke of her sweetness and understanding, her lack of the judgmental streak that ran in the family. Melissa's face was soft and her eyes sad: she had borne thirteen children altogether. Four died young. Buena Vista was buried in the Deutsch-Protestantischen Kirchhof auf Walnut Hills for the sum of six dollars. A small grave and interment for Edith cost the same.

Mildred's grandfather ran a lumberyard and stables, a business he established in 1892. His word was law in the Beamer household. He gave Mildred and the other girls in the family the job of pulling off and cleaning his manure-covered boots when he returned home in the evening. He came from an Ohio clan of farmers, strict teetotaling Lutherans, but in spite of his own strictures against alcohol, he was a hard drinker. And a hard man. He was infamous for trying to remove his bunions with carbolic acid and for breaking his own fist by punching a disobedient horse in the face.

Roy Beamer, Mildred's father, was a genial, ruddy-faced, sandy-haired man who went into construction work and before the Depression owned several apartment buildings. He always wore a big smile on his round face; his cheeks were the color of pumpkin and his eyes black as seeds.

Watching the lively three boys and two girls at her father's house, but never really belonging, Mildred never stopped thinking of herself as an orphan, unwanted in spite of her grandmother's love. She was guilty of her mother's death, she thought, because her mother had died giving birth to her. As a child in the big house on Windsor Street, she once overheard her Aunt Ninnie crying and seeking comfort from Melissa when her son died of the measles Mildred had given him. "Why couldn't it have been Mildred," Ninnie asked, "the child nobody wanted?" Though she was cheerful and energetic most of the time, Mildred never got over her aunt's words, never got over being the outsider looking in. In her last few years, she wrote about her early life, trying to come to terms with it.

Mildred's many aunts and uncles formed a background chorus with a plethora of opinions on the raising of Mildred and the other cousins. Odessa, Lester, Ninnie Esther, and Ethel were religious zealots, becoming Jehovah's Witnesses and God's Bible Students. They disapproved of card-playing, dancing, alcohol, cigarettes, and sex. Ninnie was once arrested for selling *Watchtowers* on the street.

Mildred's favorite aunt took no part in this religious fervor. Louise, whom Mildred called "Auntie," was beautiful, vain, and strong-willed. She was fond of diamonds and her "bird of paradise" hat—an elaborate headgear with an entire snow-white bird perched on top. The oldest of George and Melissa's children, "Auntie" was a good cook and ran a farm in Anchorage, Kentucky, while her husband Willis worked in Louisville as an engineer. He was the only professional among these construction workers, brick layers, and contractors.

Mildred spent many summers with Auntie on the farm. Auntie cooked for the fieldworkers; she raised cows, St. Bernard dogs, and parrots, as well as two children. She was her father's daughter. She locked her children in the closet when they were disobedient and struck her cows on the head with a large board to get them to follow her orders.

Auntie made a pet of Mildred, who always tried to please. Early on, Mildred developed the charm and tact that helped her survive in her stepmother's and grandmother's houses. When she smiled, her green eyes were full of light and life. Her teachers called her "Little Mary Sunshine."

Melissa encouraged Mildred, who no doubt soon proved herself the bright one among the cousins, to express herself through writing and drawing. After Mildred graduated from Windsor Elementary with honors, Melissa sent her to a performing arts academy. The school was run by its "directress," Helen Merci Schuster Martin, who was no doubt a strong model of feminine accomplishment for Mildred. (With the air of a grand actress, mother frequently reminded us children that she was a bona fide graduate of the "Schuster Martin School of Dramatics and Elocution!")

Mildred loved acting and excelled at it. Her diction was clear, emphatic; her vocabulary came straight from the plays, movies, and poetry she adored. Playing parts increased her natural tendency to observe and analyze others. She was sharp at detecting human foibles and "idiosyncrasies" — one of her favorite words.

As a young woman, Mildred was a flapper. She and Pearl and Alice, along with Bud's wife Marie, cut their hair in the twenties style, wore short skirts, danced, and smoked. They sneaked into the bathroom to have a cigarette, always worried that the smoke would waft out into the parlor and into the nostrils of the grandparents.

Mildred's first crush was on her oldest step-brother, an earnest, intelligent young man who put himself through school and became a public accountant and high-ranking member of a large accounting firm. Elmer remained Mildred's ideal man: educated, mild-mannered, successful. The two shared books and played tennis together.

At seventeen, Mildred married a prizefighter, a man she didn't love who convinced her that he loved "enough for two." She was ecstatic at having her own apartment and soon a baby. She doted on the infant boy, made all his clothes, and decorated his bassinet with satin and ribbons until it was "a work of art." Within four months, the "King of Babies" was dead. Again, Mildred was guilty: she had started the car in the garage and left the baby for just a few minutes to run back into the apartment and turn off the lights. She knew nothing about carbon monoxide. Her life, she thought, was over. Eventually, she divorced her husband and moved back to her grandmother's house, where Bud was now in charge because of George's drinking.

That was when Marie, Bud's wife, took on the task of cheering up Mildred. Marie was unlike the other aunts and was never accepted as their equal or quite up to the mark. While Odessa, Ethel, Ninnie Esther, and the others were hard-working high-principled wives and mothers, always putting family first and living by the solid Germanic ways of the Beamers, Marie was fun-loving and lazy. She would go shopping every day with her girl friend while Bud was at work, then rush to the kitchen and be standing over a hot stove perspiring when Bud walked in. Melissa, the peacemaker, did Marie's share of the housework and protected her daughter-in-law. As Mildred told the story, "At least once a week Marie and her friend inveigled their husbands to let them out at night. Their favorite amusement was to go up the river on the big steamboat to dance. They knew the captain, pilot, mate, and all the orchestra men. They asked me to go with them one night, telling me how good looking the mate was. Mom insisted that I go. It would do me good. He was a bachelor, I knew, a man-about-town who never passed up anything, not even the colored maids. I know he didn't pass up Marie's girl friend. All the women were crazy about him. I couldn't have cared less."

4

KONJOLA MAN

THE *ISLAND QUEEN* was lit by seven thousand lights at night: they doubled as they were reflected in the water, making the Cincinnati wharf a fairyland. She had been proclaimed the finest steamer in the world, unsinkable because of her metal decks. Four thousand people could ride the *Queen* on her trips to Coney Island, which ran from late morning until midnight. When the mate lowered the gate across her gangplank, the passengers raced off the wharf boat and up the grand staircase to claim the best seats by the rails. There were five bright white tiers to spread out on, from the ballroom to the porch, where rows of rocking chairs waited, to the open decks, where families ate their picnic dinners. Some people were on the boat just for the fun of it: to watch the dark shores slide by, drink a beer, dance, or watch the canoers who followed in the boat's wake, riding the deep waves she made. Young people rode on the open top deck, which after dark was a favorite spot for necking.

There were other excursion boats at the wharf: the *Princess* also went to Coney. But the *Island Queen* was the biggest and grandest. There was a crew of eighty: watchmen, deck hands, and porters. There were cabin boys to serve the crew quarters needed for "tramping"—one-night cruises to other cities after Coney closed for the year. She cost twenty-five thousand dollars to build.

This was the boat Marie had finally talked Mildred into riding. The two women, dressed in short skirts, cloche hats, and high heels, took the streetcar to the cobblestone wharf just under the suspension bridge. It was crowded with Model Ts parked on the slanting stones lapped by the water. They bought their tickets on the wharf boat where the *Queen* was tied off, and then walked across the short gangplank and onto the boat. They might have caught a glimpse of Harv supervising the untying of the *Queen*—or maybe they met him later when he had time to hobnob with the girls. Whenever it was she first saw him, Mildred fell completely, madly, in love: "He *was* good-looking. Immaculate. And besides, he had a black eye."

Mildred became a dedicated steamboat buff and took more and more trips to Coney Island: "I fell in love! No one could change my mind. I tried all the tricks I knew and had learned in books, even to making myself faint to attract his attention."

Mildred's family did not approve of her new love. His reputation was lurid. He was thirty-two—ten years older than Mildred. He had never settled down. "A rolling stone gathers no moss," was one of the stolid Beamers' favorite shibboleths. Why didn't he have a home by now, live in one place for life as they did? All the Beamers clustered around the Windsor Street house, in the same neighborhood, and saw mostly each other for holidays and occasional parties.

But Mildred refused to give in. She was going to marry "Jim" (he was never Harv to her). Though my father always claimed he was "not the marryin' kind," the wedding took place January 3, 1927, at Wesley Chapel, a small Methodist church on Cincinnati's Fifth Street that stood until the fifties. In spite of the family's doubts, they gave Mildred a nice send-off. Ninnie Esther and Lester attended, and Marie and Bud were witnesses. Mildred wore a blue brocade and velvet gown and carried an armful of orchids, a Harv Coomer touch.

Mildred stayed deeply in love. When her new husband went to work, she buried her face in the shirts he left scattered about their apartment. But she could not forget all the stories she had heard about Harv even before she met him. She suffered terrible jealousy when she saw him talk to another woman on the boat: "Women were always asking him questions to get acquainted."

In the *Queen's* off-season, Mildred and Harv lived in Chicago where he sold "ladies' lingerie" to department stores. He needed winter employment, and the job as salesman came along at the right time. The money was good, and the firm he worked for wanted someone nice-looking to promote their line of garments. In this new career, as on the boat, he was often in the company of women—the buyers for stores, whom he took to lunch or dinner. These "business duties" added to Mildred's jealousy: "I could hardly wait for him to come home."

KONJOLA, "THE NEW medicine of the West that restores health," was being talked about in the hotel lobbies and barber shops where Harv hung about. It was making big money. It was supposed to be good for the stomach, liver, kidney, and bowels; it cured rheumatism. Harv got a job selling Konjola, and he and Mildred began traveling from one town to another throughout the Midwest, living in hotels and rooming houses. Harv would pick out a drug store and give his spiel to the customers. In exchange for running their picture in the Konjola newspaper ads, he'd talk them into giving testimonials about how Konjola cured their ailments: the drug stores got a percentage of all the bottles sold. Harv became the star salesman and was featured in the newspapers as "The Konjola Man."

He enjoyed the theatrics of the job and the constant change. He often bragged about being able to sell ice to Eskimos. Mildred was miserable. She missed her family, especially her grandmother and Auntie. She missed the lunches in town with Marie, the giggling and gossiping with Pearl and Alice. Now she was alone, dumped in some strange room in Kansas City or Indianapolis. The couple stayed about three months in each town, until Harv got Konjola going, and then the company sent a second man to take over.

Mildred was happy when she learned she was pregnant. A baby would be a companion for her. He would replace the child she lost. James Harvey Coomer, Jr., my brother, was born in Wabash, Indiana, in March of 1928. His crib was a dresser drawer. Mildred was happy, but there was no one to croon over him and share the excitement. Wabash was soon left behind, and the family moved on: I was born in Clinton, Illinois, on October 29, 1929, nineteen months after Jim and the day the stock market hit bottom. It was five days after "Black Thursday," the collapse officially marking the worst economic depression in American history. Mildred was depressed, too. Harv claimed he had to push my baby carriage and take care of two bawling and crying females. Jim gave me my name, after a baby in an upstairs apartment. He translated for me when I began to talk: "'Oopagah,'" he said, "means she wants water."

Konjola was still doing well. A Clinton newspaper wrote: "The introduction of Konjola in Clinton has been a tremendous success and is now strongly endorsed by many. It is restoring health to thousands of people." Harv continued enthusiastically touting the stuff. When Mildred would wheel me into a drugstore in my perambulator, clutching my tiny bottle of prune juice, Harv would point me out and say, "See, even the babies love it!"

Konjola remained popular, but the owner began to neglect the business. He went to Hollywood, chased after movie actresses, and began buying racing cars and yachts. The company was soon in financial trouble, and Harv and Mildred saw fewer paychecks.

Harv was out hustling, and Mildred was cooped up with two young children in one rented room after another. At one point, life became unbearable for her: "I was left in Milwaukee and Jim started back home to straighten things out and I didn't hear for a long time. A few dollars and scanty letters was all. He was in Chicago working for a while. Knowing my husband's poor management of money, I was not surprised. If he had money, he spent it. There was no tomorrow."

Mildred occasionally made fifteen cents apiece ironing men's shirts in her room, but the money didn't go far enough to support herself and two babies. A neighbor, a girl who worked at night, offered to let Mildred move in with her. During the day Mildred took the children to the park so the girl could sleep. "I never told her how hard up I really was or, no doubt, this kind person would have fed us also."

Mildred was ashamed to admit she might have been wrong about her husband, but she wired her father, asking for a loan. He wired back, "You made your bed, now lie in it."

His response was typical of the Beamer outlook: "Sink or swim," "God helps those who help themselves." The rules were strict, and fathers did not believe in bending them. Roy Beamer's brother Clint refused to speak to his daughter Edna for twenty years because she married a divorced man. Roy was the most easy-going of George and Melissa's children, but he shared the rigorous code taught by the Lutheran preachers of the family's Germanic background and the Ohio farm country where the Beamers began life in America.

Furthermore, the Depression had hit the construction business, and Roy had had to sell the buildings he owned. He was down to one truck, hauling brick and lumber.

Mildred took Jim-Boy by the hand, put me in my buggy, and walked down to the river. She stood at the water's edge. She would jump and it would all be over. She held her breath, summoning the nerve to push the buggy over the wall and follow it with Jim. She glanced all around. There was a group of men loitering nearby on a picnic bench. They were looking her way. Watching her.

She turned away from the river, embarrassed, and leaned down to Jim, pretending to point out something on the water's surface. She glanced at the men again. They were still watching. Ashamed, Mildred went back to the apartment. She thought about turning on the gas, but when she opened the apartment door, she stepped on an envelope: it was a telegram from her father with money in it.

The telegram urged Mildred to leave Harv and come back to Cincinnati. Instead, with her father's loan, Mildred went to the Chicago hotel where Harv supposedly was living, but found that he only picked up his mail there. She waited in the lobby for hours for him to come in. When he finally arrived, he begged Mildred not to go back home.

Mildred stayed with him. She did not want to face her father and all the relatives with their "I told you so's." She later claimed she wanted her children to have two parents.

Until Konjola completely folded, the family kept moving from town to town, via the Greyhound bus. As he always did when in trouble, Harv turned once again to the river. He got a job as master (captain) of the *America*, a packet that had been turned into an excursion steamer. His younger brother Joe was mate. The family moved to Jeffersonville, Indiana. Harv worked all day and late at night, taking the boat out for afternoon and moonlight trips.

Sometimes Mildred and we children went along. Auntie lived nearby, and Mildred could visit her. At the farm, Mildred could enjoy her beloved trees and the family life she had missed so.

In September of 1930, with Harv, his brother Joe Coomer, and Jim Jr. on board, the *America* was on the way from Louisville to Fulton to tie up for the winter. The crew was putting out wire lines and setting spars when a fire broke out in the texas deck (officers' quarters). Harv called up all hands to try and put it out; the pumps were started and the men squirted the flames with fire extinguishers, but the blaze was too intense. Even the firemen who came to the scene could not get the fire under control, and the crew had to scramble off the boat. No one was injured, but the boat burned to the water's edge and the hull sank; it was a total loss.

Earlier, Harv could have gotten another berth, another job. He had never worried. Even while Konjola was going out of business, Harv kept his optimism, his jaunty air of being above it all. He always jingled change in his pocket and whistled as he walked.

Now, because of the Depression, steamboat work was way down. In 1936 the last packet on the river would make its final trip.

Auntie insisted that Mildred and we children stay with her in the country. She disapproved of Harv, the "rolling stone"; in return he gave "Mrs. Kennedy," as he called her, a kind of grudging respect along with a good deal of teasing. These two strong-willed characters never got along, although at times Auntie had to laugh at Harv's jokes.

Auntie's own husband was a thoroughly tame man. He was educated and polite, no match for Louise's imperious ways and lumberyard upbringing. He was tall and bald, with deep-set eyes and a perpetual frown.

He looked forbidding and often appeared to be out of sorts. He seemed fond only of his wife and the cute and charming Mildred, who as a child had spent so many summers with him and Auntie. She had long ago named him "More-Pop": her father and grandfather were both "Pop," so Willis Kennedy must be "More-Pop."

More-Pop detested Harv. In fact, he liked few people, including many of his wife's relatives, her son and daughter by a previous marriage, and the son's wife. But he was thoroughly cowed by Louise and forced to tolerate them all. Auntie gave him the man's place of honor at the table, the most comfortable chair in the house, and very little respect. The truth was something she doled out sparingly, her philosophy being "What he don't know won't hurt him." She usually called him "Mr. Kennedy," unless he looked as if he might be about to explode, then he became "Petty." "Now Petty," she would say, and More-Pop would stifle his anger.

Auntie was queen of her domain. Though she was fonder of Mildred than of her own daughter—she had not had the responsibility of bringing Mildred up, and Mildred's usually sunny nature appealed to her —Auntie imposed her will on everyone. When she didn't approve of something Mildred did, she called her "Lady Jane." If Auntie wanted Mildred to remain at home instead of indulging in an evening or afternoon in town, she would fake a heart attack. She constantly reminded Mildred that if she stayed with Harv she would always be broke and never have a permanent home.

In 1933, Mildred sued for divorce. She took a job, and Harv lived in town.

Jim and I were taken to see him in his hotel room. He looked very white and somehow injured with the scars that marked his shoulders. We did not want to go near him. He was a stranger.

And then we were all living together on the *Valley Queen*, snug in the cozy cabin of the great empty steamboat encased in ice.

LOOKING FOR A HOME

1934–1939

5

POSSESSED

WHEN THE *Valley Queen* went down, Daddy's navy-blue-and-gold uniform and captain's command went with it. The freedom of the river was traded for the confines of the Del Mar hotel and the Omaha streets. Daddy wore a scratchy wool suit, old spectators, and a hat with a yellowing band. He was still living on wages from the boat, but after a long dry spell got a job selling jewelry on commission. When he made a sale we paid our rent and Mom got her hair marcelled.

Daddy was away from the apartment most of the days, working or hanging around the barber shop connected to the hotel. To him the world was a small town, and he would strike up conversations with whomever he ran into. In the evening he would sit in the lobby of the hotel and argue with the other men. They covered politics and the Depression; they traded fantastic success stories and tales of stern boyhoods. Sometimes the chef from the adjoining restaurant would come in, and Joe the desk clerk would look up from his work and add a comment.

We children were occasionally allowed to stay up late and sit in the lobby with the other Del Mar residents. Some came and went, others stayed on as we did. There was an unhappy adolescent living with his mother; two old bachelors, Mr. Sticks and Mr. Smith, whom we children loved to visit; a nightclub singer Daddy always called "Sophie Tucker"; and a couple with a little girl named Ginger who were somehow connected with racing. There was also Jean Jackson, a woman who owned a diner left to her by her husband. She was remarkable among the tenants in that she was not only solvent, but doing quite well. She drove a bright red roadster with a rumble seat. The men, especially our Harv, looked up when she walked into the lobby.

We heard the name Roosevelt a lot and a velvety voice on the radio and Daddy saying, "He's telling us what a great man he is." We asked Mom who he was talking about. Did Daddy like him or not? Mom said the president, and Daddy did like him; he just couldn't resist being sarcastic. He always claimed Roosevelt was the only president who ever did anything for the common man. Actually our father liked any strong man: he loved to imitate the deep voice of John L. Lewis, the president of the coal-miners' union, and talk about the hardships of the workers before "ole John L." came along.

The addition of Mrs. Jackson threw a certain amount of tension into the lobby colloquiums. Daddy could barely stand the thought of a woman running her own business, and kept asking her when she was going to get married again. We could feel Mom bristle.

"Tell me," he would harangue, "if women are equal with men, how come all the world-famous artists are men, and all the best writers and politicians, business tycoons, even the chefs? Even to design women's clothes? Who does it all? Men."

"Women haven't had a chance," Jean would argue. She had a funny way of talking—we later found out it was because she came from New England. "They're too busy taking care of the big babies."

"And being *mothers*," Mom would chime in. "I think women would be superior to men if they didn't have to take care of children. Besides, behind every man there's a woman. They're the power behind the power. And we're content with that, aren't we, Jean?"

"Darned tootin'—anyhow I'd like to see any man do a bettah job on my dinah than I'm doing."

"I could point out some pointers"—Daddy.

The battle never got serious until it became private and then all Daddy's tension over Jean was directed to Mom and Mom's troubles directed to Daddy.

Our small rooms were a kind of crucible. Filled with the parents' disappointments and our developing dreams. With the demands of four wills and four egos. Daddy's voice was so loud and he seemed so big, we feared he might actually hurt our tiny mother or us. But he was the less likely of the two to use force. He never spanked us, while Mom would lay on with the hard side of a hair brush. She was never mad at us, just "disappointed." Anger was for beasts. She made you walk to her, and bend over her knee on your own. She never chased or grabbed you and always claimed, "This hurts me more than it does you." We never believed her. With Daddy, his voice commanding you to "be quite" or threatening to "set ye afar" was enough.

We lived in fear of Daddy's sudden blowups. He was furious when Jim, a curious and inventive child, took apart a fancy steamboat model he was given (just as he took apart alarm clocks and anything else he was interested in). One dull afternoon, Mom was dolling me up, putting makeup on me and using a curling iron on my super-straight locks. Jim begged to get in on the fun. Mom painted his fingernails and curled his hair. When Daddy came home, he took one look at his son and pushed him away roughly. Jim tried to explain that he had just been joining in a game. "No son of mine wears curls!" Daddy almost threw Jim out of his way.

When I tried out Jim's and my newly discovered favorite epithet, "you idiot," on my father, he did not speak to me for two days, just turned away as though I were not in the room.

Both children loved our Dad's bedtime routine with us: he would come into the kitchen where we slept and throw us onto the bed—we'd bounce up and he'd throw us down again. Then he'd make us hit him on the back as hard as we could. Great fun. The ritual came to an end very soon, and after we were school age, our father rarely touched us at all. He simply did not believe in coddling or cuddling; to express his affection he might say, "You're okay—when you're asleep."

Mom had rolled up a little snowball of philosophy containing rocks and sticks made of newspaper advice columns, magazine items, odd poems, and fragments of things heard in the past in the cadence of her grandmother's voice. She quoted Edgar A. Guest and Bernarr McFadden, anyone who preached the doctrine of onward and upward, positive thinking, the American Dream. From her collection came gems like "Laugh and the world laughs with you." And with one finger pointed to heaven, she could pronounce to a recalcitrant four-year-old standing before her for some misdemeanor, "AS YE SOW, SO SHALL YE REAP!"

Daddy's code was simple. In the hills, the man was supreme, women and children secondary. When he said it was time for bed, he meant it. We were never to "talk back" to adults or be obtrusive in any way: "Children should be seen and not heard."

At dinner time, when the parents came together each day, their culture clash grew loud. Unlike Daddy's belief in silent, totally obedient children, in her more liberal phase Mom thought kids should "express themselves." She believed in the perfectibility of man, while Daddy held to total depravity. "Appease 'em. Appease 'em," he would shout when she tried to achieve conformity through negotiation. "When you're old, you'll fall down in the gutter and they won't lift a finger!" Mom would counter, "I don't want my children to take care of me when I'm old—no—I don't want to be a burden. I shall go to an old people's home with other people of my age."

Mom had life all planned out. She wanted to be cremated, not "buried in the ground" after an expensive funeral. She would never be an interfering mother-in-law. We had no idea what cremation was, or a mother-in-law either.

Jim's and my meal-time peccadillos usually consisted of fighting, blowing bubbles in our milk, or tipping back in our chairs. If Mom countermanded an order given by Daddy, or we "talked back," he would bang his fist on the table and shout, "Don't contradict my word!" If kids got too far out of line, Daddy would make a loud hissing noise like an angry bull goose: "SST! SST!" Discussion closed.

Both parents were fanatic about clean plates. "Waste not, want not," Mom would intone. You could always hear the echoes of her ancestors in her more sententious sayings. She would bring up the proverbial starving Armenians and Jim would say, "They're welcome to my share of this stuff," which would set Daddy off on the poor diet of his boyhood and how lucky we were to be eating three meals a day. As to manners, Daddy ate with abandon—a little grease running down his chin did not detract from his enjoyment of a pork chop—while Mom ate primly with Emily Post decorum, her demeanor that of a princess forced to live among swineherds.

Daddy spent more and more time out of the apartment, and became an almost intrusive presence in our lives. Mom and Jim and I formed a little group of dreamers. She took us to parks and to the Joselyn Memorial, a small art museum a few blocks away. It was marble and had marble sidewalks, which later were great to roller-skate on because the surface made a satisfying hollow sound. Mom worshipped the old masters. "Michelangelo" she would breathe before a drawing—it was like an incantation. She ridiculed Dali's limp watches, though I thought they were rather interesting.

I was bought a little wooden table that sat by the big bed in the room our parents slept in. I was busy as an elf crayoning, neatly filling in the shapes in my coloring books. When Jim joined in, he scribbled outside the lines. I was pronounced an artistic genius while he was considered hopeless (we both became artists in adulthood among other professional incarnations).

We went to the library and looked through the stereopticons: the Grand Coulee dam, the Taj Mahal, the Pyramids, the Great Wall of China—all the seven wonders of the world. We took out books—everything from *Winnie the Pooh* to *Moby Dick*. Melville was way beyond us, but we loved him anyway: we liked to hear about the sea, and Mom's dramatic reading made everything interesting.

Daddy never joined in the reading. He held himself aloof from "book learnin'." All he needed to know, he maintained, could be gotten from the newspaper, that is, what was going on in the present. He praised Mom's neat little figure, but ridiculed her aspirations to culture, calling her poetry "poultry."

Because we were only nineteen months apart in age and so closed in with each other, Jim and I fought a lot. Most of our contretemps were verbal—of the "did not"/"did too" variety. Occasionally they escalated, as when Jim tried to take over my coloring table. I once threw a pocket knife at his back, and on another occasion bit him on his festering vaccination, an attack that Mom assured me would probably give him "blood-poisoning" and a swift death. He kept me locked in "half nelsons," a hold he had picked up from a wrestler who occasionally stayed at the hotel. "Hush, you'll disturb the neighbors," Mom would say, and make us sit on chairs until we calmed down.

In spite of the situation she was in, Mom kept up with all the middle-class standards that she could. She always managed to have the conventional things on the conventional holidays. On one memorable Thanksgiving Day at the Del Mar, she set up card tables in the bedroom and juggled furniture until she had room for a groaning board, i.e., the ironing board placed across the overstuffed arm chair. The washstand made a place to set a tray with ice water and glasses. She spent the morning in the kitchen baking, basting, cleaning celery—entirely and sublimely happy. Anything that reminded her of home she clung to desperately; she would observe all the holidays and rituals, regardless of her situation. Working with the food, answering the questions of the children who hung around the kitchen, this she loved—only to be informed at the last minute that Harv had invited Jean Jackson to the family party.

"You might have warned me," she hissed when Daddy came up to the apartment a few steps ahead of his guest.

Mom was too gracious and polite to say anything to embarrass anyone, and she welcomed Jean politely. Jean was dressed in jodhpurs and a blouse showing deep cleavage, which fascinated us children. Though she was very obviously female, she had a deep voice and the hard jaw of a man. She was attractive, but had none of the airs and graces of our mother.

"Gee," she said, "I feel really bad barging in at the last minute."

"Sit down," Daddy commanded. As he always did, he told everyone where to sit and rearranged the chairs. Mom brought the turkey, neatly carved and ready to eat, into the room, and we all passed food and filled our plates. Daddy kept passing turkey and dressing to Jean, insisting that she eat more and more. As it inevitably did when Jean was around, the talk eventually turned to her business.

"I never had a job befoah, and the place was in terrible shape—now it's going very nice."

"You'll get yourself married again soon, I'll bet," Daddy said.

"Oh no." Jean had a loud braying laugh. "Oh no you don't. I'm quite capable of taking care of little Jean at this point. No more marriage. If Bill hadn't of died, I would of killed him."

"Oh hell. I expect he was a good man. Maybe you just don't know how to appreciate a man"—Daddy.

Jean: "Oh I appreciate them, but I'm not going to get tied down evah again."

In the most cultured and polite tones that the Schuster Martin School of Dramatics and Elocution could produce, Mom said, "Would you care for more celery, Mrs. Jackson?" She offered the relish tray.

"No thanks, honey, I'm stuffed. That was certainly a good dinnah."

"Me? I prefer a good mess of beans." Daddy invariably said this at any formal meal.

"Is that so?" Jean said. "I guess I like New England food. I miss the sea food n' so ahn."

AFTER THE luncheon party the parents had what was becoming their usual quarrel.

"You humiliated me," Mom sobbed. "You needn't think every woman you see is crazily looking for a man. Some women are quite capable of earning their own way in the world. If it weren't for the children, I'd be one of them. My brother-in-law Lawrence offered me a job with him any time at home. Anyway you were talking about things that were none of your business."

"Oh don't get your feathers all ruffled up."

"And your idea of being a good host is to practically *make* people eat."

"She took the second helping. . . ."

"Well, who wouldn't when it's forced on them?"

"Oh hell," Daddy said airily, smiling, "just because a good-lookin' woman is attracted to me you're . . ."

"You conceited—egomaniac!"

"Well she sure acted that way."

"Oh really."

Harv was up to his old tricks.

As the flirtation with Jean Jackson wore on, Mom became really suspicious. The joking had gotten rougher and rougher, and Daddy pretended that he actually found Jean repulsive.

"She's too much like a man," Daddy would say.

"Oh Jim."

"I mean it. If she didn't stick out in front, you'd swear she was a man. When she wears those jodhpurs she looks just like a man from the back. I swear I came up behind her the other day and said, 'Say, buddy, have you got a match?'"

"I'll bet you did *just that.*"

"Well, I was fooled. Honestly." Daddy chuckled at his own wicked-
ness. "What does she wear those things for anyway? She never rides a
horse."

AFTERNOONS AND evenings alone with Mom became hard to get
through. If Daddy was late for dinner or late coming in at night, she complained. When she asked where he'd been, he'd say "Out."

"I hate him," she said one day.

"Not hate," I reminded her, carefully schooled that hate was wrong
and anger was for beasts.

"Yes, hate."

Other times she would mutter and keep looking out over the back
porch to see if she could see Jean's red car.

"I *hate* suspicious people," she'd say. "I always said I'd never be one
of those wives who suspect everyone. I always wanted to trust and be
trusted."

She buried her fears and read her magazines, creating higher and
higher ideals of marriage for herself and vowing to do her "end of the
bargain." When Daddy was expected home, she would put on lipstick,
fix her hair, and apply the mascara she always wore when she was dressed
up. But she could only gift-wrap her anger. It was always there in the little
rooms, no matter what effort she made, unmistakable, like a bicycle or a
three-headed lamp that someone has tried to cover in tissue paper.

One evening when Mom seemed particularly coiled and was dressed
alluringly, she popped us children into our pajamas early and whisked
away our dinner plates before we had finished our food. She was planning something. Her lips were tight and smiling as she opened the door
to her husband.

"Hello, dear," she said brightly.

"Well," Daddy boomed, "what do we owe this to?"

"Nothing. I just thought we'd have a leisurely dinner for a change.
The children are all bathed and fed and ready for bed."

"And wait till you see the surprise I've got for you," he said. "Is it a
honey."

"What is it?"

"Just be patient. I told you 'Stick with me and you'll wear diamonds,' didn't I?"

"Yes."

"Well this isn't diamonds, but it's really style. Come out on the porch."

"Why the porch?"

"You'll see. Look down there. What do you see? Do you like it? Ain't she purty? What do you think of the old man now?"

Across the street was a bright red roadster just like Jean Jackson's.

REPOƧƧEƧƧED

JIM AND I loved that car. We would go whizzing around the roads outside the city with Daddy at the wheel. Mom would hardly agree to ride in it because of what it symbolized to her. When she did ride, all her time was spent predicting how soon the payments would lag and calculating how far behind in the rent we already were. "Oh Millie, stop your worryin'," Daddy would say. He sped over the countryside, dodging ditches and policemen.

"Slow *down*." Mom clutched her handrest and held on tight.

We drove along the river and to a park where we got to run free. We ran up a favorite hill, then rolled down and lay on the earth, smelling the grass.

And then, like so many things in our nomadic life, the car disappeared. Things came and went for us: fathers, rivers, homes. No one ever explained what became of them and we never asked. What happened to Skipper and Jerry when we left the river? And what happened to Jean, who provoked the car episode? I imagine the shiny chariot that meant so much fun was repossessed.

Other events besides installment payments and Daddy's wandering eye took over our lives. Central School was just a block beyond the Joselyn, and we could walk there easily. Jim at first was horrified. He came home complaining at how rude the children were. They would walk right in front of you and not say "excuse me." We had been with so few children that we weren't used to the roughness and noise of a playground. We both hated group games and forced physical contact; Jim refused to take hands with his classmates.

When I started school, at four, I was so tiny I was put into nursery school until the principal, Miss Edith Hall, whom our mother had already made friends with, rescued me and placed me in the kindergarten class. The kindergarten teacher was a large, forbidding woman. Her name was Miss Hamilton and she wore a white wig, which she adjusted frequently. I was too afraid of her to ask to "be excused" and made a puddle under my chair one afternoon; her response was to shout at my seat mate Harlan Huff, "You don't have to drop your blocks in it!" I was completely humiliated. The kids I walked home with, though, assured me that my horrible experience happened to almost everyone.

By first grade, I loved school and was teacher's pet. I was dismayed by any but perfect scores. I was devastated when I was caught coloring after the teacher said to stop and had my crayons confiscated.

Reading and writing were easy for me and Jim. I was the better student because I could sit still and was more conforming. Both parents were proud of my progress. Daddy was especially impressed with my handwriting. He once looked at my penmanship and kept saying over and over, "You wrote this? You wrote this all by yourself?" He couldn't believe a little girl could write so neatly and so easily. His own signature was a bold, childish scrawl, and he never wrote letters. Maybe he still didn't "read and write very readily." He did read the newspaper, but never fiction or magazines. I don't think he ever read an entire book in his life.

Having been assured by Miss Hall that her children were "superior," Mom was determined that we have brilliant futures. We had to "make something of ourselves" and "be somebody." "You can be anything you want," she preached. She shared her books of drawings and poetry with us and we thought her work marvelous. She was a good draftsman and made charming little sketches. Her poems tended to be on the sentimental side; I realized this even as a young child. Perhaps Daddy, a master of sarcasm, had already instilled a touch of irony in us.

Mom's photograph album, which had black pages and little holders that were supposed to secure the pictures by the corners, continued to be the source of stories. The photos popped out when we turned a page. Mom told us about her relatives in Cincinnati: her grandfather thought tomatoes were poison; Uncle Clint had a wife in the asylum. During Prohibition, Uncle Acey made gin in his bathtub, and Uncle Chester went blind from drinking wood alcohol.

The relatives had interesting faces, especially the older ones with beards and mustaches, long dresses and frockcoats. They seemed to have a dignity Mother's generation, in cloche hats, bathing suits, and swingy dresses, lacked. Our relatives were all merely pictures, a one-dimensional family.

Among the stories about them and the enchanted friends in *Winnie the Pooh*, Mom wove tales about her life. She could turn from the cheerful, creative artist to a mournful victim, quick as the mask of comedy can be reversed to the face of tragedy. She would tell us how she had tried to kill herself and us by drowning, how seeing the men made her turn away. How she planned to use the gas, and then received the letter with money from her father. Was God not in his heaven and all right with the world after all? Mom could eclipse the sun.

But then it would shine again. We would see Mom sitting in Daddy's lap while he admired her legs in her silk stockings and high heels. We'd all take a ride in the red car, or go to a "picture show."

Just across the street from the Del Mar was a movie theater called the Muse. Mom started us going when she read about *Anthony and*

Cleopatra, starring Claudette Colbert. Because of its historical theme, Mom considered it educational. She and Jim and I went to see it, and we children were hooked for life. I can still see Claudette sitting on her throne saying, "Bring me the asp," then holding the box with the poisonous snake to her bosom.

After that first exciting movie, Jim and I were allowed to go alone to matinees and even evening shows at the Muse. One night, a friendly man offered us children a bag of candy, which we eagerly accepted. He asked to sit next to me. I felt odd as he slipped his arm over my shoulder, but we were taught that adults knew best. His hand crept up my skirt and into my underpants. I thought this was perhaps not right, but sat still. The feeling of his cool fingers was not unpleasant, but as I realized that what he was doing was definitely not right, I brushed at my skirt. By then, the man was gone.

On the way back to the hotel, I felt shame. Increasingly sure that what happened was not good. I told my parents nothing, but clung to them more than ever. For some time I would not go across the street by myself, nor would I let strangers help me cross. The experience stayed way back in the last rows of memory and only rose to the surface, like an infected splinter, many years later. It did not dampen my enthusiasm for going to the movies for long.

I saw every Shirley Temple movie that came to the Muse. Shirley was so adorable, the ideal every little girl compared herself to. I had Shirley Temple paper dolls with ermine coats and muffs and ruffled skirts. I had a Shirley Temple mug: blue glass with Shirley's image in white. My mother, in a totally misguided moment, curled my lank locks and entered me in a Shirley Temple look-alike contest, in which I received the twenty-fifth and last prize. When she went to the beauty shop, Mom took me along, dressed in my best Shirley Temple frock, a full-skirted taffeta with velvet bows attaching the skirt to my wrists, so that when I moved my hands the pleats spread into a gorgeous fan. I was oohed and ahhed over by the beauty-shop "girls" while feeling like a butterfly pinned and mounted for display.

I still preferred Jim's less "cute" leather jacket and functional knickers, so the clothes were not what I envied about Shirley Temple; it was the way that, in story after story, through the sheer power of her personality, she brought her parents together and mollified crusty grandfathers who had cut their daughters off for marrying the wrong man.

Daddy seldom attended a movie.

WE HAD so many interesting things to do and so many interesting people in our world. Mom made a character out of everyone from Joe the desk clerk to Mr. Sticks and Mr. Smith. I loved to sit in the lobby, watching the people come and go and making up stories about them. One woman came rushing in regularly wearing a blue cape, slingback shoes, and a red hat. She always headed directly to Joe and had a brief, anxious-looking conference with him, then left quickly. I decided she was waiting for a letter and money from her father.

There was always the Depression. It was just outside our rooms. We heard so much about money and the lack of it that one day I put all my clothes away in a drawer to save them in case we became poor. Both Mom and Daddy assured us that we were undeservedly privileged. Daddy compared us to the hard-working kids of his boyhood, and Mom insisted that we should think about those "less fortunate than ourselves." One of her favorite sayings was "I cried because I had no shoes until I met a man who had no feet." It made sense, but caused you to stow away your feelings as totally invalid. They just weren't big enough.

I was afraid of everything: of being left at night with only a bellboy to look in on us or even during the day when Mom figured the neighbors would hear us if anything happened. One afternoon, standing alone on the porch, gazing into the alley, I was suddenly hit by an animal falling from the porch above. For one second, I held it, thinking someone had sent me a pet squirrel; then, staring into its awful terrified eyes, I realized it was a rat. I dropped the thing and ran screaming to the upstairs neighbors. I refused to go back to the apartment until the rat was gone. Daddy came home and killed it.

I was afraid of kidnappers. We had heard about the killing of the Lindbergh baby. I often saw men in the street who I was convinced would try to kidnap me. Walking with my father one evening, I spotted a man coming toward us and begged Daddy to cross the street away from him.

"What's wrong, Duchess?" Daddy said.

"That man might try to kidnap me."

Daddy had a good loud laugh.

"Nobody's going to kidnap you, Duchess!" he said. He held his sides.

"Why not?"

"Well, kidnappers are out for ransom, and I don't have any money."

After that I felt safer, if less valuable.

JIM AND I had been separated somewhat by school, but he was still my model. When he was sent away for a week to the "Pest Hospital" where scarlet fever victims were quarantined, I was listless and bored. When he came back, my world was whole again. I was jealous of the three little girls who were fighting over him in first grade.

Jim was a natural-born ladies' man and a dreamer. Sent to the store for a bottle of milk, he would come home with a squishy paper bag full of broken glass, having idly bumped it on each lamppost he passed.

Mom later told us she cried as first Jim and then I went off to school. With time on her hands, she started taking part in activities at a YMCA city mission, the Neighborhood House, where she acted in skits and did all kinds of handicrafts. She made a complete set of clothes for a doll of mine named Edith Ann. On weekends and vacations, she and Jim and I continued to be a close threesome.

For a while, Daddy was coming home a little more on schedule. You knew when he was near by the sound of his whistle and the jingling of change he carried in his pocket; it came from way down the hall. He began to shed his clothes on the way to the apartment. By the time he reached the door, his tie and jacket were off and he would be tugging at his shirt buttons. He always took his pants off immediately upon entering the room and hung them neatly on a hanger so they would be presentable for the next day's work selling jewelry.

One night he came home jauntier than usual.

"Well, I'm through with that damned set-up," he said.

"What do you mean?" Mom dropped a pot she was holding.

Daddy sat down heavily in the armchair, still fully dressed.

"I quit."

"What?"

"I quit."

"Oh Jim." Mom's face moved in all directions, like ice breaking up in a river.

"What do you mean you quit? What for?"

"There's other jobs. That was peanuts." Daddy tried a swaggering dismissal of his wife's questions, but it didn't come off.

"But the debts—you couldn't."

His bravado was beginning to break, and she wasn't going to accept the attitude that he had probably worked on all the way home.

"I'm through," he said, more loudly. "Now make a big argament out of it." His rough Southern twang became more pronounced when he got excited.

"Well, I certainly *am*. I most certainly *am* going to make an argument. Do you think the rest of us have no interest in what you do? It just so happens that we're your family, remember?"

"Yes, but I'm not going to work for anybody that doesn't show respect. That Maury called me a blockhead."

"Oh dear." Silence. "But couldn't you just take it once? Which is more important, your pride or the children and me?"

"It's not a question of that," he said. "The thing is, nobody calls me a blockhead. I just don't take it."

Daddy sat in the arm chair tapping one foot, tapping, tapping, fuming. You could smell his hat band as he twirled his hat in his fingers. His hair was plastered to his head with the heat, pressed like fine baby hair against his skin.

"The son of a bitch."

"Maybe if you go back and—" To Mom, pride was a luxury that goeth before a fall.

"I'm not a goin' back."

We children stood dumbly by, staring at Daddy, who finally stood up and took his pants off and hung them on a hanger.

We were on his side. Children understand pride. Nobody should call our father names.

47

7

PICNIC

INSTEAD OF going to his job, Daddy went out every day and looked for work. Mom and Jim and I spent hours out on the cement porch counting the cars that whizzed by. We listened to the radio endlessly: "Jack Armstrong, the All-American Boy," "Little Orphan Annie," "The Lone Ranger." Mom preached education and ambition more fiercely than ever, but my greatest desire was to taste Ovaltine, the drink advertised by Orphan Annie, and to send away for an Orphan Annie Secret Decoder Ring. Movie money was scarce now, and we only got to the movies on "Potato" or "Canned Goods" night, when you could get a ticket by bringing a potato or a can of corn to give to the poor.

Mom walked the floors a lot at night, and she wrote more and more poetry. She told us her sadder tales more often. She drew pictures of a woman with a bucket over her head.

Every night we waited anxiously for Daddy to come home. Did he find a job? We knew the routine well: Mom would have dinner all cooked and waiting on the stove, becoming more and more tense as mealtime neared. Finally he would be heard, the jaunty whistle, the jingling change. He would pitch his hat on the bed. Mom would try not to jump on "The Topic," but she couldn't help it.

"Did you get a job?"

"For Christ's sake, Mildred, can't I even sit down? By God, I've been walking the streets all day and you can't even say hello."

"I'm sorry. I'm worried. I can't help worrying. I'm sorry, but did you get anything?"

48

"No," he would bellow. "No, no, no. Now will you leave the subject?"

She would sigh fearfully and go back to the kitchen.

"You don't have to worry. I'll get something. Just leave it to me. I've always got something sooner or later."

Each night we all hoped things would go smoother, but someone always said something wrong.

"The dinner's cold. It's been ready an hour," Mom might say.

"Now what does that mean?"

"Nothing."

"No, no. You never do mean anything. You're too subtle for me. I never went to school." His voice took on a speech-making eloquence. "I graduated from the lowest class there is. I never even got to first grade. I finished the Chart Class though. Do you kids know what the Chart Class is? That's like kindergarten, only we didn't play. We learned to read. I *can* read. *The McGuffy Reader.*"

"Oh Jim, *stop*," Mom would beg. "What are you trying to prove?"

"Oh nothing, nothing," he would say airily, "just that I'm not as *goddamned* stupid as you might think." His voice was quite an instrument as it changed from a light to a guttural tone.

"I didn't say you were stupid."

"You don't *have* to."

"Are you ready for supper?"

"I don't give a damn."

"Now look." Mom was mad now. "I've taken about all I can take. I cooked this supper and had it ready when you came home. Are you going to eat it or not?"

"What difference does it make to you?"

"Jim, you might consider the children."

"You're the one who might—when you ruin a man's day for him by coming to the door wringing your hands."

"It's not me who ruined it. I only asked a question."

"Only."

And so it went, all through dinner. Daddy watched us all for the slightest display of ingratitude for the food. He went into a tirade about the state of the world. He damned the government, the Republicans, the bankers, the weather; he shook his fork and thumped his fingers rhythmically and constantly on the table. We children dawdled, fiddled, blew bubbles in our milk, slipped sillily into withdrawal. Turned on the radio.

Our old Victor with the great flaring speaker was our greatest pleasure. We could always forget our troubles and be carried away to another world by our programs. Then one afternoon as we were sitting on the bed, listening to Jack Armstrong, a man came to the door. Daddy answered, and soon we heard loud voices. The man demanded Daddy return our radio to him. We watched, terrified, as Daddy argued, then finally grabbed the man and pushed him out the door.

"Don't come to my home, in front of my wife and children! Get out!" Daddy chased him down the hall, bellowing at him. Jim drummed his feet on the radiator by the bed. I sat like a stone as the voices receded down the hall and died away. The radio played on:

Raise the flag for Hudson High, boys, show them how we stand.
Raise the flag for Hudson High, boys, we're the best in all the land.

DADDY BEGAN to dream about going back to the river. We could live fine on a little houseboat. We took walks to the river bank and Daddy began collecting oil-drums to make a boat. We thought it was a great idea; we could have a dog and a cat again and more freedom. We children and Mom sat on the stones by the water and watched Daddy march round and round his oil drums, thinking and planning.

On the way to the river, we had to pass the city dump. People lived on the mounds and hills of garbage in little tents erected here and there, moving on like Bedouins as they picked up broken furniture, rags, bits of food, whatever they could salvage. They were covered with gray dust, ashen, like the little fire-worms that crawl in the papery charred wood of a fire. We talked to some of the children who came down to the river to play; they had punctures on their skins where rats had bitten them in the night. They seemed almost too tired to play. They were vague and withdrawn like sick animals, and the water reflected back in their flat, vacant eyes in an almost impossible reflection and re-reflection of emptiness. We seemed like lucky people: the wealth of our life, our play and our reading, our radio—truly there were those "less fortunate than ourselves." Here they were. We, on the other hand, had a father who, for all his problems, was looking healthy in his torn jacket, marching round and round his oil drums, looking lively and strong enough to build us a boat. We all liked to do this—we had plans!

Suddenly, Mom began packing, as we had seen her do many times before. It was quite a ritual. We didn't have a lot of things: our clothes, our radio, my play table and chairs, unused groceries—that was it except for Mom's boxes of stuff. She carried these with her everywhere; they were her memories. Her photograph album had to be packed, and as she placed it in a cardboard box we got at the grocery store, she thumbed through it and told us once again some of her favorite stories: how she'd almost died as a child and been given up for lost and an aunt had nursed her back to health, the time she let a prize canary loose, and the time she coaxed her half brother to swallow a watch as a magic trick.

Mom read her old poetry once again and gazed at her grandmother's picture. "How I wish I'd been better to her," she said. "Her running up and down stairs in that old house doing all the work. I used to complain about helping, now I wish I had the chance."

Mom added the photograph to the things to be saved, along with the albums she kept of our report cards and school drawings. As we finished our packing, the small rooms began to lose their lived-in look. The clothes were gone from chairs, the closet doors neatly closed. The half-used soap powder was covered with a towel, the drinking glass washed and put away, the books and toys all packed. All our things were arranged in the middle of the room waiting for Daddy to come and get them.

Mom worked all morning. She cleaned the rooms so no one would think we were dirty people. Her hair was hanging in her face, and her energy, which always seemed to increase when she was faced with a challenge, burned and snapped in her eyes.

"Where are we going?" we asked.

"I don't know. Daddy's rented something."

She looked out the window and drummed her fingers on the sill the way he did.

Jim and I were getting bored. "We want to *do* something," we complained.

"Oh dear, just wait. Sit in a chair. Play Riddly-Ree can't you?"

"I'm tired of waiting," Jim said. "Isn't he ever coming?"

"Oh be still."

When we didn't stop complaining, Mom said, "Hush or I'll spank your bare bottoms right now."

"Let's go."

"We can't go till he comes."

"I wanna go."

The afternoon was spent trying to live around packed boxes, waiting for the phone to ring. For a snack, we had to dig into a box for peanut butter and bread.

"Naturally it's at the very bottom," Mom said.

Hours went by. We got sleepy and mean. The room grew hot. We curled around the suitcases and paper bags on the bed. Mom joined us.

Just as we were falling asleep, the phone rang. Mom talked groggily for a minute or two. When she turned from the phone she was crying.

"We've got to go now," she said. She took each of us children by the hand and started toward the door.

"But our things," Jim said.

"We forgot our suitcases," I wailed.

"No," Mom said, "they won't let us take them. Daddy couldn't get the money for the bill so they said we'd have to leave our bags."

She jerked us out the door after taking a last look at our precious junk.

"You'd think after all the time we've been here . . . But that's the way everything is—strictly business." She raised her chin. "Don't speak to anyone in the lobby."

She marched us down the stairs and past the barber shop entrance and the desk and Joe, past the potted palms and the people sitting in the lobby.

"Keep your head up," she whispered. "Act like we're going on a picnic."

HARNEY STREET

MOM LED us through the streets, tears streaming down her face, looking neither right nor left. We had to struggle to keep up with her. We passed the Muse, Jean's diner, several vacant lots, a Piggly Wiggly grocery store.

Finally we reached the new home, a plain red brick building. The "front yard" was dirt, shady and cold as an icebox even on this sunny day. The entrance hall was drafty, dark, covered with chewed-up linoleum.

We turned to a door on the right. "This must be it," Mom said, "Apartment One."

The door opened and a man peered out. He seemed gray all over—skin, clothes—even his voice was gray. "Are you Mrs. Coomer? I'm the landlord. Your husband told me you'd be over. Can I help you bring your bags in?"

"Oh, no!" Mom said. "We're going to get them in a taxi tomorrow. We left them at the other place."

She was shaking. We could feel it through her leather glove.

The man kept on talking.

"—and the bath is down the hall. I take care of the place. I own it, or rather the bank does, so if you need anything, just call me. I don't do any heavy work. I've got a hernia, you see. Oh yes, a bad one—got it doing—"

We noted his seedy-looking clothes and dirty finger nails, reflecting that even "landlords" might be poor. He seemed to have had a sadder life than anything we could imagine, and Mom, being a sucker for any and every pathetic story, listened to a whole recital of his poor health, bad luck, poverty, war wounds, and vicious relatives. By the time he left and we got the door closed, we sagged with fatigue. We looked around the apartment: the windows were near ground level and overlooked the tiny strips of dirt in front of the building. Heavy traffic whizzed by as the rush hour approached. The one large room, which was the bedroom-living room, contained an armchair, a scarred end table, a dark wood dresser, and a bed. The wallpaper was grayish brown and marked by greasy heads and dirty fingers. We could see that this place had once been part of a larger apartment now divided into small flats; the light fixture hanging from the ceiling in the kitchenette (the only other room) had been pushed to a forty-degree angle by the thin partition that served as a kitchen wall. What was once a large dining room was now two small kitchens, and we had been awarded the original fixture.

We looked around vaguely, losing both our sense of unity and of individuality. Jim sat on the bed and picked at the tufts of the chenille spread; Mom looked around the kitchen and peered into the icebox. I wandered to the mirror. I was shocked to look out from my world of rich fantasy and see a plain, too thin, very pale child with wispy hair around her face. This was the first time I remember ever seeing an image of my-self in a mirror.

Suddenly Mom swung into action. She poked around in the kitchen, opening and slamming the cabinet drawers.

"This place is filthy," she said.

She peered behind the stove and icebox.

"Look here. Dead roaches."

She ran her fingers over the top of the cabinet and brought forth a finger full of greasy fuzz. She opened the pantry and stripped back the shelf paper—the different color beneath proved that the shelves needed washing.

Her energy seemed to burn again. She found a broom and swept out all the dust. Her movements were precise and fastidious. When she'd sweep a large area, her eyes would spot a speck of lint like a hawk seeing a rabbit, white and innocent, miles below. She'd wet her thumb and finger and pick it up with the precision of a predatory bird. She found a bucket, a half-used bar of soap some previous tenant had left, and a stiff, twisted rag beneath the sink, stuffed in the S-curve of the drainpipe. She scrubbed down the shelves. Soon dishes were stacked all over the table, pots and pans shoved in the sink to be washed. The kitchen linoleum, though nicked and scuffed, became clean enough to eat on.

We watched, amazed, as her arms struggled against the dirty floor, her neck stiffened and glistened with sweat, her hair flew, and her eyes bulged with determination to make the place livable. When her job was finished it was dark outside. She turned on the lamp and threw herself down in the armchair.

"It's up to you children," she said. "I've tried all I know how. I've been thinking. I've been selfish. I must not be doing the right things. But I've tried, God knows I've tried."

We weren't sure what she was talking about, but she looked desperate. The yellowed lamp shade hung near her head like a faded party favor. We studied the shade, memorizing its corrugated sides, only half listening to her voice. We wondered what was going to happen to us now. We just sat frozen on the bed.

"You children are the ones now. You must do something with your lives. Don't waste it—you children must achieve something. My life is over. My life is done."

We looked around helplessly, not understanding, wishing we had our supper. It was past time to eat, and we'd never missed a meal before. We wondered if not eating was going to become a regular thing now— is that what she was so upset about?

We were hungry and bored. It was past time for Orphan Annie and Jack Armstrong. We wanted to ask when our radio would come and when we would eat, but were afraid of setting Mom off again. We stared out the window.

Suddenly the front door opened and banged, and the whole little brick structure seemed to rock on its haunches. We heard Daddy's quick step in the hall. He opened the door and came in.

"Well, I'll be God-damned," he said. "I'll be God-damned—that hotel keeping our bags!" He looked around the tiny apartment. "I've never been tossed out of a hotel before."

Mom looked at him expectantly. "Where were you?"

Daddy paced from the window to the sink.

"I've been all over town trying to borrow money! Not one of the big shots that are always bragging about their dough have got a thing—suddenly they're all poor. I haven't got a damned cent. Is that a joke! I'm broke. I am really broke."

"Oh Jim," Mom said, "didn't you get *anything*?"

Daddy dragged a chair from the kitchen and flopped down on it.

"Nothing."

Daddy held up one foot and showed us the thin spots in his shoes. "My shoes are wore out! I'm wore out!"

He glanced at the scarred end table and the lopsided ceiling fixture. "What a dump!"

Suddenly, he jumped to his feet. He rummaged in his pants pockets and came up with a single coin.

"I've got one nickel," Daddy said. He held the nickel up and studied it like an object of art. "Exactly one nickel." He pulled the linings out of his pockets and stood there like the showman that he could sometimes be, assuming his old medicine-man's personality. He threw the nickel to Jim.

"Here," he said, "you go up to that store I saw on the corner and get you some candy. Go on. You and your sister."

Jim-Boy seized the money eagerly, and he and I started to the door.

"Jim," Mom wailed. "Our last nickel!"

"Oh for Heavens' sake, Mildred, what in the hell would you do with one nickel?" Daddy waved us on. "Go ahead," he told us.

"It's a start," Mom said.

Daddy held up his hands like Lear in the storm.

"Go on, kids. I want to see what's it's like to be absolutely poor! I haven't even got a penny now—nothing! I'm busted! Nothing between me and the world, not even a god-damned nickel."

He tugged at the linings of his pockets.

"Nothing. Nothing!"

We ran into the hall and up the street toward the store. Daddy's voice rang out in the twilight as we passed the window, still orating on the twists and turns of fate.

When we came back chewing on B-B Bats and peanut brittle, Daddy was getting ready for bed.

"Where the hell are we gonna sleep?" he said. He opened what looked like a closet, and a bed came crashing down on the floor. Daddy read the label on the mattress. "Johnson In-a-Door Bed." Now I've seen everything. I've slept on straw beds and feather beds. I've heard of bed boards, bed and board, bed bugs, and bed sores, but I never heard of a bed in a door. Damn!"

THE NEXT day we had food. We didn't know where Daddy went or how he managed to get the money to buy it. Mom told us admiringly: he had walked over to the barber shop at the Del Mar and met a man he hadn't seen for a while, who luckily didn't know the state of Daddy's fortunes. He borrowed a quarter and bought a fountain pen in the dime store. Then he sold it for fifty cents. It took him most of the day. Then he bought two fountain pens and sold them for a dollar. Mom bought a pound of hamburger and some beans and fixed what would be the staple of our diet for many years to come: chili.

After several days of selling pens, Daddy had enough money to buy more food and had carfare to go and look for work. While waiting and looking, he supported the family by selling more pens and chances on a punch board. This was a cardboard game with some twenty circles to punch out; one of the customers who paid a quarter for a chance won a dollar if the circle he punched had a red dot on the inside. The other quarters went to Daddy.

It was some time before we saw our luggage. While it was still missing, Tanya, the little girl from down the hall, came to play. She was dressed in a frilly Shirley Temple frock and wore her hair in the same plentiful curls. She looked around the apartment, which was smaller than the one in back where she lived. She asked if I didn't have any dolls. I could not admit that my collection was still back at the Del Mar, so I said I didn't like dolls. Finally, finding nothing of interest to look at, Tanya headed toward our one closet.

I leapt in front of her. My shame would be revealed if she saw it was empty. I tried to coax her away, but she was relentless. She flung open the door: the metal hangers tingle-tangled in the empty space. She looked them over, puzzled, and demanded, "Where are your clothes?"

The hangers swayed meanly. Tingle-tattle.

LIFE TURNED gray on Harney Street. Every evening, Daddy would sit by the lamp, circling items in the want ads, mostly factory jobs. He struggled filling out forms, trying to find a place to fit in. Unlike those of a pipe fitter or tool-and-die maker, skills like knowing how to load hogs and horses on steamboats were not in demand. Being a well-dressed boat captain who took people out for a good time on the river was a thing of the past. Now, in his spectators, his scratchy wool suit, and his sour-smelling hat, he was just another hillbilly looking for work.

9

ANOTHER THANKSGIVING

HEAT. IT SHIMMERED on the sidewalk, mocking us with its willow-the-wisp dance. It softened the tar and came at us, flat, unrelenting. The rooms at Harney Street heated up like a boiler room. There was no cross breeze, no air except from the two windows at street level. Our beds were hot as ironing boards.

Heat. That's what I remember most clearly about Depression days. It seemed never to let up. We would wake up at night choking for air. Our little room sounded like a hospital ward with our coughing, gagging, and complaining. We went from chair to chair, to the beds, to the windows, looking hopelessly into the street and wishing for rain.

Ice was at a premium. It cost money, and it melted very fast in the wooden ice box, protected only by the tin liner of the ice chest. We children begged for pieces of ice, but it had to be conserved. No matter how careful Mom was about not wasting, the milk bottle would slowly melt into the diminishing block of ice in a strange embrace, and soon there would be only a puddle and a sour tinny smell.

We were always thirsty. The water from the tap was warm and foamy and flat. We all complained, except Mom, who stoutly maintained that ice water was not good for you anyway. She also didn't believe in electric fans.

Mom slept through the heat better than anyone. She regarded our complaints as sissified (I don't think I ever understood her until I read the Nibelunglied, the scene in which the Teutonic woman sews right through her children's flesh). Daddy never held back a gripe in his life, and would declare he was so god-damned hot you could fry an egg on him. He was more sympathetic about our discomfort than Mom: I remember his voice saying, "Go back to sleep, Punkin. I'll pat your back a while."

We all remembered the hottest week Omaha had in ten years. The temperature rose to ninety-four degrees at seven one morning and kept rising steadily throughout the week. Each day, the sun searched the back of our room and struck the mirror, lighting the parents' bed with a harsh halo. We children would get up groggily and begin to moil about and fight like puppies in a box. Before breakfast was over we'd have had at least three fistfights.

On one of the last days of this heat wave, the temperature was 104. Mom just commented to whomever she saw, "It's going to be a scorcher." We kids did everything we could to break her down.

"Oh don't take on so," she said. "A little heat won't hurt you."

We moaned and complained.

Daddy came home from job-hunting wringing wet.

"Whew!" he announced as he came in the door. He tried to pull his shirt away from his skin. He cursed the sun, the city, the apartment, the neighbors, the chili we were all growing tired of.

"Now don't you start," Mom said, "I've been listening to the children all day."

We sweltered at dinner. The red eye of the sun watched us as usual through the inadequate blind as we sat sweating over the bowls of hot spicy chili. Beads of sweat rolled down our noses and went drip, drip, watering down the food. Tears rolled out of our eyes. Our skin glistened. Our hands grew slippery on our spoons.

Finally Daddy threw his down.

"Agh! That's enough for me."

Relieved, we relinquished our spoons too and staggered about the living room.

"Well, really," said Mom, the mental and moral athlete. "You babies."

"Oh Mom," Jim whined, "don't tell me you *like* hot weather."

"No. It *is* hot. But there's nothing you can do about it. You just accept it."

"Oh hell"—Daddy.

"Think of something else. Maybe we should go out. It would be better than just sitting around."

"I'm going to bed," Daddy announced, and he began to peel down. Mom quickly got us into our pajamas, but the moment we lay down the heat became more oppressive than ever.

Daddy took a can of talcum powder and sprinkled it all over his bed, then beat it in and climbed aboard, after also powdering his neck, armpits, and knees. He got up again, checked the windows to see if they could possibly be raised another quarter inch. They couldn't. He lay down again and tried to trick himself and us into falling asleep. "Do you know how to spell Mississippi? M—I—double S—I—double S—I—double P—I." Then he tried counting sheep.

He grumbled himself into a fitful sleep.

We children lay wide awake, staring at the yellowish ceiling, resenting the heat. It should lift at night. We kept bouncing up and asking for water or to be fanned for a while. Mom gave us a newspaper and we took turns fanning each other. But that just worked up more heat.

Mom had wrapped a wet washcloth around her neck. She kept soaking it in the sink and reapplying it. We kept grumbling, sitting up and throwing ourselves back on the bed in disgust.

"Oh look," she finally said, "let's try to cool off. We'll try soaking your sheets." She let the cool water run over the sheets in the sink and then put them back on the bed. She soaked our pajamas too; now they were hot and clammy as well.

Finally we woke Daddy, and he swore that now he'd *never* get back to sleep.

"Let's try the park," Mom said. We all agreed that anything would be better than cooking in this room, and we started out, wearing as little as we could get away with.

There was a strip of grass and trees in a park two streets over from Harney, so we headed for that. The sidewalks were still warm even in the moonlight.

The stoops along the street were crowded with people. There were always a few sitting out, Grandmas and grown people, but tonight even the little ones were out way past dark, in just a diaper or a pair of underpants. On our own stoop we passed Mr. Kovacs, sitting not two feet from our window, and old Mrs. Finestein who lived with her daughter and her granddaughters, Pauline and Esther. They were *Jewish*. We thought they were quite strange: they ate funny twisted bread—and the *children* were allowed to drink coffee.

The tenants on Harney Street were a degree seedier than those at the Del Mar Hotel. We could hear the couple next door through the thin partition screaming at their four-year-old, Cathleen, as though she were responsible for everything that went wrong in their lives. Upstairs was a young couple with a baby. The woman craved company and was always trying to entice someone, anyone, to come and admire her child. She would give out jelly bread, tea, or milk and crackers for a little company. When I visited, I felt instinctively that I should love the infant, but I didn't. He was sour smelling, and had collected in the crease between his chest and stomach a stagnant pool of saliva mixed with talcum powder. When the couple began a fight, I would pretend to hear my mother calling me to dinner.

Mostly Mom and Daddy kept to themselves on Harney Street, but occasionally they drank a coke with a shot of whiskey in it with Tanya's parents. And Mom found a kindred soul in Mr. Kovacs. When he came to collect the rent, the two would lose themselves completely, happily spouting bromides. Before long, it seemed we owed Mr. Kovacs as much back rent as we had the Del Mar. He wasn't about to toss us out, though; he couldn't rent the apartment anyway, and in Mom he had found the most willing listener of his life. He'd mention our bill, just to say he'd done it, then they'd be happily off on "life."

"Times are bad, times are bad. Don't I know it" — Mr. Kovacs.

"Boom or bust," Mom would say. "That's the way it always goes. Things are bound to get better soon."

Daddy's favorite neighbor was the one Republican in the building, a poverty-stricken creature, who, with his matted clothes and skinny children, apparently couldn't get enough blows from fate to suit him. He insisted that the economy should be left to follow its natural course and that "initiative," "enterprise," and "ability" would be killed by the New Deal. He and Mr. Kovacs were both convinced that Roosevelt was really Rosenfeld. This was a popular rumor at the time. Even children passed it around.

The other neighbors were for the president. Still, they considered it a little bit shameful to be on the dole. Daddy resisted the WPA. Communism, Socialism, Anarchy were not serious movements taken part in by decent people with common sense. You were patriotic and got by through hard work (not too far off what that Republican believed). Mom was uninterested in ideas, except those that concerned her children. She and Mr. Kovacs agreed that "We'll all be dead in a hundred years." And what idea could ever compete with the firmly rooted notion that everything happens for the best?

The park was crowded, bodies everywhere like a graveyard in a flood. The benches were filled by men sitting hopelessly, staring at the traffic whizzing past. Some people were lying on newspapers and some on blankets. Some had thermoses of water or beer. There were couples desultorily kissing, not quite stopped by the heat, families trying to get their children to lie down on mattresses they had lugged over. The young children took this occasion as a holiday, and were, even at eleven o'clock, playing hide-and-go-seek. Their voices echoed through the park in plaintive minor tones: "All-ee — up-in-tree — one — two — three — coming — ready-or-not."

THE DEPRESSION meant men on park benches, vacant lots, an empty bread box. Grayness. Everything seemed without color. Our yellowed apartment walls were stained like a bag of bakery goods. The dresser and end table were scarred by cigarette burns. Mom always tried to make things nicer, but without a regular paycheck there was little she could do.

I don't know how we managed to eat with Daddy out of work. But we never missed a meal, even though our kitchen got very close to empty many times. Mom made soup out of a single dried onion: add grease and water, float in a hunk of stale bread and the scrapings from a piece of cheese carved almost to the rind. She would extend the mayonnaise for another meal by pouring a little milk in the jar and shaking every last bit off the bottom and sides. To watch her scrape the icing from the cellophane package our breakfast rolls came in was to observe a surgeon at work.

We children were always slightly hungry. We went through the kitchen cabinets whenever our parents were out, stealing handfuls of sugar, making sugar sandwiches from the soft packaged bread. We sampled everything: vanilla, which smelled so good, but tasted so bad; even EX-LAX, though we'd been warned it wasn't chocolate candy.

Just because we were hard up, Mom wasn't about to let us fall idle. Once we were settled and progressing in school, we spent our off-hours at the Neighborhood House where Mom taught sewing and crafts as a volunteer and led a group of Girl Reserves. Mom acquired a little confidence by helping others—something she was fond of preaching—and she broached the subject of getting a paying job to help out. Daddy forbade it. "You just stick to your knittin'," he would say. "I'll take care of this family!"

Nevertheless, one summer Mom got a job at the Community Chest, a camp for underprivileged children at a place in the country called Carter Lake. She was paid a dollar a day and lunch. She actually saved part of the dollar to buy life insurance. Daddy scoffed at her, claiming he didn't want to be worth more dead than alive, but every week a man in a black suit carrying a large book would come to the house and for a dime write our names in the book of "Providence" or "Everlasting Life."

Though we never considered ourselves underprivileged, we went with Mom to the camp. There was a good-sized lake and a big central building where the kids ate and did crafts. We hated it. The food was wretched, endless baked beans and bread with margarine. All the campers hated the food: the Italian kids said that at home they had root beer and watermelon for lunch, a menu I still remember, for our mother was big on wholesome, well-balanced meals. Mom never never never permitted sweets before meals (one of my strongest memories is of a maid at the Del Mar who gave me a whole Power House candy bar and let me eat it before dinner!). Mom considered the mix of ethnic backgrounds at the camp—Italian, Black, and "Us"—educational. She was a complete liberal, considering all people of equal worth. Somehow, Daddy never caught wind of our mixing with other than "White" people. Had he known, he probably would have raised the roof—Burnside was not hospitable to outsiders and had a homogenous population of Irish, Scotch, and English descent.

Each day as we rolled out of bed, Daddy would be sitting by the window "figuring," as he put it, wearing a pair of glasses he had bought out of the bin at Woolworth's Five and Dime. The newspaper was folded to the want ads, and a cup of coffee was at hand. As he read down the list of jobs he might check out, he stirred sugar and evaporated milk into his coffee. Pet Milk: a tiny can with a pair of holes punched in it, which, as the sweet, sticky milk collected, looked like two runny sores. On the label was a fascinating picture of a cow within a cow within a cow. Before we left for school or play he'd be on his way, wearing his one decent suit and the hat and shoes that were growing more rundown each week.

One Thanksgiving when we lived on Harney Street we were too low on cash to have a turkey. Mom accepted one of the baskets the Neighborhood House was giving out. Instead of turkey, it contained a chuck roast; there was also a can of cranberry sauce, some paper Pilgrims and turkeys for decoration, a pumpkin pie, and candy corn.

The day started pleasantly; we had a ritual to perform. Everyone kept saying, "It seems like Sunday." Father home, kids out of school, "Young Widder Brown" on the radio (the heroine had pulled out of an amnesic trance just for the holiday).

We had the celery to clean and sweet potatoes to bake, which made my mother, and in time me, happy. To stand at the sink and scrape fresh celery, the little curly leaves and straight stalks smelling so fresh.

The cranberry sauce was slid out of its can and plopped onto a dish, and, with Daddy's usual litany about "store bought" things playing softly but steadily in the background, we proceeded with contentment. The smell of the roast, the dishes of cranberry and pickles, the table cloth: it was all very pleasant. Even Daddy seemed to relax and enjoy it.

The chuck roast was very good and we all praised it highly. Of course, Daddy had no idea that it had come from a charity basket. Mom had thought it best not to tell him. We all dug in, agreeing that it was better than turkey any old day. Then one of us children let slip where the stuff came from.

Off Daddy went. He railed against "Charity! Do-gooders! Old maids! Meddlers! Social workers! WPA bums!"

We paused, chewed a little slower.

"I can support my family myself! I don't need charity!"

"Well, it made a good meal, and there wasn't a cent in the house," Mom said. "Would you rather starve?"

"Nobody's going to starve."

"For Thanksgiving only, I took a basket."

"I can eat chili!"

"We were all enjoying it so—why spoil it?"

Daddy got up from the table and banged his fist on it, making the chuck roast bounce on its platter.

"I don't need Charity! I don't need Charity! I don't need Charity!"

He walked out of the apartment and slammed the door.

"Go ahead and eat," Mom said. But everything had soured, become dry, lumpy, impossible to chew, stomach-hurting lye-in-the mouth, poison, and finally stomach pains.

10

PENNY SAVERS

THE TEACHER passed a graham cracker and a half-pint bottle of milk with a straw to everyone in my first-grade room except me. It was snack time and the crackers and milk cost five cents. I yearned to be included. I didn't even like milk. But I liked graham crackers—and straws. I tried to look away from the kids sucking and munching their treats.

Probably there were other children in my class who couldn't afford to join in at snack time, but this is the way I remember it. I was so humiliated, so close to tears, I had no heart to look around me.

The children at school often asked Jim and me what our father did for a living, and we would go dumb and embarrassed; we didn't know there were so many other people without jobs—we were such a small, tight unit. Mom told us to just say "Unemployed."

She, who had always been pretty and loved clothes, got any decent outfit she had to wear from her step-sister Helen in Cincinnati. Daddy often looked exhausted, though he never stopped whistling his familiar tune or jingling whatever change he had in his pocket. He still made a joke of everything, even a horrible dish he created out of sardines and spaghetti, the only food in the house one evening when he cooked.

We knew Daddy felt deeply about being out of work from his frequent angry outbursts; after all, his father had been a man of some standing in Burnside, and Daddy had held important positions on steamboats. Daddy was never nostalgic, though. Mom offered to move back to Burnside with him if he wanted to go home, but he had no desire to return.

Mom yearned for the hills of Cincinnati—"my home." "Omaha is so *flat*," she said. She talked about how green her city was, how beautiful with the river running past it.

THE GRAYNESS and feeling of being stuck and trapped in a colorless world hung on. I grabbed at every bit of color that life offered—pictures in a magazine, any book or toy or ornament that was bright and pretty. I looked for beauty everywhere, spending much of my time drawing and cutting out paper dolls. My friends and I drew clothes for them endlessly, making little tabs to hold the dresses on.

The bleaker our situation was, the more intense were Mom's efforts to instill ambition in her children. She marched us all over the city on long walks and preached the importance of education. "You must go to college," she'd lecture me. "You'll get a scholarship. You will go to college. If I have to scrub floors, you will."

I was to be a famous artist, Jim a great scientist or maybe president of the United States. It was all up to us. The future was everything, the present only a preparation for what was to come. She sent us to the surface like bubbles.

Her ideals were the Central School principal, Miss Hall, and her teacher friend Dorothy Fisher. The two women lived together in a neat, well-furnished apartment and traveled the world during the summer holidays. We loved to visit them; they let us handle the treasures they'd collected from their trips: little ivory figurines, fans, shells, tiny boxes, straw and wooden dolls, marble eggs.

Daddy thought Mom's pretenses to culture were funny, her aspirations confusing and strange. When he made fun of her poetry writing, she'd put on her grandest Schuster Martin air. "The children like it, and they're going to be educated people who understand such things."

"I didn't say anything against it, that's fine," Daddy would counter. "I hope they do. But just don't forget the most important thing on earth: Get that buck!"

"Oh Jim."

"It's true," Daddy would insist. He'd rap his knuckles on the table. "Course, maybe if y'all do get educated, you can use your head instead of your back, like me—and you can make a fool outa your old man."

THE SAVING thing for us children during the Depression was that we didn't live entirely in this world. On Harney Street we were quickly incorporated into the sidewalk games kids played then: jump rope, hopscotch, Mother-May-I?, Kick-the-Can. We played Robin Hood on the church steps, running in and out of the grimy, pigeon-dirtied pillars, and cops and robbers in the parking lot of the insane hospital. We had lots to talk about, too, as we sat in little clusters on the cement steps: what did "Flaming Youth" mean on the movie poster plastered to the side wall of the grocery store?

We debated the relative merits of freezing to death or burning to death. This was argued with scholastic fervor as one child, perhaps a partisan of freezing to death, learned a new and horrible detail about burning to death. Comic books and boys' adventure magazines revealed new aspects of one or the other terrible demise that could be used for argument.

We played a game called Druthers, somewhat like Lil' Abner's "druthers" (Lil' Abner was the hero of a comic strip about "hillbillies" — all we knew of our father's background). Druthers was started by one child who might say reflectively to another as they walked slowly around the block, "Wouldjew druther be dipped into hot boiling wax and be made into a stachoo, or have red hot needles stuck under yer fingernails?"

This conundrum would occupy the other player for some time. It was nearly impossible to make up your mind. The reflecting child generally countered with another question such as, "Wouldjew druther be out on the desert dying of thirst and come to a pond, and it's ol' stagnan' water fulla bugs and slime and garbage — wouldjew druther drink the ol' stagnan' water or die of thirst?"

We played imaginary games with our paper dolls, simply rearranging our world in a more pleasant way than what reality offered. We would sit together on the sofa or floor and decide: "You be Jeannette MacDonald and Nelson Eddy and I'll be Dick Powell and Joan Blondell." And so it was.

We sat on the hot sidewalk waiting patiently for the iceman to come and deliver ice to the lucky neighbors who could afford it: large blocks he held on his shoulder with tongs. We'd beg for a chunk to eat. If the iceman was in a good mood, he'd chip off a piece. It always had little bits of burlap on it from the bag that he draped over his shoulder as he carried the heavy blocks into various apartments. He'd given all the housewives cards that said "ICE," which they were to put in the window if they wanted him to stop.

There was a lot of status in having the sign displayed—it meant you had an actual icebox and not a window box. These cardboard or wooden boxes, stuck in whatever shade the building offered, were messy, with the milk getting cheesy, the butter melting, the food going bad.

Penny candy was the Depression's affordable treat. For a penny we could buy three Mary Janes or two B-B Bats, sweet artificially-flavored taffy on a stick—chocolate and banana. I can still smell the cloying banana. Licorice cigarettes came in a pack of twenty; they tasted like rubber, but were fun to pretend to smoke and lasted longer than some of the tastier treats. We took our time spending our hard-won penny (Mom: "Money doesn't grow on trees"—"I'm not made out of money"). Looking into the grocer's glass case full of possibilities, we'd slowly decide: did we want a Guess What, a wrapper containing two chewy kisses and a novelty prize, or a flat piece of Bubble Gum that tasted only slightly better than the baseball card that came with it? A penny could buy a small bag of peanut brittle—maybe that was the better choice—or a jawbreaker you could gnaw on for a long time before reaching the soft center, or a small box of red-hots that would turn your tongue red for about twenty-four hours.

Religion brought little comfort. My mother alternated between belief in a cruel deity who was punishing her for some unknown sin and a sunnier deity, a "just and merciful God." But her idea of the afterlife was "When you're dead, you're dead." She saw no use in visiting cemeteries or elaborate memorials: "Life is for the living." Daddy clung to "the Almighty Dollar." Jim and I were sent to the closest Protestant Sunday school. We saw little difference in the denominations, learning the books of the Bible, the Apostles' Creed, and the Bible stories in all of them.

In spite of our family's casual attitude toward religion and our dearth of cash, we always had the conventional things on the conventional holidays. One year I dreamed we didn't get any Christmas presents, but our parents always managed somehow to come through for us. Our tree on Harney Street was strung with popcorn, cranberries, and silver paper from cigarette wrappers.

We made presents at the Neighborhood House for "our relatives" far away: shellacked wooden door stops in the shape of Dutch girls, lopsided ashtrays. In return we got some presents from out of town, most notably boxes from Auntie: little wads of sugar pressed flat and stamped with a pecan, tubs of fudge, divinity, and cookies of all shapes and sizes. We lived in a fit of frantic greed, counting the days until the tissue paper could be ripped off and the packages under the tree would be in our possession.

Every year Daddy delivered a running lecture on the commercialization of Christmas: bought presents, rummies dressed as Santa Claus, pre-cut trees.

"Y'all will go out and *buy* a tree," he'd complain. As though we could go and cut one off the sidewalk. Christmas cards! A racket, a swindle!

But we didn't care whether the stores were gypping us: we were full of the wonderful sentiment of Christmas, humming Christmas carols, planning, scheming, hoping, and feeling true love for our fellow man. We went to Kresge's dime store or Woolworth's for the few things we bought; the "five and ten," though small, carried everything from shoes to pots and pans and canary birds. A woman hawking sheet music sat at a piano and plunked out popular tunes. The aroma of hot dogs filled the air.

On Christmas Eve we went to bed as relaxed as six-day bicycle racers. We were never among the heretics who opened their gifts on Christmas Eve. We waited until morning so Santa could make his deliveries (Daddy dutifully ate the cookie and drank the milk we left out for Santa, thus proving the absolute reality of St. Nick).

Finally, in the wee hours, we slept, dropping off into the darkness like the more stubborn needles on our tree, scuttling off into restless dreams. In the morning we awoke suddenly and completely, eager and anxious. We were allowed to rifle our stockings, but Mom could never bear to give anything away without a struggle; pleasure must always be postponed, if possible to the breaking point, ideally after some heavy task or soul-redeeming obstacle was overcome. So the presents waited until breakfast was eaten, cleared away, the dishes done, we children absolutely frantic. At the word, the gifts were snatched up and ripped open, the pretty wrappings thrown unnoticed in a pile. Mom tensely gathered up "perfectly good ribbon" to save for another day, and Daddy had the time of his life making comments about how little he got. "It's Papa who pays," he chanted. He made treats out of the oranges in our stockings by inserting a peppermint stick into a slit in the skin.

Jim and I were each alone in the search for our own name on packages, uninterested in what the other got, slightly dejected when we had to hand a package over to some one else. When we did get a present, we dug into the box, inspected the contents with the cold-blooded detachment of pawn brokers, perfunctorily placed it in our growing pile of toys, and lost interest.

The living room was a mass of tissue, as if a giant Kleenex box had blown open. Then came ribbons, candies (squashed and whole), seals of little Santa faces, candles, deer, bells, holly, and envelopes carefully rifled for dollar bills. We stepped in boxes wherever we turned, tripped over ribbon, and crammed ourselves, as if at one last orgy—it was the only time there would be candy between meals—with fudge and nuts, caramel, fondant, hard sour balls and peppermint sticks, licorice and chocolate. We sampled everything and spit jellies behind the couch and chairs. Even in January, when we were down to the last dregs of the Christmas candy, we wouldn't eat jellies.

All morning we listened to carols over the radio—groaned out and syrupy, by Bing Crosby. We stayed frantic until noon, then Mom urged a cleanup. No kind of orgy, even a happy Christmas, should go on too long.

Daddy drank a glass of whiskey, and we knew the biggest part of the holiday was coming to an end. He always looked grimly at the mass of stuff and litter, paper and seals, Santas and bells, and passed judgment on the day.

"Do you know what Christmas means?" he would say.

"What?" We always fell for his traps, played the straight men every last time.

"The rich are richer and the poor are poorer."

With this he had a good chuckle.

"Suckers!" he said.

JANUARY AND February brought snow piled high, dwarfing us on our way to school. With it came colds and croup and fear of pneumonia. Daddy mixed up whiskey and honey in a jar with some sort of gourd. Mom slapped "mustard plasters" on our chests and smothered us with blankets, trying to "sweat it out" of us. Mom declared most ailments "All in the mind." Daddy swore she would say this to a cancer victim or a total amputee. The one thing that scared her was infantile paralysis: polio. We saw pictures and heard stories of iron lungs, and President Roosevelt headed a charity for crippled children. We were told, if we had a sore throat or a cough, to bend our neck forward to make sure it wasn't stiff—a sure sign of polio.

A doctor was called only when all else failed. Mom always dressed up a little and combed her hair when one came to the apartment; even though his ilk were pill-pushers in league with the druggists, he must not think we were needy and low class.

She wished Jim could be a doctor.

SOON IT was time to move again. Daddy got a job as a salesman for Penny Saver bread, a soft, packaged loaf that got its name from a large picture of a penny printed on the wrapper, which was redeemable for one cent at the grocery store. Daddy was unable to fool himself about the quality of the bread, though he was probably good at selling his customers on it. At home, he would hold a slice of Penny Saver up to the light and say, "You can read a magazine through this stuff."

Nevertheless the Penny Saver loaf brought a steady salary and a move to an apartment across the river in Council Bluffs, nicer than Harney Street.

We followed the usual ritual of packing, once again going through the family album, staring at Mom's grandmother's picture, packing her one good possession, a small bisque figurine of a little boy sitting on a cushion. Daddy was always off somewhere while Mom got us and our stuff onto a Greyhound and settled us into new rooms.

The apartment in Council Bluffs had a small courtyard and a spot of shade (something I always loved). Our movie house was called the Liberty; the public library (our salvation) was nearby. We were soon enrolled in school. I was in second grade and Jim in third. The school was like all the others we eventually entered: a playground; noisy halls with cut-outs done in art class along the walls; the familiar portrait of George Washington, floating in clouds, above the teacher's desk; the pull-down maps on the blackboard. I loved school, I loved its very rigidity: the bells that told you when to come and go, the clock above the classroom door that seemed to suddenly jump to the hour, the predictability of going back to school after a sometimes long and boring summer, my report card telling me I could do something right.

The name of the school we attended in Council Bluffs is lost in the blur of moving, for we were soon on the go again. The year must have been 1937, the year Mom's grandmother, Melissa Beamer, died. Though our relatives were still just pictures in a book, I cried along with Mom when she got the news.

Leaving Council Bluffs, we as usual didn't know where we were going or why. Daddy simply announced his decision to move on and we headed for the bus station.

11

MANAWA

WE COULDN'T wait to get up in the morning. We had our own little room across the hall from our parents'. We'd look out the window and see the sun coming through the trees in the long backyard: time to get up and play.

The house was a big white frame, the kind you saw in pictures, with a front porch and a back porch and lilac bushes all around. It was located on a shady lane next to a smaller house in Lake Manawa, a community somewhere near Council Bluffs. Daddy called the town a broken-down summer resort. We had two bedrooms, a kitchen, living room, and dining room on the first floor, and two bedrooms we never used and a bathroom upstairs. The backyard was grassy and included an outhouse, a walk-in dollhouse, and, in the center, a large spreading apple tree just waiting to be climbed. A vegetable garden was at the back of the lot, and alfalfa fields bordered the property on two sides.

Jim and I lived in the apple tree, lolling on the branches to read, swinging from one limb to another like monkeys, eating our bread and syrup (Karo syrup on white Penny Saver, our favorite lunch) high above the ground. We had a dog, another Jerry, and a plethora of cats. The one we brought from Council Bluffs seemed to reproduce overnight, and soon there were some twelve kittens mewing and purring about the yard.

Where this place came from or how we got there is a mystery. Daddy was always the instigator of moves, so he must have seen the house for rent and moved us in. We children, of course, never gave a thought to details. Manawa was simply our new home, and we loved it.

When we weren't in the apple tree, we were on the garage roof. Jim and I convinced the neighbor kids—a boy named Charlie Knott; his pesky younger sister, Sandra; and Bill Bates, the local pariah—that we were the only ones who could handle the electric wires connected to the house, due to our mystic powers. We would dare the others to touch the fatal coils as we did. Of course, the wires in question must have been dead, but how did we find that out?

It must have been Jim's scheme; he was the leader in all our play. I grew frustrated always being Maid Marian while he got the title role in games of Robin Hood. But he was bigger and stronger and always a year ahead. We had many fights, like a pair of little spouses. Though I enjoyed the excitement of following around an adventurous boy, I often wondered how mother could possibly love him.

He knew his power and how to exert it. He built a wooden airplane, with no motor of course, and talked me into being the "test pilot." I actually felt honored until I sailed off the garage roof on two wobbly pieces of wood roughly tied together into something resembling wings and crashed into a lilac bush.

We were forbidden to go alone to the lake that gave Manawa its name, and we actually obeyed this rule, only going when Mom or Mrs. Knott, Charlie and Sandra's mom, took us. Daddy did not swim—in spite of his river background, he avoided getting into water. He never went near the garden either, though surely his forbears grew at least their own vegetables.

The garden yielded a few tomatoes from old plants, but most of it went to seed, producing feathery asparagus bushes and curly pea vines with no peas. I ventured back there one afternoon and discovered a large black spider and a single poppy. The flower was a vision: bright red-orange, soft as tissue paper or aged skin. The spider seemed to be a kind of omen, and I flew from the abandoned garden in terror like Miss Muffet.

The country could be frightening, as when the porch awning flapped in the rain like an old wet ghost. It was beautiful in spring, when we saw the white apple blossoms drop away, creating snowdrifts beneath the trees, and the inchoate fruit bulge from the dark lashes at the heart of the flower.

The difference between boys and girls acquired interest as we grew and had opportunities for a bit of experimenting. Our little gang all dropped our pants on the garage roof to show "everything we've got." For some inexplicable reason, we all decided to pee in a large jar. We were quite proud of our production, a vessel brimming with yellow liquid, foamy as beer—until our mothers caught us and we got a good spanking and a lecture.

We learned how to curse. Daddy, the old steamboat mate, swore a blue streak when he was mad. But his language was always profane, never scatological. Jim taught me a new vocabulary of "bad words" and exhibited me to the neighborhood as a kind of prodigy. These performances came to a stop when mother heard me call Jim a "dirty asshole." She was wise in so many ways, and this word, she simply told me while I was bathing, did not sound nice. As she didn't get into a fit about my peccadillo, I accepted her advice to watch my language. In other ways, I remained a total tomboy and hoyden. The parents were always trying to get me to be more ladylike. Mom suggested more feminine activities; if Daddy saw me with my skirts in the air, he would give them a tug and say, "A little dignity."

In matters of sex, our parents were opposites as usual. We knew their life together was highly sexual and charged with male-female tension. It was a matter of what should be revealed or hidden. Mother loved to answer questions about sex, and in fact sometimes told us more than we wanted to know. Daddy thought all matters having to do with gender or reproduction should be ignored. When Jim called me a "morphodite" at the dinner table, he went flying across the room.

"I won't have such talk in my house," Daddy stormed. "As God made little green apples . . ."

Getting back on his feet, Jim said, "Well, I didn't know it was that bad. What does it even mean?"

"Well dear," Mother said. She turned to Jim with her expression of sweet reason. "Such a person . . ."

Daddy cut her off with his angry hiss.

"SST-SST."

"But Jim."

"Not another word on the subject."

Young Jim muttered something.

"Silence! Silence!"

While life in Manawa seemed like a perpetual summer, Jim and I at some point attended a one-room country school where I finished second grade. Otherwise, as usual, we lived pretty much to ourselves and carried our culture with us. We had just two encounters with the world outside Manawa.

Mom got a job with a family of huge Germans named the Katzenheimers. They owned a grocery store in a nearby town, and Mom helped out there on Saturdays. Daddy must have temporarily relented about women working because we heard no storms over the issue. We visited the grocery store, impressed by the size of the Katzenheimers; even their cat was enormous and attacked our poor little Jerry, who was never the same after Oscar swiped him rudely across the face with a giant paw. Mom fell in love with this family because they were so close; the entire clan played Monopoly on Sunday afternoons, and we were initiated into this most American of games. Daddy declined the invitation to join in.

A girl dropped into our world from some exotic place, challenging my cockiness. Daddy invited a business associate and his daughter to the house for a picnic dinner. They were *Jewish*. This fact was made much of. Daddy was uneasy with all ethnic peoples except the ones familiar to him in Burnside. He seemed to assume the guests were ashamed of their heritage. We were to be especially nice—after all it wasn't their fault.

There was much anticipation as the day of the picnic drew near. Daddy set up a nice spread of food on the picnic table under the apple tree and decided that Jim and I should keep the flies at bay. He made wands out of sticks, with shredded newspaper attached, and showed us how to sweep them carefully above the table. It was like something from plantation days, maybe a chore Daddy had seen performed on the Mississippi. We felt like slaves and didn't last too long at our work. At last the guests arrived. They were different from any Jewish people we had met before. Pauline and Esther from Harney Street were even less refined than we were. Their grandmother, an immigrant from Palestine, spoke little English and squatted on her front stoop like a peasant. Mr. Handfelt, the owner of the *Valley Queen* and provider of Juicy Fruit, had had his face shot off some years after we left the boat. This man was sleek and his daughter was beautifully groomed and cared for. She was like an exotic doll, with perfectly braided black shiny hair and flawless olive skin. She was obviously not accustomed to swinging from the branches of apple trees. I wondered what she thought about us: would she have liked to join in with us savages, or stay miles away?

I didn't exactly envy this girl; she was too perfect, too quiet. But I certainly felt inferior. And different. I had overheard Mrs. Knott explaining to a visitor that I was "more like a boy than a girl."

Life at Manawa went on in its lovely way. During our time there, the parents got along better than they had before. They even cooked together, turning out a sandwich cake made of soft bread and a variety of fillings. Every Saturday we kids got a whole nickel's worth of candy, our reward for staying away from the lake and being good while Mom was at work. We would lick Holloway suckers, or sample a mix of marshmallows and caramels while lying on the living room floor reading "Mandrake the Magician" and "Lil' Abner" in the funnies. Bliss!

We set up a lemonade stand, drinking most of our product ourselves, as few people wandered down the lane in front of our house. We gathered wagons full of apples and sold them door to door. We visited a nice old couple, Uncle Ought and Aunt Maude, who let us ransack their pear tree. We caught batches of sunfish in the lake and Mom fried them to a crisp.

I remember one perfect day: we went swimming and returned home cool and happy. We sat at the dining room table and had dinner, corn on the cob and beets and tomatoes still warm from the garden. The room was like a Vuillard painting, low-lit and cozy. We got all the way through this one meal, the only one I can remember, without a quarrel. We talked little, and quietly. I felt sleepy and contented.

Then, one evening in the very depth of summer, we were sitting in metal chairs in the front yard. The heat was kept away only by the great trees: the June bugs were careening around, and lightning bugs were flashing their tiny spots of fluorescence. The cicadas had started their whirring, the crickets were clicking, and we could hear the frogs croaking in the fish pond near the rock garden.

"There's no place noisier than the country," Daddy said. "You can hardly hear yourself think."

He slapped away a gnat. He held up his hands and observed a mosquito boring into his flesh.

"I've got a different kind of bug on every one of my ten fingers. It's time to get the hell out of here."

WE WERE right back on Harney Street. The hopeless feeling of the times came back like a chronic disease. The heat pressed down and the money worries ate away at everything good. The only place you could get cool was in an air-conditioned movie theater. You would get a whiff of comfort walking past one. The sign out front advertised, "20% cooler inside." But dimes were harder than ever to come by.

One minute we kids were the hope of the future to Mom, and her best buddies. She would encourage us in calisthenics, demonstrate the Charleston for us, teach us to stand on our heads. The next minute we were "millstones" around her neck. She tortured herself for being a failure: "Oh God, why hast thou forsaken me?" she'd demand, eyes turned upward. She called on the heavens to explain our bad behavior—fighting, making too much noise, annoying the neighbors, forgetting to lock the door or to be home from playing on time. She read us a poem about a family of children who promised to do things for their mother and didn't come through—all but Little Sally. The refrain was "Which one loved their mother best?" If she really wanted to get us feeling guilty, she would sigh and say, "Of course, I never had a mother. . . ."

She blamed herself and Daddy for the family's situation. After all, her relatives were living on the same block they always had, in their own homes. Daddy blamed everyone and everything but himself. Their war resumed.

"You think everybody is out of step but you," Mom would charge. "You're a law unto yourself."

Daddy just shrugged.

The contretemps over women working was again suspended when Miss Hall got Mom a job working in the student lunchroom at the University of Nebraska at Omaha. Mom was open with people about her predicament and willing to accept help. Daddy would never admit he was anything but in charge.

At work Mom was "Little Mary Sunshine" once more. She loved being on the university campus. She listened to the students' dating problems and their academic worries.

Daddy was out of work again, and the family's finances must have gotten desperate, for when I was in fourth grade and Jim in fifth at Central, we were told we'd be leaving for Auntie's in Louisville. Mom was by then so popular at her job that the university gave her a big party and a locket with her name on it and she was written up in the campus newspaper.

I was glad to be leaving Omaha. Anything would be better than Harney Street. I pictured Kentucky as one great horse farm with rolling green hills and white fences and Loretta Young riding thoroughbred horses amid the lush trees and meadows.

The *Valley Queen* at the height of her glory as an excursion boat, ca. 1930.

The *Valley Queen* iced in, Missouri River between Omaha and Council Bluffs.

Jim-Boy, wearing the envied aviator cap, and Dot (the author) on the *Valley Queen*, 1934.

Dot, Jim-Boy, and Daddy on the *Valley Queen* pilot-house steps, 1934.

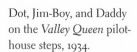

The family with dog Jerry on the *Valley Queen*, 1934.

The *Valley Queen* sinking on the sandbar, Missouri River, May 17, 1934.

Harv's father, Marshal John Coomer, in black with badge, with Burnside
friends, ca. 1900.

Charity Noe Coomer,
Harv's mother, ca. 1900.

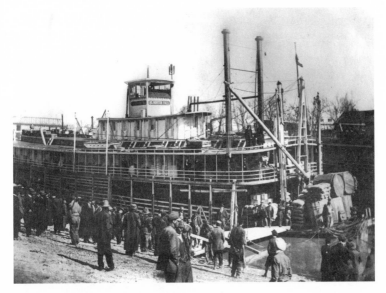

The *Jo Horton Fall*, one of the packets Harv served on in his steamboat days. She was refitted as an excursion boat in 1926, becoming the *Valley Queen*.

The *Idlewild*, one of Harv's favorite steamboats, ca. 1928.

Mildred as a young woman, ca. 1927.

Mildred as a young woman, ca. 1927.

George and Melissa Beamer, Mildred's grandparents who raised her, ca. 1890.

Melissa True Beamer, ca. 1900. This photograph always had a place of honor wherever Mildred lived.

Willis Kennedy and Louise Beamer Kennedy (Auntie and More-Pop), with whom Mildred spent childhood summers and with whom we lived during the school year of 1938–39.

Auntie in one of her fancy
hats, ca. 1905.

Roy Beamer, Mildred's father (*l.*), with cousin Asa Beamer (*r.*), 1929.

Mildred's aunts and uncles who helped raise her: Morris (Bud), Ethel, Ninnie Esther, Roy, Odessa, Clint (hidden), Lester, Louise (Auntie), ca. 1930.

James Harvey Coomer in "Konjola Man" days, holding baby Dot.

Jim and Dot, Kansas City,
Missouri, 1933.

Mildred (*r.*) with Jim, Dot,
and friend on a steamboat,
Kansas City, Missouri, 1933.

Dot dolled up for Shirley
Temple contest, 1935.

Dot at the Cincinnati Zoo,
ca. 1939.

Roy and Lulu Beamer, Mildred's father and step-mother, ca. 1940.

Mildred's stepbrothers and stepsisters Elmer, Helen, Ray, Mary, and Freddie, Bevis Avenue, ca. 1940.

The *Island Queen* delivering passengers to Coney Island, ca. 1940. *(From the Paul Briol Collection, Cincinnati Historical Society Library, copy by Public Library of Cincinnati and Hamilton County.)*

Harv, probably on the *Island Queen*, ca. 1940.

Yacht club main boat (our cabin up top), ca. 1939.

Yacht club float.

Daddy, Dot, Drift on float.

Daddy at yacht club.

Flood, East End, ca. 1942.

Shanty settlement, the last in the area, on the Licking River bank ca. 1984. *(Photograph by the author.)*

Shanty boats in Licking River ca. 1984. *(Photograph by the author.)*

ALONG THE OHIO

1939–1942

12

AUNTIE AND MORE-POP

THE GREYHOUND BUS. How familiar the elongated dog on the side of the carrier seemed, the maw where luggage was tossed, the pulling out of the station for yet another journey, the sound of the air brakes softly sighing. We piled into seats, our socks squishy from a soaking in the rain on the way from the streetcar. Mom could relax now, at least for a moment. She had gotten us and all our earthly possessions through the terminal. Her hands, as always, shook as she bought tickets, steered us to the right line, and sent us to the restrooms for one last pee. She had just enough cash for one cup of cocoa, which we split three ways, Mom staring down the incredulous waitress. I suppose Daddy was on the bus as well, but somehow he was never around for the grubby work of traveling.

The trip seemed unending. Jim and I were not yet at the age where we could sit still for very long. Nor could we resist trading punches. I was carsick as usual, and saw, close up, the grimy floors of rest rooms from Nebraska to Iowa and Illinois.

When we came through Indiana, the trees along the ridges were beginning to show their leaves. I had never seen anything so beautiful. Mom was thrilled. Her beloved hills. Not yet Cincinnati's, but close. So close.

We must have been a strange sight when Auntie picked us up at the bus station in Louisville: a man with a black mustache and receding hair nervously snapping his fingers; a tiny worried-looking woman trying to keep an eye on the children and the "luggage," a tied-together suitcase and a bunch of lurching cardboard cartons; a towheaded boy in knickers, one of which was falling toward his shoes (the rubber bands he used never worked for long); a frazzled, too-thin girl with long pigtails and a worried look just like her mother's.

Jim had been running around and had acquired, as usual, a row of sweat pearls above his upper lip like an extra set of teeth. I had a stomach ache.

Auntie had gotten really fat. She had always had heroic proportions. Now, at a little over five feet, she weighed a good two hundred pounds. She had brown hair permed to a frizz, glasses, and a big welcoming smile. She had written many letters urging us to come home, and seemed actually glad to see us. She kissed Mom and us children and glanced at Daddy and said, "Hello, Harvey."

We got ourselves and our stuff into Auntie's long black Buick and headed for the house on West Main Street. As we drove I stared out the window, hoping for some note of glamour in Louisville. Instead I saw a very ordinary, dowdy city, older than Omaha, with miles of undistinguished commercial buildings. We arrived at a tiny shotgun house opposite a city jail on a pleasant shady street.

We entered the backyard from an alley. Auntie had moved as much of the farm to this suburban spot as was probably legal: the yard, which was long and completely fenced in, contained a pen full of rabbits and a wire chicken coop with a dozen chickens, all clucking and clacking away. The garden was overgrown with watermelon vines and squash plants and tall corn stalks. Apples littered the ground around a fish pond. A pair of Pekinese dogs romped about, and a fat Persian cat was stretched out on the steps of an enclosed back porch. Inside, a bright green parrot —just like the one we remembered—was squawking at a cage full of yellow and turquoise parakeets.

More-Pop sat in a chair on the porch. He was tall, with deep-set eyes, a bald head, and a slight frown. He was wearing a hat, though it was not cold; we soon found he always wore a hat to keep drafts off his head. He smiled at Mom and nodded at Daddy. His look told us children to keep our distance.

The house was full of reproductions of paintings and photographs— a stag being held at bay by dogs, moonlight on the ocean, a child posing as Cupid, large twin photos of Auntie and More-Pop as young marrieds, she in her "bird of paradise" hat and he looking distinguished and hirsute.

The living room furniture was deep red plush trimmed in dark wood, and the tables were covered with soapstone birds in bird baths. Beneath a fancy table were the only two books in the house, huge volumes of *Pilgrim's Progress*. The living room was at the front of the house and was kept scrupulously clean for company or visits from the Fuller Brush man.

Auntie's domain was headquartered in the rooms having to do with food and the creatures, human and animal, that she fed. Besides a large dining table and sideboard wedged into the tiny space, the dining room held a stove with a stovepipe attached to the wall and a floor-model radio. Then came the kitchen, crowded with pots and pans, a table and chairs, a huge refrigerator (wealth!), and a gas stove. The back porch was where Auntie and More-Pop lived: he in his rocker, invariably wearing high-topped leather house slippers, and Auntie in her rocker, surrounded by tatting, knitting, crocheting, and sewing supplies. The room was so quiet, you could hear the chiming Seth Thomas clock in the dining room ticking. Every hour, it went "dong, dong, dong, dong — dong, dong, dong, *dong*," followed by the number of hours.

We found Auntie to be as sugary as the confections, pastries, and breads she created. She worked in the hot kitchen every day, turning out the lightest and most delicious pies, cakes, and doughnuts. She canned and preserved as though still feeding a crew of farm hands. She never minded the company of children. Just as butter and sugar were laid on in her cooking with a generous hand, she never called us simply "dear" or "honey," but always "Honey-dear" or "Honey-doll."

More-Pop said very little and left the house most days, only to return to his porch rocker, the one thing that was all his in Auntie's kingdom. He did some kind of work at the fairgrounds. We knew he had been to college in engineering and that "Sister Kennedy," his only sibling, a teacher, was also a college graduate.

We children left More-Pop pretty much alone. Like the dogs and cats, we attached ourselves to Auntie — the little Pekes would growl at More-Pop if he came near her, and the cats cuddled in her lap, enjoying the voluminous pillowy softness. We found that lap comfy, too: Auntie would scratch your back for hours, and she let you train the electric fan right on you — she didn't believe, like Mom, that ice water and moving air were bad for you.

She seemed to have missed the Beamer stoicism that maintained discomfort was "all in the mind" and that pleasure should not come easily. All but sexual pleasure it seemed. She once told us that no one, least of all More-Pop, had ever seen her in less than her girdle. We had observed this formidable garment, made up of stiff stays, long as barrel staves, held together by thick cotton and rubber and endless laces and eyes. It could stand on the floor all by itself.

Auntie had never absorbed the maxim "Cleanliness is next to godliness," subscribed to firmly by Mom, Melissa, and the rest of the Germanic aunts and cousins. While she was a superb cook, she was not interested in housecleaning. A child getting up at night to go to the bathroom had to step gingerly around the black water bugs that populated the kitchen in the dark.

Auntie never let her bulk slow her down. She was constantly in motion. On the days she didn't bake, she would build herself a new set of kitchen shelves or make her own noodles—she would roll out huge paper-thin sheets of dough on the dining table; cut them into strips the length of the table with a noodle-cutter, a sharp wheel on a handle; and then hang the strips on a clothesline to dry. Everything she created was perfect: each pie rich as sin and light as air, the crusts punctured with fancy curly-cues and perfectly fluted at the edges; doughnuts lifted lovingly from boiling-hot fat to rest on a paper towel only until cool enough to eat.

Her Sunday dinners were prodigious. Up at six, she drove to the icehouse for dry ice. Since we were around to help, she might let Mom or me pack the ice cream freezer with the ice while she stirred up a mixture of cream, sugar, and peaches picked from her backyard tree. She packed the freezer with salt and deputized me and Jim to take turns cranking it. While we lazily worked in the yard, Auntie would emerge from the house with an axe held high in her hand and a determined expression on her face. She eyed the chickens in the wire pen appraisingly, went in after a few, and dragged the unhappy squawking fowls to a stained wood block beside the fish pond. There was a struggle, but Auntie always won. She held them down and gave them a purposeful whack: the severed heads were soon lying on the ground with their eyes half open, sleepy-looking, surprised; they clucked faintly. The headless bodies flopped wildly in Auntie's hands and even stirred in the pail of boiling water into which she plunged them to loosen the feathers.

I watched, fascinated, while Jim ran around the yard holding a chicken head high, pulling the tendons that dangled from the neck to make the mouth gape like a puppet's.

"Come on, Honey-dear," Auntie would say to me, and I'd follow her back into the kitchen where she dipped the chickens into another vat of hot water and scooped out the purple, yellow, and red guts. The chickens were washed, cut up into parts, dipped into batter, and finally gently lowered into a skillet of hot grease. While the chicken cooked, Auntie would turn her attention to the pie or cake to go with the ice cream.

"Give that bag a turn," she would tell her acolyte, me, and I would twist a dripping bag of curds tied to a drawer. The run-off sourish milk went into the chicken feed; the stuff left in the bag was *smearkase*, or cottage cheese.

Vegetables, bread were easy. Mom and I could help chop carrots or de-string the string beans and make salads. Loaves of bread dough had been set out the night before in pans covered with white cloths; they had been slowly rising since we went to bed and now swelled like pregnant stomachs. Auntie pulled off the cloths and popped them into the oven. All the while she worked, she drank cold coffee from breakfast and sang "Take Me Out to the Ball Game" in an inimitable style: "Ta-yke me out to the ball game / ta-yke me out with the crowd. Bee-eye me some peanuts and cr-*rack*-er jacks / Eye—ee don't care if I *niver* get back. . . !"

Everything was ready by twelve noon, and More-Pop and any and all relatives who happened to be in town were invited to a dining table set with Auntie's prize set of Haviland china. Every dish, cup, serving bowl, and saucer was covered with pink and white roses. Delicate crystal glasses held ice water or iced tea. After the dessert, More-Pop would rise from the table, lay his napkin down neatly, and say, "Thank you, Mother."

When Auntie canned, the small kitchen became a factory: bushel baskets of green beans, lima beans, apples, cherries, peaches, cucumbers, corn, tomatoes—everything that could be preserved—lined the kitchen, waiting to be cut up and boiled, made into jelly or succotash, pickles or chow-chow. Vats of food and hot wax to seal the containers bubbled on the stove while Auntie lifted steaming mason jars from another large boiling kettle and set them out in rows. Boxes of rubber rings and caps were lined up and ready to go. The room grew hotter and hotter. Big dark stains wet Auntie's underarms. Her hair frizzed up in the humidity. She worked as though these store-bought bushels of produce were from her own fields and had to be laid in for a long winter—when they would just be added to the hundreds of jars of pickled beets and tomato relish already crowding the shelves in her cold cellar. This dank place beneath the house even contained preserved chickens and eggs stored in a liquid called "water glass." It was eerie: an occasional jar swelled and broke like blasted corn, and the pink fleshy chickens floating in juice looked like fetuses.

Maybe Auntie was the only one of Melissa and George's children who remembered the farm life of their forbears—she was a goddess of plenty, surrounded by fruits and vegetables flowing from cornucopias. Everything she touched flourished: her sunflowers, nodding in the backyard, were tall as men; her red, magenta, and yellow hollyhocks marched along the fence, growing in numbers throughout the summer.

Cooking in her kitchen, Auntie wore a faded cotton dress, an apron, run-over black Edna Jennick shoes, and brown cotton stockings. But when she finished her chores—and she was always finished in record time whether working in the kitchen or at her ironing board or sewing machine—she got dressed up and took off in her black Buick to visit country friends. Then she wore a black silk dress with a white lace collar, her ample bosom bedecked with a set of diamond pins; she wore more diamonds on her ears, and a large black straw hat like Scarlet O'Hara's. She sailed out of the little house, looking every inch a lady of means.

WE COOMERS were the poor relations. Mom tried to be helpful around the house, and Daddy made himself scarce. He had a traveling job, selling pants pressers, a near useless gadget made of two flat pieces of metal that you ran down the knife pleats in trousers to sharpen them. Even Daddy didn't believe they had much potential, but he took to the road and loyally tried to send money to us at Auntie's. Though Auntie made us welcome, More-Pop remained dour, and we felt as though we were on probation in his house.

I loved Auntie, but I was constantly afraid of something going wrong. Jim was always leaving the back gate open or taking the funny papers out of More-Pop's *Courier Journal* and getting the pages mixed up. Mother worried and fretted over these crimes.

So when Jim, who had somehow acquired a golf club and ball, set up a tee across the street from Auntie's front room, I had the terrible feeling of something dreadful about to happen. I'd seen people in movies swing such clubs and send the ball sailing high into the air. I glanced across the street from my position near Jim. I could see through the window: More-Pop was sitting in the big red plush chair. I tried to grab the club from my brother.

Whack! I saw the ball go sailing high over West Main Street toward the window and More-Pop's head. Smack! The window glass shattered and fell to the ground in a shower of lethal spikes, along with my hopes of staying with Auntie.

13

THE LANGUAGE BARRIER

WHEN THE glass of Auntie's front window fell to the front lawn, Jim and I didn't know whether to run toward the house or away from it. We stayed frozen in place. Mom rushed out of the house, yelling, followed by Auntie, looking stern.

"Whatever possessed you to do that?" Mom demanded.

Jim looked sheepish. He couldn't deny anything with the golf club in his hand. Mom grabbed him by the shirt and marched him across the street.

"You'll apologize and pay for the window." Something like that would, of course, take him about twenty years.

More-Pop was looking through the window at the damage with a puzzled expression.

"I'm so sorry," Mom told him. She was close to crying.

More-Pop glared at Jim, his deep-set eyes stern. Jim smiled his sheepish smile. The world went into slow motion.

"I didn't mean to—" Jim began.

Mom wrung her hands.

"What were you thinking?"

"Now Little Bit," More-Pop said. "Don't get all upset."

He looked Jim over as one might a dog that has dug up the lawn.

"Boys will be boys," he said. "I guess."

AUNTIE AND More-Pop stayed mostly to themselves on West Main Street. More-Pop probably knew no one. Auntie occasionally chatted with the people on either side of her house. The couple to the right were enormous people who made Auntie look tiny. They were big and loosely covered with fat, like two polar bears. Their combined bulk—for some reason they were sharing the outhouse that still stood on their lot—broke the wooden seats of the privy, and they went crashing into the muck. A fire truck and ladder came to dig them out, a scene we children thought hilarious.

The Goodins on the left were always on the verge of disaster: Mrs. Goodin had a raft of sons, daughters, and daughters-in-law who came and went, eating up the groceries and leaving poor Mrs. Goodin, a passive, mildly complaining sort who spent her time rocking on the front porch, to mull over their troubles. Her son Red pushed his wife down the steps when he found out she was pregnant (by him); the other son was in jail. I spent some time with Red's wife, who taught me to paint my fingernails with "Chinese Black" polish and make flirtatious eye contact with men in the street.

We children went to school, this time J. B. Atkinson Elementary, where I finished fourth grade and Jim fifth. We entered according to the usual procedures: Jim was given a ritual beating by the local bullies, I established myself at the head of my class and attached myself to yet another "best friend." I always picked the most outstanding and prettiest girl in the class and clung to her. I was always the lover, never the beloved. There was Jean, Michaela, Mary, Betty, and now Laverda.

The kids at J. B. Atkinson were still fighting the Civil War, and we were staunch Unionists. Our greatest hero was Abraham Lincoln. These children were used to segregated schools. Whether *de facto* or by policy, they had never attended classes with black kids and were furious when we argued that our "Negro" friend Arthur from Omaha, who played the violin, was every bit as smart as they were.

We had difficulty understanding their speech. "Grass" and "out" each had at least two syllables. I could not understand the teacher when she asked me to "spay-ill pah." I had to ask her to repeat herself several times until I understood her request, and then probably annoyed her with the precise diction and long *i* of my retort: "Oh, you mean 'spell pie.'" The kids made fun of our Nebraskan accents. We said "eye-ee," while they said "ah." Our bookish vocabularies always made a hit. When I would say something was "simply beyond my comprehension," a fellow student would marvel, and not in envy: "You musta swallered a dictionary!"

The language barrier notwithstanding, we entered the world of the neighborhood kids, which was more or less like that in Omaha. Children then had a long-established culture of their own—based on street games and superstitions—which I think may be all but dead. Everyone knew red rover and statues. I still try to avoid stepping on sidewalk cracks and gas meters: "Step on a crack, break your mother's back."

In summer, we had endurance contests to see who could walk longest on the street tar that all but bubbled in the sun. When we were all raw-footed, we begged some mother (all the houses had mothers) for ice cubes. We went to the movies as we always did when there was someone to cadge a dime from (now it was Auntie). A whole bunch of us would walk the few blocks to a theater in an old warehouse, stopping at the corner of West Main to buy an ice ball from a man with a cart bearing tall mounds of ice: grape, lime, and lemon, yellow as doggie pee in the snow. We started a club and sent ourselves threatening notes from The Black Hand.

We didn't really miss our father. I suppose we were used to his comings and goings, and we were relieved at the absence of tension. We assumed that without him to upset her, Mom would always be her best self—the one that cheered us up and thought up things for us to do and shared her reading with us. We wanted her to be more like the other mothers, not sexy and pretty the way Daddy seemed to like her. I even fantasized having parents like Uncle Ought and Aunt Maude at Manawa, or even Auntie and More-Pop: quiet and sexless, able to sit together in peace. (If there had been battles between Auntie and More-Pop, she had long since won.)

When Daddy was at Auntie's, the grownups played endless games of cards. Jim and I had played 500 rum with Auntie many nights, and she always won. It took Daddy to point out that she cheated. We were shocked. We were so law-abiding. Jim was always in trouble for some mischievous prank, but never anything against the law. I was terrified of committing even the smallest crime, for fear the entire family would come apart—if not the world. Defacing a library book was about the worst thing I could even think of, and I was careful never to even turn down a page corner to keep my place.

WE FINISHED out the school year at J. B. Atkinson, an academic experience in my case more memorable for my lunch pails than my achievements. With Auntie packing our lunches we had the best spreads in the whole school. I can never forget the sound of the lid being pulled up, wrench, and the smell of food confined all morning in tin: sandwiches, fruit, cookies, cheese, celery and carrots, pickles, and slabs of Auntie's special fudge. It was creamy and full of black walnuts; we ate pieces the size of small coal chunks.

It's a wonder we didn't grow fat like Auntie. Only Mom seemed to be gaining weight. She was wearing her blouse outside her skirt instead of tucked in.

I found out why one day when I came home from school and overheard her crying. She and Auntie were in the bedroom where Mom and Daddy slept. I peeked in and saw Mom sitting on the bed in a bathrobe and Auntie patting her on the back and crooning, "Now Petty, everything happens for the best."

Mom was crying hard, and I went into the room and threw myself at her feet, bursting into tears myself. "What's wrong? What's wrong?"

It took Mom a while to pull herself together, and Auntie said "Shhh," and shook her head at me, warning me off. But I wouldn't go away. Mom was the earth I clung to on the spinning planet that we lived on.

She patted me on the head.

"Don't worry," she said.

"But why are you crying?"

Mom sighed. "Do you know what a miscarriage is?"

I nodded yes. I was pretty sure I did know. It was being pregnant when you didn't want to be. Something like a miscarriage of justice.

"Are you going to have a baby?" I said.

Mom looked startled at my question. I obviously knew less than she thought I did. She drew herself together to explain.

"It's when you are pregnant and—lose the baby."

A terrible picture formed in my brain.

Where was this baby?

Mom must have seen my alarm.

"It wasn't far enough along to be a baby, just sort of a bit of blood."

Auntie was gazing out the window, embarrassed to death.

"What did you do with it?" I said.

Mom paused and sighed. "Flushed. The bathroom," she said. She started crying again.

"Let her alone now," Auntie said. "You run on out to the kitchen and get a piece of cake." I was almost relieved to be dismissed. I bypassed the kitchen and ran to the comfort of the porch. More-Pop was sitting in his chair. I sat opposite him in Auntie's rocker. We stared at each other, neither saying a word. The birds fluttered their wings. The parrot squawked. One of Auntie's clocks chimed: dong dong dong dong—dong dong dong *dong*: dong! dong! dong!

I resolved never to feel.

14

===

YOUR MOTHER'S
RELATIONS

WE FOLLOWED the Ohio River all the way on old Highway 42, through Carrollton and Warsaw, Kentucky. Auntie drove us in her black Buick.

When Mom caught sight of the hills of Cincinnati, and we crossed the suspension bridge, she breathed "my *home*." I felt a little jealous. Didn't we have a home? I supposed we didn't—nor could we ever replace the family she talked about so constantly.

To us children, Cincinnati was a shock. It was so *old*, so dirty. Omaha had been new and clean, and it took us a long time to appreciate the beauties of hundred-year-old brick and stone.

"They tore down the incline!" Mom pointed to the western hills with dismay, then cheered up to see that the Mt. Adams incline was still going —two bright yellow streetcars were passing each other on the steep hillside leading to Eden Park.

"The hills—it's so *green*," Mom said.

She was right. Cincinnati was hilly and had an awful lot of trees.

Meeting the relatives was like having Mom's photo album come to life: there was Pop Beamer with his ear-to-ear smile; Mom's stepmother, Lulu Neiderhelman Beamer, a rather gray, droopy woman. The great aunts and uncles, who had lived at Windsor Street and helped raise Mom, looked just like their pictures. We met Uncle Morris (Bud) and Aunt Marie, he with a black mustache, white hair, and a cocky gleam in his eye. Marie, the woman who had introduced our parents, had gotten fatter, and immediately established the fact that she wasn't "well"—nerves and Saint Vitus's dance.

One after another the relatives invited us to their homes for dinner. They all lived within a sort of Beamer compound on Bevis, Hewitt, and Wabash Avenues in the suburb of Walnut Hills. Uncle Bud and Marie had a very pleasant house on the corner of Hewitt and Wabash with what seemed at the time a large wrap-around porch. Trees and awnings kept it shady. Uncle Bud worked at the Milling Machine and "made good money." Aunt Marie owned a fur coat and had her hair done regularly. Uncle Bud served fancy cocktails before dinner, and Jim and I were fascinated by the "girlie" magazines that he kept in the rack in the living room.

Next door Aunt Ethel presided over a small white stucco bungalow and a mild-mannered husband, Uncle Fred, who matched the house: he had white hair, white skin, and the personality of a big, sweet rabbit. Everything was perfect in Aunt Ethel's house, from her delicate crystal, lace tablecloth, and heavy draperies to her small lawn and flower garden. As we got to know her, we found that she, along with Ninnie Esther, who lived in Memphis, regularly predicted the end of the world from charts and diagrams provided by the Jehovah's Witnesses. This apocalyptic obsession did not, however, prevent Aunt Ethel from going about her business as a housewife, keeping the overfurnished rooms spotless and everything under control. She faithfully read the *Watchtower* and *Photoplay*, a movie magazine.

Uncle Lester, who lived just down the street, was between wives when we arrived in Cincinnati. The Jehovah's Witnesses were not strict enough for him, and he had thrown his lot with Judge Rutherford and the God's Bible Students, creating a small schism in the family.

Later on, we lived with Uncle Lester for a while: Mom kept house for him in exchange for room and board after one of his wives left. Lester was a small man who looked like a solemn monkey; his smile was as tight and begrudging as Pop Beamer's was open and sunny. He was one of the reasons Daddy resignedly referred to the whole Beamer clan as "Your mother's *relations*."

Lester was so parsimonious he would boil a whole box of Quaker oats at once and cut slices off cold to save on the gas bill. He worked hard hauling building supplies in his truck, then would come home every day at the same time, take his shoes off in the basement steps, sigh "Work, work, work," eat dinner, and retreat to his chair by the front window. There, beneath a large portrait of Judge Rutherford, he would read religious pamphlets or the Bible and drink Pepsi-Cola laced with water.

We met Ray, Mom's middle stepbrother, whom we knew from a photo of him leaning rakishly against a roadster with a rumble seat; blond, blue-eyed, active, he was handsome and mischievous. Mary was the hefty girl we had seen standing on the very steps of the Bevis Avenue house (a victim of "glands"). Freddie, the baby of the family, was dark-haired and smiley. Helen, the older sister, had married and was on her own; she and her husband Lawrence seemed bland—nice but distant. Elmer, Mom's one-time "best friend," was the bright one, working as a CPA. Ray worked at a garage, and the women worked at drug stores. Elmer and his wife Esther were the only Beamers with college educations. Esther was writing a book; the pages were all laid out on a card table in their dining room, and we all tiptoed around this mysterious project in awe of her brilliance (it was about secretarial work).

People in Cincinnati said "Please?" when they wanted you to repeat something and "anymore" to mean "now." All but Elmer and Esther. Lulu called pretzels "bretzels" (the German way). Pop explained that we were in the city of the three B's: baseball, beer, and bretzels.

In honor of our visit to Cincinnati, we were taken to the zoo, to the "flower house" (Krohn Conservatory) in Eden Park, and to Coney Island on the *Island Queen*. We had never been treated to such hospitality, and we said to Mom, "Everyone's so *nice*." We thought Cincinnati was always a constant round of parties, but Mom explained that life here was not always quite so exciting—we were simply being welcomed back to the family, a one-time event.

AFTER JIM and I finished our year at J. B. Atkinson in Louisville, our family foursome moved to Cincinnati to live with Mom and Pop Beamer. As usual, we children were given no reason and we just went along like good soldiers.

The house on Bevis was bulging: Mary, Ray, and Freddie all lived at home. But Pop and Mom fit us in. There were just three rooms on the ground floor of their house: a small living room, dining room, and kitchen. Upstairs were three bedrooms: one for Pop and Mom, one that Mary and I shared, and one for our parents. The two uncles and Jim were relegated to the attic.

Jim and I were enrolled in a small school a few blocks away called Horace Mann. Fifth and sixth grades were in one room, so Jim and I had the same teacher. He and I were a debate team on the topic of whether radio programs should have commercial sponsors. We won, taking the affirmative. Jim got in his usual amount of trouble by passing off as balloons a bunch of condoms he found in the street.

Horace Mann was on the border line between a white and a black community and had more black students than we'd ever before encountered.

I was given the job of drawing a chalk mural of Mount Vernon on the blackboard. Standing on a chair, I debated with myself whether to make the slaves the same color as Martha and George Washington. Would there be hurt feelings? Should I as an artist always stick with the best I could accomplish in terms of verisimilitude? I went with the artist's obligation, filling in the Washingtons' faces with chalk and leaving the board color showing through in the slaves' faces. After school, walking down a dirt hill to the sidewalk, I was suddenly pushed to the ground. Standing over me was a tall black girl named Mary. She didn't like the fact that I'd made the blacks look different from everyone else. I apologized, confused.

At Bevis Avenue I went from being the adored, indulged darling of my Auntie to being a nuisance to my grandmother (who can blame her for being impatient, with all those people descending on her?). Lulu was as spiritless as Auntie was full of spunk. While Auntie never rested, Lulu was tired by eleven in the morning after a two-block walk to the grocery store, at which time she and her black cocker spaniel Patsy would sit in the kitchen and have a slice of coffee cake. Everything about Lulu drooped: her hems, her lower lip, her hair. Mom said, "She's a good old soul," implying she was not much on brains.

We were her prisoners, again the poor relations, and while Lulu could be nice on occasion, she did like to carp. All one summer I wore sunglasses (the better to shut out reality), and Lulu complained I would ruin my eyes. My constant reading was sure to drive me crazy by over-taxing my brain. I was too thin and ate like a bird.

I did eat like a bird. The Beamers loved sauerkraut, huge sausages, blood pudding, rutabaga, cabbage, everything redolent of the pot, any-thing that sent gas charging through the pipes. Lulu served endless skil-letsful of *goetta*, a German dish of meat scraps and oats; I hated even the name. She tossed sugar into everything—coleslaw, potatoes, gravy—and, while it was not an official ingredient in her recipes, Patsy's black curly hair appeared in most every dish. I learned to eat cautiously. If the offend-ing strand was not in the goetta, it was in the gravy, or it might turn up in the butter. I was not only a "picky eater," but soon declared "nervous."

Lulu baked cakes that weighed three pounds. She would cover these monstrosities with chocolate icing and decorate them with little silver-colored sugar bee-bees that could break your teeth. I didn't even like the special-occasion dishes like *sauerbrauten* and *hasenpheffer*—a dish made of hare, which too strongly suggested Patsy's participation.

The radio at Pop's was always tuned to baseball. The players names resounded through the small rooms in the relentless voice of Red Barber: "Ernie Lombardi, Bucky Walters." No one had to ask who was the sub-ject of the question "What are they doing?"—a frequent question at the Beamers' house. It asked whether the Cincinnati Reds were winning or losing. Conversations between Pop and Mom and their generation con-sisted mostly of homilies like "You can't eat just one potato chip" and "It's not the heat, it's the humidity." Polite conversation might consist of "Hot enough for you?" and "Think it'll rain?"

Mom Beamer's life scared me. Was it the five kids that wore her out? Or having lived the traditional routine for women: Monday, washing; Tuesday, ironing; Wednesday, mending; Thursday, baking; Friday, can-ning; Saturday, cleaning; Sunday, sermon. Lulu didn't go at her chores as Auntie did. They were joyless. Once I helped her wash the beige lace curtains that covered the dining and living room windows and smelled of dust. In the dark basement, we ran them through the rollers of the washing machine, always fearing an arm caught and mangled (everyone knew someone to whom this had happened), and then stretched them on window-sized frames covered with nails, crucifying them stiff as lace valentines.

Mary and Freddie and Ray encouraged us kids to climb in their laps and investigate their double chins or their Adam's apples, or to sit in the front porch swing and play "Scissors Paper and Rock," or fall for their magic tricks, or tag along when they walked to the corner drugstore for a coke. Mother was always pulling us away from them. We must not bother anyone. We must be quiet and especially must be polite. We were popped into bed promptly at eight o'clock every night, much earlier than other children our age. We felt that if she could put us in a basket and push it under the bed she would do so. We were kind of embarrassing, dependents whose father was off somewhere, sending only sporadic payments for our room and board.

Mom tried to bring in some money by ironing at people's houses. I admired her willingness to work, but was embarrassed, for some of her clients were my friends' mothers. Mom would come home exhausted and give me a lecture on my need to attend college. Was she drudging just for me? What about Jim, and herself?

We became more and more attached to Ray and Freddie and Mary. Ray took us for rides in the rumble-seat of his car. Freddie took us to Mammoth Cave and Cumberland Falls in Kentucky (we didn't know we were standing above the very waters where our father started out in steamboating). Mary began a romance with the clerk at the corner drug store, and I was seized by giggle-fits when they took me for a ride in his car.

I had a crush on Ray, and would beg him to "swing me around"— hold me by my arms and whirl me in circles. I helped him wash his car, he in his undershirt and tight jeans, me in shorts that showed my still-spindly legs. I daydreamed of us getting married. Me sitting in the living room in a halter top like the woman across the street he always whistled at, and Ray admiring my large breasts (the reality was less than a bee sting). The family, seated around us as spectators, marveled at how desirable I was.

WHEN DADDY made his occasional stops at the Beamers, he arrived in a used Chevy with a decal of President Roosevelt on the back window. To the Beamers, being a Democrat was like devil worship: ornery as ever, Daddy proudly announced that he had bought the car solely for the president's picture. This was our Pop.

But as time passed and we saw less of him, he began to seem like a stranger. He was so stiff and formal compared to Freddie and Ray. We weren't sure whether to obey him or not. On one visit, he reached out to hug me, but I felt so confused, I pulled away. Finally, I was ordered—by Daddy or Mother or someone—to sit on my father's lap. I sat there tensely, answering his questions as quickly as possible so I could get loose.

"How's school?"

"Fine."

"Are you drawing much?"

"Pretty much."

I squirmed, could not look at him.

"Well, talk, Duchess—what do you know?"

"Nothing."

He loosened his grip on my arms.

"Well, hell, go play then."

I jumped down, so grateful to be free. Now I felt like a rat.

"We did go to the zoo," I volunteered. "On zoo day. We had fun."

"O.K." Hurt, no further response.

"Well, I've gotta go wash my hands for supper."

"All right."

"See you later."

ONE DAY the Bevis Avenue house was empty when Jim and I came home from school for lunch. On the kitchen table was one of Lulu's monstrous cakes, all covered with silver bullets and waiting for dinner. For Jim and me there were two glasses of milk and a plate of sandwiches —a few scraps of leftover ham on white bread. They were the last bites of a huge joint that had been appearing on the table for a good week. Lulu had griped at us for not cleaning up the meat leavings like good beggars.

I suddenly put my fist right through the middle of the cake. Like Jim when he shot the golf ball at More-Pop's head, I didn't know what to do next. What I had done was unforgivable. What would be my punishment?

Jim helped me pat the cake back into shape.

I sat through dinner sweating with anxiety. Surely someone would notice the lurch of the cake, the smudged icing and sagging center. But everybody gobbled it down, not noticing a thing, just as they never noticed Patsy's black strands in the goetta.

15

DADDY'S PEOPLE

WE WERE going to Burnside. Just Mom and Jim and me. Daddy's sister Edna had invited us to spend a week with her. Jim and I had a lot of fun deciding how we should act. We pictured Daddy's hometown as being something like Dogpatch in the "Lil' Abner" comic strip we read every day. There was Lil' Abner himself, a handsome, earnest, not-too bright mountain boy, and Daisy Mae, his ultra-sexy girl friend who wore a polka-dot off-the-shoulder blouse and a mini-mini skirt. Pappy and Mammy Yokum, Lil' Abner's parents, were tiny wizened people, and Mammy smoked a pipe. On the annual "Sadie Hawkins Day" the girls got to chase the boys to win husbands, and for years we had been following Daisy Mae's attempts to catch Lil' Abner. He preferred a tougher "gal" because she could compete with him in "bar' knuckle wrasslin'."

We practiced our accents and corn-pone ways. Daddy had given us material to go on, with his "cain't" for "can't" and "far" for "fire." He sometimes referred to mother as "your Mammy." Though in a light tone, he stressed the toughness and primitiveness of his birthplace. He often claimed that Burnside women didn't go off to hospitals to have babies; they had them right in the fields where they worked, then went on hoeing.

When Mother caught wind of our nonsense, she advised us to just be ourselves and be polite and try to learn what we could from the experience. She never prejudged people and respected everyone's ways (except Daddy's). We settled down, and the Greyhound took us about a hundred and eighty miles south of Cincinnati and even further from the Beamers.

We had never seen such tall mountains as the ones we came upon as we neared Burnside—the Cumberlands. Omaha, Council Bluffs, and Louisville were flat by comparison, and Cincinnati's soft hills were nothing like these. We approached the town via a bridge over the Cumberland River, built into the rock. There were only a few small buildings on the highway through town: the bus station, the barber shop, Matty's grocery store, and Singleton's. Burnside seemed dusty and neglected, a contrast to the neat, controlled neighborhood where the Beamers lived.

The relatives who met us at the bus station were all smiles: Edna, her husband Joe Fitzgerald, and their two children. Edna was tall for a woman (to us, anyway, with our four-foot-eleven mother). Joe, who worked on the railroad, was solidly built, with an open, ruddy face. Joanne was a quiet little blond about five years old, and Jim Ed (Jim and I nudged each other) looked like a typical little country boy in denim overalls; he had black curly hair, clear blue eyes like marbles, and a ready-for-anything expression.

The Fitzgeralds seemed genuinely glad to see us. We were startled to hear Daddy referred to as Harv, because Mother always called him by his first name. We had dinner at the Fitzgeralds' small house on a hillside. Just beyond the kitchen door was a large garden bulging with cabbages, tomato plants, corn, and beans propped on poles. A wooden outhouse stood by the back fence.

Over the next few days we made the rounds of the town. Every excursion beyond Edna and Joe's involved walking up and down a steep path. I had an infected boil on my knee, and walking hurt. The whole town seemed to know about my problem. As we passed houses of neighbors, people would call out, "How's your bawl?" along with "C'mon and set a spell."

Mother returned the town's friendliness. She listened to the stories of the people she met and asked about their ways, and, like all those who ever met her, they seemed to appreciate her interest.

Daddy's eldest sister, Alma, joined in our many walks. She was heavy, deep-voiced, a chain smoker, tough as nails, on her second husband. She asked Mom about the latest fashions. "I'd rather be dead than out of style," she said. I couldn't tell whether she was kidding.

The houses we visited were mostly old, frame, always with a front porch, many needing paint. There was a row of neater houses up on the hillside overlooking the Cumberland River that seemed more prosperous, but we didn't know the people who lived there. We did meet several little old ladies who smoked pipes and one who dipped snuff. She'd rub it on her gums, savor it a bit, then spit into a nearby tomato can.

Matty's store was unlike any we'd ever been in. Everyone knew the proprietor by name; she was part of the community. In Cincinnati, Lulu exchanged "good mornings" with the butcher at the corner grocery, but never personal gossip as the customers did at Matty's. Singleton's General Store was another revelation. The range of stuff for sale! Everything from farm equipment and feed to candy sticks and bubble gum.

We saw the house our Dad was born in: an ancient frame that had once been the headquarters of General Burnside, the union commander who occupied the town during the Civil War. It had a doubly interesting past.

We hiked up in the mountains to visit a relative whom Edna and the others often took care of: the Fitzgeralds watched the children, sat with the woman of the family through sicknesses, provided food. The cabin was isolated and rundown. Several under-nourished children and lanky dogs loitered in the yard. A lizard crawled over one of the children, and he hardly seemed to notice. The mother was thin and stringy and the cabin smelled of sourish corn and smoke from the stove. A man in a back room was counting the hundreds of cigar bands he had collected. While the adults talked on the porch, Jim and I sat off to ourselves and wished ourselves back at Edna's or almost any place.

The kids in Burnside were O.K., if somewhat strange, we decided. Like Jim Ed, the boys all had double names, a tradition we found hilarious. Their talk sounded quaint to our book-trained ears: Jim Ed's best friend, Billy Bob, accused of some crime or other said, "I didn't done it!" "What went with my slingshot?" asked where it was. All the boys wanted to take Jim on—I was glad I was a girl so I could avoid the fisticuffs.

I did follow along when Jim Ed's little gang engaged in the sport of tormenting pigs. We climbed onto the pig pen fence near a tree—for support and escape—and jumped up and down to enrage the hogs. They came grunting and snorting violently toward us—and slammed into the fence hard, almost knocking us off and into the pen. These man-eating monsters were not my idea of pigs. I hung on tight to the tree as the hogs rushed us. I was terrified, and I jumped down after the first few onslaughts.

We went to a number of houses for noon dinners and suppers: fried green tomatoes, cornbread, chicken and mashed potatoes, and always biscuits and sweetened iced tea. The women stood during meals and served the men and the guests. They seemed very different from the Beamer women. The Cincinnati aunts might pretend to take second place to their husbands, but they ran the show. "Any old day, I'd let a man tell me what to do," was one of Auntie's frequent boasts.

The Burnside folk were friendly but not jolly like the Germans. They were gentler in many ways. Their sympathies were completely with, instead of against, the sick; every family had its own invalid, like the man with the cigar bands, and was tolerant of him or her. To the Beamers, poor health was a sign of moral weakness. Mom, Auntie, and the others never believed Aunt Marie was anything but a lazy malingerer. The Burnside people were clean, but not fanatical like the Cincinnatians; they did not try to scrub away their connection to the earth.

When an electric line went down in a storm, they did not race to get it repaired as the Germans would have done. They talked about it, marveled at the mayhem it caused. Talked it over.

Where the Cincinnati Dutch traded homilies and bromides, the Kentuckians told stories and laughed at even the most painful things. They liked being seen as "wild Kentucks" and bragged of the number of shootings in the county.

Which group did Jim and I belong to? Neither, it seemed.

AT ONE OF the homes we were invited to, we stayed past dark. My mother, my aunts, little Joanne, my brother, and I walked down a bumpy old dirt lane together. The trees blocked the moon from time to time and we picked our way carefully over the rocky ground. Head-high weeds along the way allowed only an occasional glimpse of the mountains beyond our path. We heard a faint rustling, stones being dislodged by some approaching person or thing. We all cowered together, imagining robbers or bad men, even Civil War ghosts. We were so close to whatever was there we could feel the vibrations of the tall weeds from its passage and hear its breath. Then we heard a faint bell, and then we were staring into the wide brown eyes of a nice friendly old cow. Laughing together with the other humans in this remote mountain place, I felt, for just a moment, a part of Daddy's old world.

That night we sat around Edna's kitchen table, looking at her photographs and mementos. There was a large tinted photograph of Daddy and Edna's mother, our grandmother, a handsome woman wearing a blue dress. She had died just a few years previous. Daddy had never mentioned her death. Or her. There was also a black-and-white photo of her in a long dress: she was slim and erect and strong looking.

And there was our grandfather, long dead, killed by a stranger with no real grudge against him. His feet were wide apart and his hands on his hips in a determined pose. He wore a black hat at a cocky angle, a black vested suit, and the silver badge of a U.S. marshal. Edna had been just four years old when he died. From a box wrapped in wax paper, she drew the collar he was wearing the day he was shot. The bloodstain was rusty brown. I touched it with my finger—blood shed almost forty years before, long before I was born.

Edna spoke of her other brothers, Stafford and Joe. We had never met them. After their steamboat days, Daddy and his brothers never wrote one another, called, or visited (only much later did I discover that Joe lived near Cincinnati in Evansville, Indiana). All we knew of the eldest, Stafford, was that he had once met Daddy accidentally on the street in St. Louis and said, "Your shoes need shining." That was all.

With the cicadas making our ears ring and the rustling of corn stalks coming through Edna's back door, I felt a kind of poetry in this place: the nearness of animals, the mountains and the river, the fir trees high on the ridges. I always afterward wished I had known more of my father's birthplace. But life took us into other worlds.

Daddy never went back to Burnside until he had a good suit, a diamond ring, and plenty of money.

16

—

MORE RIVER DAYƑ

Down by the O-hi-o
I got the sweetest little Oh-my-oh!

THE CALLIOPE shrilled out the tune. The big boat huffed and puffed, working up steam. She looked beautiful, all five decks of her, her big side wheel churning up the water by the wharf. We ran down the cobbled landing, late as usual—Jim and I, Mom and our aunt Mary. Daddy was watching for us on the lower deck, back in uniform. He had his old job again as mate on the *Island Queen*. We ducked under the rope he held up for us to sneak under.

We got a whiff of elegance from the officers' quarters, imagining the white tablecloths and good food that the finely turned-out mate, captain, and pilots enjoyed. We felt special, being allowed to ignore the "Keep Out" signs and run up to the pilot house where Captain Harry Doss, the pilot, welcomed us. Captain Doss was tall and lean and always had a half-chewed cigar in his mouth, gummed until it resembled a brown grape leaf. The tobacco juice went flying into a brass spittoon on the floor nearby. With the big wooden wheel of the *Queen* behind him, the monkey that was his mascot swinging at the window, he talked to us about his invalid wife, occasionally stopping to hurl a curse at the calliope playing right beneath his window. He especially liked Mother—as all men did—and by the time I reached high school age and began to fill out, he enthusiastically claimed a kiss from me.

Everything on the boat was brass and polish, trim and white, neat and well-designed. I've heard steamboat buffs say the *Island Queen* was not a beautiful boat; true, she was rounded off in the bow and did not have the classic steamboat proportions, but she was big and impressive, and the whole city loved her. Everyone loved to hear the calliope and the low, deep groan of her whistle. We children ran from deck to deck: from the humid boiler room where she made steam and the giant pitmans turned, to the open sunny top deck. At the stern, on the lowest level, we watched the canoers who followed in her wake: the waves were deep and moving fast and could easily pull a canoe under. The *Queen* smelled of hotdogs, beer, and popcorn. She was our good-time girl, the one we suspected the *Valley Queen* of being on those summer nights we weren't allowed to board her.

Leaving Cincinnati and going to Coney Island upriver, we got to know the Ohio. We'd leave the old cobbled landing and the wharf boat behind and make the large bend just beyond town, passing St. Rose's church, a beautiful pink brick building right on the water with a huge clock on her steeple that told the river men the time. A tall gauge painted on the wall facing the water marked the levels of the various floods, with the 1937 mark at the very top. We passed a water-station of the gas and electric company that looked like a miniature castle on the Rhine and a set of permanent concrete icebreakers the shape of pyramids. The waste disposal plant, another landmark, pushed garbage and human waste into the water. But no one worried about it. The river and hills were beautiful, with lush greens and blues and relatively unspoiled banks of feathery willows.

At the river entrance to Coney Island, the crowd pushed through gates beneath a fake lighthouse. The quiet of the shady picnic grove by the water was punctuated by the *pocketa-pocketa* of the roller coaster cars climbing the trestles and the screams of the riders as they dropped down the curves. On the midway, planted with geraniums and bright red cockscomb and thousands of pink begonias, we would hear the organ-grinder melodies of the merry-go-round, the sound of raucous laughter from a huge fat-lady dummy who bent double and boomed out her "ha-ha-ha" every few minutes, and the voices of the game barkers calling: "We got a winner—*right down here!*"

There was a lake for rowing and canoeing, and there was dancing at

Moonlight Gardens, where the biggest bands came to play. Everyone who ever visited Coney would agree that it served the best Creamy Whip cones ever made; they were nothing like the dairy whips of today, but rich, smooth, and really—well, creamy.

Closed down in the winter, Coney was like an abandoned city. Wind was the only noise, whistling through the game pavilion. The laughing lady was doubled over and silent. The Ferris wheel and roller-coaster cars were covered with canvas. Jim, his friend Reedy, and I got there one February day on Reedy's boat, the only customers in the whole park. We picked up a few gray-black baseballs left on the concrete near the pitch-into-a-bottle game like motley fruit fallen from a tree. Then we saw our great adventure: to climb to the top of the Shooting Star, the biggest of the roller coasters. It was easy: we just pulled ourselves up on the slats across the rails. They made a good ladder. What a glorious feeling—to reach the summit and stand looking over the silent park, the river in the distance. It was our own little Everest. Until the loud voice of a security man commanded us to get down and get out of the park at once. We ran to the boat, dropping baseballs out of our pockets as we headed back to the water.

During the time Daddy was on the boat, we moved to a small apartment in Covington, Kentucky. It had a shady side yard with a broken fountain and a wrought-iron fence. We could walk from there to the river—just a few blocks—and sit in the riverside park and go down to the water's edge and skip stones. This was another of those brief moments, like Lake Manawa or the *Valley Queen*, when things seemed to be looking up. Then it was over. Daddy was to be the harbor man at the Cincinnati Yacht Club, a marina in Cincinnati's East End. I sort of liked the sound of it: "Yacht Club"—it had a touch of the glamour and grandeur of my fantasies.

WE DROVE there in a taxi on an early fall day in 1940. Daddy was excited. He talked all the way about the early days on the river as we followed the same route the *Island Queen* took past the city's riverfront. Along the water on Eastern Avenue were dilapidated houses, kids playing on the sidewalks, cars on blocks. Mixed in were wooden houses with gingerbread trim that looked as if they had once been pretty and well built. A little brick church stood on a corner next door to a house with a silver ball on a pedestal, several bird baths, a whole slew of windmills, a herd of pink flamingos, and flower beds in rubber tires. As Eastern turned away from the water, we continued east on Kellogg, still following the river.

We arrived at a large open field and turned down a cinder road to a group of trees and a parking lot many feet above the water. Moored to the bank below was a three-decked old steamboat turned boat club; it was white with blue trim around the windows and rails. Perched on the top deck was a small cabin with a porch. At the boat's bow, facing the city, was a string of empty wooden floats to which, in the summer, scows and runabouts would be tethered in wooden stalls.

Daddy jumped out of the cab and grabbed our suitcases.

"Thanks, cap," he said to the driver, and over-tipped him on our dwindling money.

"Oh Jim," Mom murmured. Her mouth tightened whenever cash changed hands. When she opened her purse, her hands trembled.

"Hell," Daddy said. "Let's go. Don't spoil it now."

He breathed in the air of the place.

"River's in pool," he remarked professionally.

We looked down at the steep blacktop path we were to descend with our luggage.

"Here, I'll just scoot this down. Jim-Boy, get down to the gangplank and catch it!"

Daddy launched a suitcase down the steep embankment. Mom and I shuddered, picturing our clothes floating down the river and sinking into the mud.

"See that thing there that looks like a telephone pole on its side?" Daddy asked. "That's the spar. Holds the boat away from the bank."

We wended our way down to the gangplank, watching our step, Mom's high heels catching in the rough surface. Then it was over the rattly gangplank, a swingy metal-and-wood arrangement that sang and clanked as you walked. The last step was a metal plate; the noise it made was like the clang of a garbage can lid.

We went up a flight of stairs and paused on the open deck to look up and down the river; it was very empty. In every direction were banks of solid green trees with hints of buildings beyond them. We could see a few shanty boats along the shore to the east. A dog barked from their direction, the only sign of life. The water looked cold and forbidding, the air was whipping up, and whitecaps were beginning to appear. We all shuddered, and looked at the long drop to the water: how far down the flat mudbanks seemed. This was the end of the world.

We moved on, through a large storage area, the main part of the second deck, where canoes, old boat equipment, lines, and cables were kept; there were two restrooms, one on each side of a short, narrow stairway. We climbed the steps, lugging our awkward parcels and heavy suitcases. Daddy fumbled with the lock and finally pushed in the door.

My whole world turned gray. The first thing I saw sitting right opposite the door of the dingy little room was a toilet—naked, unmistakable, terrible. There was a bed, which almost filled the rest of the room, and a nicked-up dresser. The room beyond was also small and contained a kitchen table, a sink, and a potbellied stove that was cold as death.

I don't know if either Daddy or Mom had seen these quarters before Daddy accepted this job. But they proceeded to move in as though this were not the most awful place in the world.

Mom immediately dug an old shawl out of her luggage and threw it over the toilet; she placed her one good piece of china, the Bisque boy, on the tank, turning it into a little altar. She inspected the cabinets above the sink, which were dirty and gray and peeling.

"We'll paint those and put some decals on them," she declared.

Daddy fussed over the stove, which the previous occupants had left covered with soot and bits of kindling wood.

We looked out the window at the river. The water was a cold gray as the sun set over Cincinnati, now hidden and far away beyond the Ohio hills.

Mom dug into one of the boxes she had brought along and opened a cabinet. It too was dirty, so she left the half-box of rolled oats, the can of Calumet baking powder that had followed us several places, and the Zesta soda crackers in the cardboard container. The closest store was up on Eastern Avenue, about a mile from the river. Mom found a can of Campbell's tomato soup and announced that we'd have a picnic of soup and crackers and go shopping tomorrow. She heated the soup on the small electric plate that, along with an equally tiny electric oven, would serve for cooking.

The river darkened as we ate our soup and crackers, and for a moment or two the whole world seemed dark. It was nicer now, not seeing the toilet or the grime on the walls. Only the lights from the outside came into the little cabin: moonlight, the lights of a plane heading for Lunken, the searchlight of a passing towboat. The room rocked as the big tows left their wake.

At bedtime, we had to turn on the ceiling lights. And there was that hideous thing in the middle of the bedroom. Mom began to put sheets on the big bed, then she noticed how alive the springs and mattress were.

"Eww, bedbugs!" we screamed.

"We need kerosene," Mom said. Daddy searched the second deck and came up with a can of kerosene, and Mom made a rag torch which she applied to the unlucky vermin daring to attack the bed of a Cincinnati Beamer. Presumably she and Daddy slept on this ill-smelling resting place. We children were handed two army cots and told to set them up. They were stiff, recalcitrant, bony—like old people who can't stand straight. Trying to jab their long joints into canvas was like trying to dress arthritic patients. This chore we accomplished every night for most of the two years we lived at the Cincinnati Yacht Club. The name made it sound so fancy, and it could be—for the members who owned boats for summer rides, but lived in houses in the hills.

The gentle rocking of the boat lulled us to sleep in spite of our dismay and depression. But in the middle of the night we awoke to a horrible cracking sound.

"Oh my God, what's that?" Mom said. We thought the floats had torn loose or that we were about to be swept away in the current.

"Go back to sleep," Daddy said. "It's just the cables stretching."

The creaking kept up all night, and we soon got used to it—just like the creaking and groaning of an old house.

In the morning, Mom prepared to wash everything in sight, but discovered there was no hot water; it had been turned off for the winter. There was no drinking water either, only river water that came up through the pipes for washing floors and windows and decks. The drinking water was on the hill where the taxi had delivered us, about a hundred steps straight up.

"C'mon Jim-Boy," Daddy said. He handed Jim a bucket, found two for himself, and proceeded to climb the hill. The buckets had to be filled at a lonely little spigot springing from a wooden base, carried back down the hill and up the three flights of steps to the cabin, and emptied into a ten-gallon tin can next to the sink. Young Jim complained and protested the whole way, but Daddy pushed him as you would a puppy you were trying to train. Mom, busy measuring the windows for curtains and boiling water, could not bear the carping and yelling.

"Oh I know I abuse the pore child," Daddy shouted.

"Naturally he doesn't want to do that. Those buckets are heavy."

"They're heavy for me, too."

"If you'd just go about it more calmly!"

"Appease 'em, appease 'em. I'm tryin' to make a man out of him."

Daddy poured the fresh water into the large can, then prodded Jim into another run up the hill.

As they started for the door, a huge tow passed by, sending its churning wake to the shore. The waves were like a poltergeist at work: an empty box scuttled across the cabin, a dish crashed onto the floor, and the little Bisque boy fell off the back of the toilet.

Mom was holding on to the edge of the sink. "Jim, I think I heard something give way."

"Naw."

"Maybe you should go around and check."

"Just stick to your curtains, Mildred. I'll take care of the boat."

The dipper in the water can clunked against the sides like a miniature buoy. Warning, warning.

17

THE EAST END

SCHOOL WAS a big Victorian building between Eastern Avenue and the railroad tracks. It was the oldest school building in the city, with wooden beams in the gym and chutes to slide down as fire escapes. We all longed to try them, but fire drill was just a march through the halls and onto the playground.

The playground was only feet from the trains that chugged by regularly, throwing soot over everything. When we kids played kickball we came away looking like end men in a minstrel show. Also in the blacktopped yard were the "shacks" where the "dumb kids" went. These were separate barracks manned by the strongest and most fearless teachers and populated by the hopeless.

There were smart kids and dumb kids, fat kids and skinny kids, bad kids and good kids. One of the boys in my sixth-grade class was a Down's-syndrome child; the other children called him Dopey after the dwarf in *Snow White* and teased him without mercy. Howard, a tall, handsome boy, had a horrible smell, a smell so bad no one would be his buddy in line or take his hand. No one did anything to help these children. Our teachers were old maids, usually with iron-gray hair. They dressed in subdued colors and sensible shoes. They loved their subjects and encouraged the alert and motivated. They had no interest in social problems or the unprepared. Howard probably never knew what was wrong.

Every kid had a nickname, usually based on his or her worst feature: there was "Tits," a boy who had pronounced breasts, and "Warthog" and "Meatface," both struggling with pre-teen acne. I was dubbed "BBD" for "Big Butt Dorothy."

We were seated by level of achievement. I was soon competing for the first seat in the first row by the door. Poor Howard brought up the rear in the very last seat in the last row by the window. In between were rows of dozing kids as the teacher lectured on the Constitution and "Initiative and Referendum."

Even singing class was hierarchical: the sopranos were "Bluebirds," the altos and tenors were "Robins," and the basses and lower-voiced were "Crows," a nomenclature that obviously favored the higher registers.

In spite of my standing in the class, or maybe because of it, I felt out of place. I was the new kid on the block once again, a kid who talked like a book.

Though I might have been smart, I was still a "River Rat." I hated writing down my address: "Boat, Foot of Donham Street." I wanted a house number and a street name, something solid and respectable. Everyone else lived in secure homes that stayed put on the small shady streets of the East End, while I hiked up to school from the river.

I spent hours in the library at the corner of Donham and Eastern reading Louisa May Alcott and the Brontës. The Brontës gave me romance, but Alcott gave me more solid dreams. I wanted to have a family like Jo's: intelligent, peaceful, loving, and living in New England in a shingled house with lilac bushes and apple trees. Half headachy from print (I was always suffering various aches and itches) and due for dinner at the yacht club, I would walk a block down Donham, then often be held up by a stalled freight train. To get by, I would climb through a coupling or crawl under a car, fully prepared to hit the dirt and lie flat if the train started.

The kids of the East End were quite aware of the area's low-class reputation and soon taught us not to mention where we were from if we went outside the neighborhood, to the skating rink or downtown: "Just say you're from Hyde Park or Mt. Lookout."

In spite of the neighborhood's lack of wealth, the part of the East End around McKinley School was quite pleasant, like a small river town. There were shade trees along Eastern and some houses with historic charm. I was chosen to appear on a radio program featuring school children from various neighborhoods, and learned that the East End was originally called Columbia and was the first community in the city to be settled. The riverfront was once the town of Fulton, where steamboats were built. We had a pioneer cemetery near Lunken Airport and historic residence built by Benjamin Stites, an East End founder.

Clustered around the school on Eastern Avenue were a supermarket, a beauty parlor, a clothing store, a bank, a movie theater, a post office, a diner, several bars, a chili parlor, and an old-fashioned notions store with pull-down stools. Everything families needed could be found there.

In the days we lived there people paid little attention to the river, unless it flooded or gave up a dead body or did some other asocial thing. We roller-skated and hung around in the school yard. There were parks in the lower East End, toward town, but we never went to Turkey Ridge or below because the kids there were rumored to be really tough.

Mom warned us to stay away from tough kids and told me not to let the older boys get me alone anywhere: "They may have desires you younger children don't know about." True, there were a couple of boys in the school who shaved or had chins black with stubble, but they could be avoided. We ran pretty free in our own nearby streets, never worrying about bad areas or hoodlums. We went to the movies, Jim and I, at night, along with some kids who lived right next door to the coal yard near the tracks.

Back down on the river, I practiced kicking the kickball in the field above the marina. More than anything, I wanted to be a good player, but I was never more than a bunter. Occasionally I wandered over to the woods where the shanty boaters lived. Nettie and Annie went to McKinley, and their brother "Pig Iron" was receiving his education in the shacks. Their boat, an old scow with no motor, was moored among the willows. Their bathroom was a seat over the water and a bar of soap on a rope. The family grew their own vegetables on the small bit of land where they moored, and they kept chickens. Clarence, the father, fished for their dinner and made his own "raisin jack." He and the other shanty-boaters "rolled coal" for their stoves from barges that were tied off across the water. The minute a towboat left a barge full of coal on the ice breakers—to be picked up later—and puffed out of sight, an armada of small boats surrounded it. Clarence, along with his cohorts, was out in his skiff filling it with chunks of coal. He would come back from a raid so weighed down, the oarlocks of his boat were at water level.

Mom thought shanty-boaters interesting and colorful and encouraged me to make friends with them. But when Daddy got wind of my visiting them he forbade me to go back. To a steamboat man, the shanty boaters were thieves, riff-raff, no-account.

As usual, I depended for company on Jim, who was willing to let me tag along with him until more interesting male companions came along. Mom needed my services to help cook. Chopping cabbage for coleslaw, our usual salad, and frying pork chops were chores I enjoyed. I hated trying to make "oleo margarine" look palatable, like butter. We squeezed a tiny glob of red dye into a pound of nasty white lardy stuff and kneaded it in. We did everything to the accompaniment of the radio, our one link besides school with the world beyond the river. We sang along with the endlessly played soap ads: "Rinso white, Rinso bright / Birdies sing all day long." We would never forget the slogans: "Ipana for the smile of beauty, Sal Hepatica for the smile of health."

Soap operas played constantly: "Backstage Wife," "Lorenzo Jones," "Just Plain Bill," "Life Can Be Beautiful." I believed in the last one, utterly.

CABIN FEVER

WE NEVER knew what to expect in the morning when we got up. Some days the mist was so thick we could barely see the river; then it would rise slowly and subtly and here and there reveal a touch of brown.

It was like a nice morning in a warm kitchen. Other days the water would look fresh enough to drink, sparkling and clear, and we wondered why people complained about the dirty Ohio: it was blue and green and silver and reflected the sun in a million facets. White clouds might drift over, their images in the water like a herd of fluffy sheep. The next day the river would be flat as a stone, the next the exact color of milky coffee.

Nothing on the water remains stable. Paint peels more rapidly than it does on land and, like an old sunburn, drops strips and little dandruffy bits onto the surface of the water. In winter the surface freezes and then cracks, then the chunks go hitting the hull, cl-clunk, cr-runk: the big pieces and chunks go grinding downstream, working each other into a mush and then disappearing. The river is always moving, swiftly, slowly, changing its depth, its content, forever altering the things placed on shore to keep the boats in place: stakes, lines, cables, spars. The gang-plank walks up the hill like an old man pushing a wheel barrow, inching along. The mud oozes, the stakes loosen, the cable goes slack like a jaw dropping in surprise. The wind pulls and tears and washes drift against the lines or puts a hole in a rowboat left in the water for five minutes.

It was Daddy's job to keep all this under control and to get the club members' boats into the water in spring and out in fall. He was on the job twenty-four hours a day, but had long stretches of nothing to do between emergencies and mundane chores. This life on the river did not appear to be the wonderful return he had hoped for. He was older now than he had been when he was on the packet boats. His hair had thinned out and his fingernails were thick and discolored. Nostalgia had gilded the satisfactions of rugged toil, the constant demands and frustrations of the river, the naked war against heat and cold and wind and water. He didn't enjoy being at the beck and call of the club members, a hard-drinking group he had little respect for.

Mom was stuck in the tiny cabin, cut off from contacts with friends or family. At first there was the job of making the place livable. After Daddy caulked the windows and porch doors with felt to keep out the wind, she made white and blue curtains to match the club-boat colors and embroidered little anchors on them. She bought decals at the dime store and supervised me as I floated the designs off their paper and onto the cabinets she had painted white. She painted the walls. But when the moving in and fixing up was finished, she had endless hours on her hands. She watched the towboats go by and wrote down their names and their time of passing.

She had little to excite her imagination except her novels and an occasional Bette Davis movie, from which she would come home charged with fire and drama, making perfect Bette Davis turns and spitting out challenges to the "male ego." By morning she would be back at work trying to keep her cramped home neat. With the stove, table, four chairs, radio, a big bed, two bunks (later built in by Daddy), a sink and water can, dresser, the awful toilet-altar, the coal bucket and kindling—one item out of place in the cabin and it looked like a rummage sale.

Mom picked up all day. She mopped at the sink top and the table. No sooner would she get the tiny rooms clean and in order than Daddy would come clumping up the steps in muddy boots and mess up the floors. He hung about the kitchen drinking second and third cups of coffee. He stirred it and stirred it, watching the condensed milk rise in powdery little swirls, sloshing it with his spoon, making a sticky pool on Mom's just-wiped table. He smoked quietly, letting the ashes fall carelessly. He figured on paper: how much money he would have if he'd never smoked and instead saved the price of daily cigarettes. The war debts from the First World War: he brooded over the countries that hadn't repaid their loans. Mom stood by with a wet cloth, wiping up the coffee rings as Daddy picked up his cup for a swallow.

He criticized her cooking: "Salt the meat *before* it's done!" "Add more grease."

He stoked the stove.

"Are you finished with that coffee now?" she'd ask.

"Why?"

"I want to wipe off the table—*once and for all!*"

"Oh hell, leave it dirty."

MOM DID the laundry on a washboard in a galvanized tin tub and let it dry on the porch when the weather was decent. On rainy days she hung it on the second deck among all the junk. Ironing was done with two heavy flatirons heated on the wood stove. You pressed with one while the other was warming up. Bathing was done in the same tub as the laundry; there was barely room to squat. If the water was warm, one part of you was comfortable while the part not in the water froze. If an elbow shot out too far, water cascaded all over the floor. If you bent over too far, you were in jeopardy from the red-hot stove that Daddy stoked with coal until it turned translucent. Mom was terrified of the stove. She always pictured it blowing up or choking us all with fumes.

An alternative to the tin tub was a shower in the rest rooms downstairs, but the trek down was cold and lonely, and the enormous shadows from the stored boats loomed. The toilet-stall doors banged on their hinges as the boat lurched. The floors were like ice and the water equally cold. Being clean dropped in importance. Jim and I developed crusts on our ankles. We saved showers for spring and summer.

The little cabin was sometimes snug and secure as we sat through the long winter evenings listening to the radio; at other times, with the four wills and egos grating on one another, our voices got so loud the roof, like something out of an animated cartoon, must have jiggled up and down. We could argue about anything. Daddy bragged (half in humor) that he was an "authority on any and all subjects." Mom, for all her claims of submissiveness and meekness, never backed down in her life and, indeed, had mysteriously endowed her opinions with a sort of "rightness," so that to disagree was like cutting oneself off from the Church. Jim and I were learning things in school and held everything that came from the teachers infallible, every statement from a school book fact. Imbued with a few nuggets, such as "the first colony at Jamestown was established in 1603," and zero wisdom, we felt superior to our parents who were "uneducated." We didn't know Mom had been an honors graduate from Windsor School, though we knew, because she reminded us often, that she had been a student at the "Schuster Martin School of Dramatics and Elocution."

We fought about everything. A tiny remark and someone, usually Daddy, would pick it up. We argued about the length of my hair. "Hair is a woman's crowning glory"—Daddy. We argued about whether it was better to live in a big or small house. Daddy favored a mansion with many rooms.

"Well, how would you wash all those windows?" Mom would demand.

"For God's sake, Mildred, if you had a big house, you'd hire someone to do that."

"Just give me a small house, *paid for*," Mom would counter.

Our radio was a source of pleasure, information, and conflict. Jim always wanted to tune in "Blondie," but Daddy insisted that "Cavalcade of America" was more educational. "Mr. District Attorney," "The Kate Smith Hour": we were regulars. We knew the schedules by heart.

Daddy was fond of reading little bits from the newspapers to the rest of us.

"Now," he'd say, inaccurately, "you're thirteen and twelve. . . ."

"Twelve and eleven."

"'LET'S TEST YOUR HORSE SENSE': Which of the following textiles is originally derived from an animal? One, wool; two, cotton; three, linen; four, silk."

"Let me see," I'd say.

"I shall repeat the question: Which of the following textiles is originally derived from an animal? Wool, cotton, linen, silk?"

"Wool," Jim would say.

"Mildred, what's your answer?"

"What were they now?"

Daddy would begin again impatiently, "Which of the following textiles is originally derived from an animal? Wool, cotton, linen, or silk?"

After this ordeal we'd all lapse back into our books and radio programs.

Soon, Daddy's chair would fall. Bang! His feet hit the floor. He always tilted back, one leg swung over a table or chair. Triumphantly he would read, "Unhuh, says here, 'Prize bull sells for thirty-six thousand dollars!'"

"So?" Mom would say absently.

"'So'! You never heard of a cow selling for that much!"

Daddy occasionally sold boats; after one sale he went shopping downtown. He had his picture taken in one of those booths in the dime store and brought home bags of things we couldn't afford—hair ribbons for me, silk stockings for Mom, neckties for himself and Jim, a velvet jewelry box. Mom had a fit. None of the stuff was necessary, and we needed real things like shoes; furthermore, she didn't want a picture of him at the moment. He was underfoot enough, telling her how to cook and what to do.

Mom lugged the groceries from Eastern Avenue above the railroad tracks near school. If she accepted a ride from one of the club members, Daddy would demand to know why old so-and-so was offering her a ride. What did he have in mind?

Mom called him domineering, uncouth. She couldn't stand his temper and suggested he try being "psychoanalyzed." We couldn't even pay a doctor for an earache, much less mental therapy.

Jim and I hated these fights. I was like a seismograph: I could feel the rumbles of real trouble coming miles away. It would begin with some untactful remark by Daddy, Mom saying, "Shh, for heaven's sake, stop." Jim or I would say, "Oh Daddy, c'mon." We were told to mind our own business. "Use a little discretion," Mom would say. Daddy would go into a real tirade.

"Must you be so loud?"

And they were off, arguing about his vulgarity. He would list his shortcomings according to his wife, bellow, pound his fist on the table. One night he hurled a coffeepot through the window. She was the trained actress, but he could always match her in dramatic flare.

One night Daddy got side-tracked on liquor and decided in the midst of his rage that neither he nor Mom would drink anymore. They didn't really drink much, but he'd decided that whiskey was responsible for their troubles. He got out their bottles of alcohol and climbed out to the edge of the boat. Standing precariously in the gutter three stories above the water, he ceremoniously emptied them into the river looking like a mustached Carrie Nation. Then he hurled the bottles, plop! plop! into the water.

During fights, Mom at first gritted her teeth, tightened her mouth, tried to ignore Daddy. She cajoled, she pacified, she reasoned, she endured. She would not sink to his level. Then finally, goaded beyond endurance—maybe that's what he wanted—she would let loose.

She often threatened to leave and would pack up. She would get as far as the door, then stop and declare it unfair to abandon her young children. Jim and I were relieved. We worried how the word "divorce" would sound on the playground at school. Divorce was worse than death. Death was not a disgrace.

Driven to fury one night, Mom flew apart. She knocked over the lamp and screamed that she wouldn't stand anymore. She beat at Daddy with her fists. "I'm a human being!" she raged. "I'm tired of being the goat!" Her voice grew hoarse and she rushed around the little rooms panting and knocking herself about. We followed along, begging them to stop—

"Oh Daddy."

"Now, Mom—don't," Jim begged. "Don't *do* that. Daddy didn't mean it. Did you? Did you?"

"God damn it to hell," Daddy said. Now he was scared. Before, he'd told Mom to get out when she threatened to leave, he didn't care. There's the door. Any time. I don't need you. But her madwoman fit really got him. He began to wring out wet washcloths and mop ineffectually at her face. He chuckled sheepishly and tried to make it up with us children. We had hard knots of sorrow in our throats. We couldn't think.

"She'll be all right."

Jim vaulted out the door and ran down to the second deck. He couldn't stand it.

"Jim-Boy, come back here!"

He clattered down the outside steps. We all ran out on the porch and saw him running over the gangplank in the moonlight. Heard its plunk, plunk.

"Jim-Boy, come back here this minute!" Mom screamed.

Jim kept running.

"Don't disobey your mother!" Daddy called. "How dare you. You'd better show a little respect!"

Jim was on his way to the top of the hill. Then he disappeared among the trees.

Mom started to sob and keen louder than ever. She and Daddy argued about who had caused Jim to become so upset. I went back to the dinner table and sat staring at my plate. There was a pork chop and canned corn on it. The corn seemed like great dazzling lumps. I started to eat it. Big tears formed in my eyes and I let them stay there. I tried to harden all over. I sat there for a long time, letting my teeth chatter.

Daddy was still mopping with his washcloth and Mom was rolling on the bed gasping and sobbing dryly. I went over to see how she was.

"Do you want anything?"

"No, nothing. I'm all right."

Daddy came to her with more water.

"Now just lie quiet. Take it easy." To me: "Your Mammy sure can get riled up, can't she?"

I didn't want to be taken into his confidence. I went back to the table. I wondered where Jim was and if we would ever see him again. Why didn't I go with him?

Later that night, when mother was quiet, Daddy put on his jacket and said he would go call the police. Somehow, Jim was found at the airport. He was going to run away, but he didn't have any money.

THE NEXT day, the sun came up: Mom was writing down the names of the towboats that went past, and Daddy was out on the floats pushing debris away from the lines. But Jim and I were afraid our world might come apart.

19

BIGGER BATTLES

ONE WINTER the river froze over, and we went skating. Rosy-cheeked and healthy, like Hans Brinker people, we glided over the crystal ice — even Daddy. He was the one who found the old skates buried behind a canoe on the second deck and helped us pad them out to fit.

We all loved the weather: Jim and I played games of fox and hare in the snow and had huge, organized snowball fights with the neighborhood kids. We loved the wind. Standing on the deck with me one time, Daddy looked at the white caps being whipped up by a coming storm: "I love the river when it's like this." It was one of the few times he expressed a feeling other than amusement or anger.

Christmas on the river was the same as always. Jim and I worked like Santa's helpers making lopsided doorstops and ashtrays for all the relatives. Mom saved up twenty-five dollars by joining the local bank's Christmas Club, putting a few quarters away each week into an account. We went to Mom and Pop Beamer's for the holiday. We were ashamed of our little handmade presents. In exchange, Ray and his wife Marcella, Mary and Chuck, Freddie and Lessie, and Helen and Lawrence gave us bright shiny games and toys. Elmer and Esther, the two educated ones, came up with the cheapest gifts, often instructional. They seemed to disapprove of the whole sloppy mess of Christmas.

Daddy did an entire riff on a letter from Esther after she and Elmer moved away from Cincinnati. It described her Christmas gift from Elmer, a sterling-silver candle snuffer.

"A candle snuffer! Now I've heard everything!" Daddy lectured. "A silver candle snuffer! What's wrong with putting out a candle the old way?" He wet his forefinger and thumb and pantomimed dousing a candle with two digits. Then he puffed up his cheeks and blew hard over an imaginary flame. "Whoosh! The candle's out!" He tried swallowing the flame and holding it up to a draft from the window. This went on for quite a while.

Though he never praised our efforts at homemade things, Daddy always put the handcrafted above the store-bought. He himself surprised us with a sudden show of skill at woodworking. He decided to earn some extra money by creating wooden scrapbooks: he sanded, stained, carved, and decorated the covers, then tied them together with rawhide laces. Sometimes he put decals on the cover and sometimes drew designs on them with a woodburning set. They were quite popular with the club members.

I was always drawing and painting, and made all the family Christmas cards. I attended the free classes at the art museum on Saturday mornings, at Mom's insistence—transferring twice on the streetcar to get to Eden

Park and becoming the pariah of the school for drawing "dirty statues"—the plaster casts of Greek sculptures that adorned the great hall of the museum. Both parents approved of my artistic efforts, though Daddy always added to his praise, "Of course the most beautiful sight in the world is a fine family wash hanging on a line." He disliked anything ugly or negative in my drawings, so I always drew "pretty girls" and happy scenes. "Good," he'd say. "Try to buy a hamburger with it."

Ballet lessons were out. Daddy was convinced they led girls straight to the Gayety, Cincinnati's one burlesque show.

Looking forward to Christmas, 1941, we came home from the movies on a Sunday afternoon and Daddy and Mom were sitting quietly, eating their Sunday-night Italian salami and sharp cheddar cheese (something they agreed on!). They were preternaturally quiet.

"We're at war," Daddy said.

"The Japanese attacked Pearl Harbor," Mom added.

Boy. We felt as though we'd been socked in the stomach. We had followed very little of the events leading to the war, just what we saw in the newsreels at the movies. I had fairly successfully blocked out those parts of the show, because while I'd seen images of guns and battles since I was three or four, I hated them and couldn't wait for the features about spring hats and fashions. We sat very quietly and listened to the radio.

What would this mean? A very important thing had happened. Like a hurricane announcement on the radio, we waited for it to hit. Tighten up your houses. Be ready. It's coming.

We had no memories to dip into to help us understand, only a few vague associations: Daddy's references to the last war, his uniform, a German medal he'd collected. We'd seen Kaiser Wilhelm II in the newsreels, steel helmeted, wearing his long, rigid, lead-colored army coat.

We began to ask questions. "Will we win? Can they beat us?"

"No. America's never lost a war."

"Will Daddy go to the army?" "Will we get killed?" "If they win does our country belong to them?"

The parents were totally optimistic. We would win. It was only a question of time. Our father was past draft age and we had no older brothers who would go into the army.

At school we now had war-bond drives, and every week we kids bought a ten-cent Victory stamp. I was appointed cashier and sat at a desk in the hall, counting the school pennies. Posters were all around with slogans like "Loose Lips Sink Ships" and caricatures of Hitler and Hirohito.

We kids went to work collecting scrap metal. We labored for hours, pushing an old wagon around the streets, up and down the hills. Our hearts thrilled at the sight of a few old rusty coat hangers produced by some housewife whose door we knocked on in our rounds. A car tire was a bonanza. They were really hard to come by, but occasionally we got one at the gas station. The scrap drive was set up in military fashion and we could earn chevrons for the stuff we collected. Sometimes we worked until after dark, hauling and sorting our loot, until Daddy put a damper on the proceedings.

"They shouldn't allow these kids to run around like that, collecting junk—a couple of old tires and tin cans for a week's work. That's awful." After that we contented ourselves with saving grease and tinfoil from cigarette packages. Since I couldn't knit—and handmade socks were the girls' most popular contribution to morale—I made paper scrapbooks holding pinup pictures, cartoons, and drawings (I wonder if they ever reached the front).

Aside from these efforts, we experienced the war only through the movies, the magazines, the radio—as though we could hear the reverberations of the guns, but not the actual shooting. We knew the faces of the enemy intimately: Il Duce, bloated, blustering, ridiculous; Hitler, frantic and mustached, always the personification of evil or the most ludicrous of tinhorns; Hirohito, impossibly buck-toothed, sawed-off, underhanded, Orientally cruel, speaking in pidgin English. We *hated* Hitler. *Hated* him. Hirohito and Mussolini, too. We wished they were dead. Somehow we thought that would solve everything.

Our comic books became heavily anti-Japanese. One article explained how to tell a "Jap" from a Chinese person: the former would have a separation between his toes from wearing thong sandals. How we would de-sock said person was not described, nor why we would need to differentiate between civilians from friendly and unfriendly nations.

We experienced the war through countless war movies. There was always the tough "pro" army man and "the kid" or "Junior," the sophomoric draftee who grew up by facing combat. Wings, guns, motors, hymns, team spirit, uniforms, zooming planes, death, destruction; Captain Cassidy (good old Cary Grant) leaving wife and family. Clark Gable, Walter Pidgeon, John Wayne—we watched all of Hollywood go off to war.

The war invaded our fantasies and dreams. To civilians in an untouched country, it *was* a fantasy. Still, I dreamed the Japanese crossed the bridge from Covington to Cincinnati. They weren't two feet away, and in their eyes were rape and killing.

Mostly, our sheltered lives went on, mundane activities gradually choking out the news of war. At school I continued to be teacher's pet. On report-card day, I would bring home perfect scores, while Jim would try to hide his report somewhere on the second deck, or "lose" it. He was much more adventurous than I, more likeable, capable of doing excellent work, but not of sitting still. Also, while Mom revered education, Daddy did not push it for him. Being tough and a good worker were more important. So while Jim was called on the carpet for a missing or bad report card, his sister Benedict Arnold would be enjoying the praise of the parents.

The parents worried about Jim Jr. He was such a dreamer. "What are you going to be? What are you going to do?" A bad report card filled them with dread. A lost jacket was the money burned up, thrown down a sewer. What was to become of us? What?

AT SCHOOL I supervised the class mural, starred in the seventh-grade play, and served on Student Council where I helped filibuster for the girls' right to be safety guards. Next thing I knew, I was getting up an hour earlier in the morning, trudging through the snow in the dark, and standing in ankle-high slush, holding a sign that said "Stop." Of course, I did get to wear the official-looking white belt.

Mom always kept in touch with the teachers, attended PTA, and kept track of my progress. She never let up on the need to attend college, to "excel." She could make the word "mediocre" sound like high treason.

All this excelling did not make me super popular with the other kids, and I often suffered from loneliness. I daydreamed of having a party with the few friends I acquired, but the girls never came to my "house." I was ashamed of it, and they didn't seem to want to come down to the river. It had a reputation—dirty, dangerous, a place of lurid assignations and killer-tramps.

And yet, I was too good for this neighborhood. My seventh-grade teacher, Miss Reedy, grabbed my arm one day on the street and said, "Get out. You don't belong here. You must get out of this neighborhood."

Where did I belong? I wondered. It seemed like nowhere.

20

EAƒY LIVIN'

SUMMERS, JIM and I took our cots outside on the porch. There was always a breeze there, and the rocking boat was like a cradle. The night noises were never-ending and various: tree toads and crickets among the willows, a train hooting along the Kentucky shore, the egg-beater sound of a runabout returning to the harbor, and, when all was quiet, the gentle plop of a fish. Our perch on top of the yacht club gave us a view, upstream and down, of the green growth and campfires along the banks, the open sky full of stars. Our view twinkled with the lights of planes heading for Lunken airfield, the small red and green lights of towboats. We had the best seat in the house.

The boating season began with Daddy getting the pleasure boats out of dry dock and tied onto the floats. The boats, not the supersized cruisers of today but houseboats and runabouts, had spent the winter up on blocks and had to be pulled by cables over to a launching rail and slid into the water. Daddy was most himself with the heaving and tugging and yelling, and the spring wind blowing and the river running fast with recent rains. With a crew to supervise and practical, exciting work to do, he was back to his old steamboat days.

Mom had gotten the job of cooking on the club boat, and was boiling up beans and ham and cornbread to feed the men. Jim helped Daddy. I helped Mom, and we all joined in the lunch-time feast.

Now the floats were filled, and the big club boat looked like a mother duck with a string of babies. Soon the cafe opened up. It took all of the lower deck except for a shaded sitting area overlooking the boats. It was a long room with windows on the water, tables for four, and a bar to the landward side next to a small kitchen where Mom was soon grilling hamburgers and steaks for the members.

Jim and I were constantly being thrown out of the bar. Daddy got tired of our lust for the slot machines and our ceaseless whining for soft drinks. He would tell us to go and get milk from the icebox up in the cabin, but that was lukewarm: the ice had usually melted to the size of a quarter, and the sour tinny smell of the closed box could not compete with the happy "oof" of an orange crush being opened and its bright, cold sweat. Mom would direct us to the pot of beans always bubbling on our upstairs stove, but we could smell hamburgers, french fries, and minute steaks, the odors wafting from the greasy fan over the club's kitchen door. The parents hadn't a soft bone in their bodies: one relaxation of the rules or a taste of comfort and we would be the depraved and corrupt wastrels that our basic nature would have us.

The staff of the boat club now included a bartender: one Whitey, a somewhat punch-drunk ex-prizefighter. Needless to say, he had snow-white hair, which was neat as a spool of thread atop his tough little face and broken nose. Jim enjoyed sending him into a fighting stance by creeping up behind him and banging on a pie pan.

With the opening of the cafe, the club members came back to the river like a flock of water birds. They wore bright aqua and pink "slack suits," huaraches, captains' hats with the CYC logo on them, halters, sunglasses. Kegs of beer and blocks of ice, picnic food and deck chairs slid down the hill to the gangplank.

Running errands, delivering phone messages, I had a unique view of the members' lives. The boat club was like a miniature village: every-one's windows were open, and voices carried on the water. There was the drinking set led by the Morleys, Mr. and Mrs., who looked like twins, both men. They had dimpled out-thrust chins, heavy jowls, and full eye bags from booze and late nights. The younger brother of Mr. Morley, Tim, and his wife Wanda, were softer looking. Wanda had dead black hair, a white baby-doll face, and a curvy figure; she wandered around passively, awaiting orders from her husband, unlike the older model who might slug it out with hers. The boozers had Chris Crafts and cruisers, fast, sleek boats. The prettiest woman among them, a blonde with a large mole by her mouth, rode standing on the seat of a runabout, holding a rope like a water-skier. With her hair blowing in the wind, she was like the figurehead of a ship. Then there was the group jester, Mel, who went about all summer nursing beer from a baby bottle.

There was the family set: the Stegemyers, a big clan, who actually lived in the East End. The "mister" owned a machine shop. Every few years their house flooded, and they simply scooped the mud out and re-painted the walls that the water had stained like satin.

A pair of grandparents owned a big, comfortable scow, and usually brought along a little granddaughter, whom my father declared "spoiled" and held up as an example of how I ought not to behave. But then, Daddy felt that way about every girl who got her own way and had a reg-ular allowance.

There was Doc Behymer, the club intellectual, who kept an office on Eastern Avenue in one of the most charming of the old houses. He came down mostly to fish, but spent many hours arguing politics and generally locking verbal horns with my father. Captain Jim was stiff-necked about being at other people's beck and call. He played the hill-billy when it suited him and usually took the opposite view of whatever Doc proposed.

A childless couple, not one of the in-group, came to the river early and lived on their houseboat far into the fall. She was ill with some un-known (to me) condition. Her husband was very solicitous of her, and when I delivered their phone messages or mail, they looked very cozy sit-ting together in the cabin. The man reminded Mom of her successful accountant brother, Elmer. He was a "college graduate" and therefore brilliant. "He's the kind of man you'll marry," she assured me, her tone making it unnecessary to contrast him with her own unfortunate spousal choice.

The club members were our community, our only one during the summers. Our parents talked about them the way doctors talk about patients, parents about children, servants about masters. We knew their quirks and weaknesses and saw them in moods as different as the changes in the water around us.

At the New Year's Eve party where I helped Mom serve, we were amazed at the grandparents with the spoiled granddaughter: at the stroke of twelve, he quietly poured a bottle of catsup over his wife's head, and she, with no change of expression, painted his face with mustard.

The younger Mr. Morley, Tim, who we all knew beat his pretty wife, sat watching me one day as I sat on the steps to the second deck, sketching the boats. He glanced over my shoulder and rather wistfully remarked on how good the drawing was. In fact, he raved about it, far beyond its actual worth, I knew even then. But I was touched by the praise.

Another day, on those same steps, my mother was struggling to fix my hair, which I wore in two long plaits. Mr. Morley watched her awhile, then asked whether he could braid my hair for her. He took the comb and softly combed the long curtains of hair, watching the electricity lift it and letting it flutter back into place. He was all contentment. Then he braided it into pigtails.

Soon after, this same man woke us in the middle of the night, stone drunk and yelling loudly. He was going to kill himself by jumping into the river. Mom, of course, felt sorry for him: he no doubt had psychological scars. According to her everything was explained by one's early experiences. Daddy took the cold absolutist's view. The man was disturbing the whole place with his yelling and had to be stopped. Daddy turned the searchlight on him where he stood teetering over the rail of the second deck.

"C'mon up and get some coffee," Daddy yelled. "This'll all look different in the morning."

"I'm gonna jump. I'm gonna jump!"

"Think about your wife and children, man!"

"Nothing's worth it!" The threats and offers to help went on for a while, with Mr. Morley refusing to listen to reason. Finally Daddy said, "Go ahead and jump, you Goddamn fool." He turned off the light and went to bed.

Presumably the man slunk back to his boat and also went to bed, for he appeared the next day with a glass of beer with an egg in it and a sheepish expression on his face.

To Daddy, the boat clubbers were all the same: loose-moraled and no-account. Mom made friends among them and was universally liked. Jim and one of the party-people boys became buddies and rivals. I remember us kids going on many exciting motorboat rides and houseboat picnics.

If Daddy was in the right mood, we were allowed to borrow the club skiff. Jim and I both became good rowers: dip the oars just beneath the surface, not too deep, pull back, lift out. Daddy showed us fancier ways —rotating the oars or pushing them forward. Mom fretted about our jumping around on boats, walking narrow catwalks, and being "unsupervised" on the river, but Daddy laughed and said, "Kids are like goats. They're surefooted. Don't worry. They won't fall." Besides, he implied, if anything happened to us there'd be two fewer mouths to feed.

Daddy taught me to swim by throwing me off the club boat into deep water. At first I was scared, hitting the hard surface and going down down down, but then I rose like a cork through the beautiful green depths of the water and broke the surface into the sunlight, raising my fist at my father and laughing.

I became a strong swimmer, loved diving and swimming in the cool water, sometimes battling the current and dodging the occasional turd that drifted by covered with green moss. I loved lying on the wood planks in the sun, watching the water reflections and the bright green slime on the lines through the cracks of the floats. I loved the feel of a soft summer breeze on my face and through my hair.

Jim was my only real companion, and we lived like Tom Sawyer and Huckleberry Finn—or maybe more like Tom and Sid, the sissified junior Sawyer. Jim was still my model, and, at least during the summer, I forgot I was different from him, not a boy. His most cutting insult, when he disliked something I did, was, "You're acting like a girl." We had always competed in everything, with me on the losing end of things athletic.

On the river, the contest was who could dive from the highest deck: Jim made it off the top, I only made it off the second deck. While someone rowed, we swam across the river to the Kentucky shore: Jim made it all the way, I had to stop three-fourths of the way across.

We spent hours in the skiff rowing up and down the river. We would pull in at some shady spot, tie off, and hike along the banks under the cool, lacy willows. The mud was up to our thighs and would suck at a whole leg as we tried to pull it out to take another step. We discovered other people's camps: charred branches, bits of fishing tackle, bottles, and footsteps in little nooks beneath the trees. We would sculpt cities in the mud and, resting among the trees, eat the picnic lunch we had packed.

The danger of the river only made it more attractive to us. I learned how treacherous it could be when, swimming too far out, I was caught in the current. Fighting my way to safer water was like swimming in a dream. Another time, after we had acquired a second-hand beat-up outboard motor for the skiff, I took the boat out alone. I was never good at pulling the string to get the motor started, and it stalled near the Kentucky shore, far from home base. I was trying over and over to get the string to work, totally concentrating on my task, when I looked up and saw the *Island Queen*, on its way to Cincinnati, bearing down on me.

One of those odd things happened that sometimes do when your number is not yet up. A fisherman in a small boat appeared from nowhere, jumped into my boat, pulled the string once, and jumped back into his own boat as the motor caught. We both roared off. Not a single word was exchanged. There was only enough time to get out of the way of the oncoming steamboat.

EVERY SUMMER I spent several weeks at Auntie's. For a brief time, I was back to being pampered—allowed to sleep till noon, eat all the potato chips I could hold, and spend quiet evenings with Auntie and More-Pop, invariably observing the ritual of our nightly ginger ale.

Always finished with her ironing and baking by ten in the morning, Auntie would often don her black silk dress and big Scarlet O'Hara hat and drive to the country to visit old friends. I watched the women we visited closely, trying to figure out what kept them going, what their dreams might be.

She and I frequently dropped in on a couple who lived in a large manor house that sat by itself on huge grounds behind wrought-iron fencing. The shy chatelaine of this manor seemed so old, not involved as Auntie was in the world of growing and cooking food. Her husband was stiff as a Grant Wood farmer. One afternoon, seeing me reading (I was considered a genius because I could plow through a three-hundred page novel), she took me into the library and showed me a college journal that included an article she had written: "Heredity or Environment?" She said nothing. It had the odor of stored linens saved for a big occasion that never came.

We often visited another farm, this one with working fields and a small frame house with a front porch and parlor—a "living" room unlived-in and saved in pristine condition for guests. Auntie played pinochle with the farmer and his wife, while I investigated their outdoor cold cellar, played with the kittens, and picked raspberries. One summer, their Chow dog produced puppies, and they gave me one. We'd had dogs at the yacht club, one a rather manic canine named Jerry who just disappeared one day. This one was all mine, an adorable eight-week-old, his fur soft as a caterpillar's. His gums, which showed when he flashed his teeth in a smile, were the color of blueberries. I named him Cinnamon and promptly sat down and wrote Mom and Daddy that I was bringing him home. Once again I was pronounced a veritable genius (for writing a letter to my parents!).

Somehow I got Cinnamon back to the yacht club. I rushed up the steps to the second deck, eager to show off my new pet. Jim greeted me.

"The parents had a Battle Royal while you were gone," he said.

I burrowed my face in Cinnamon's soft neck fur. Our triumphal homecoming was spoiled.

Mom was tense all that week, complaining how little she and Daddy shared. When things calmed down, I asked her why she had married Daddy in the first place. She sighed and tightened the sash of her apron, getting ready to go to work.

"Your father was a very handsome man," she said. She stood at the door for a moment, looking pensive.

"I sued for divorce once. But on the very day it was to be made final, he talked me into dropping it. He had a new job on the *Valley Queen*, and things were going to be better. They were. For a while."

I held Cinnamon tighter. He looked as if he might actually feel my distress. From then on, he went everywhere with me: on hikes with Jim where he shared our picnics, including the root beer; on trips over to the icebreakers we climbed. He would sit in the bow of the rowboat, his fur ruffled by the wind, his yellow eyes closed with pleasure. He seemed to be listening to the creak of the oar locks, the drip of the paddle lifted from the summer-tranquil water.

21

FLOOD

MALE AND female, Southern and German, water and land. They seemed so different and yet they overlapped. Both parents had hills in their background, and each loved the river in his own way.

But he was the tough one and she the soft one. Wasn't that so?

Back in school, in the seventh grade at McKinley, I came home one afternoon eager to get together with my beloved Cinnamon. When I got to the gangplank he always came trotting over to me with his lopsided smile and his rump wriggling. He would jump on me with joy and I'd pet him until his fur crackled.

One afternoon, he didn't appear. I ran up the steps to the cabin: no Cinnamon. Mom was not there; she periodically got jobs at dime stores and was probably still at work. Daddy was down on the floats, poking around. The boats were out of the water now, and up on the hill. He was wearing his old duster and hat and grappling with something in the water with a long pole.

"Have you seen Cinnamon?" I asked.

Daddy seemed preoccupied.

"Not for a while."

I took off for the trees between the yacht club and the shanty settlement, calling and whistling at every step. I couldn't believe Cinnamon would leave his home base. He was still a puppy. I went into the thick weeds, pushing back vicious strings of blackberry bushes. Maybe he was chasing a cat.

I went down to Nettie's and Annie's shanty boat. "Nettie," I called out. "Anybody there?"

A head poked out of the boat's front door: Annie.

"Have you seen my dog? A little Chow?" I asked.

Annie shook her head.

I moved on. I went to the gas station at Kellogg and Donham. The men there had not seen a small dog.

I ran all over the neighborhood, at each stop describing Cinnamon, showing with my hands how big he was. I even crossed the tracks to Eastern and inquired at the beauty shop. At almost twilight, a terrible sick feeling came creeping over me. I went back down the cinder path to the yacht club and met Jim near the boat.

"Is Cinnamon back?" I said. "Is he upstairs?" I pictured him returning home while I was foolishly tearing around the river front: he'd be lapping up water with his little black tongue.

Jim shrugged. I raced up the steps and burst into the cabin. Mom was at the stove starting a skilletful of pork chops.

"Is Cinnamon back?" I said. The cabin seemed horribly empty.

Mom turned to me and pulled the skillet off the burner onto a hot pad.

"I have to tell you something," she said.

That sick feeling took over my whole body.

"Cinnamon is gone."

"He wouldn't run away!"

"No—he's dead, Dot." She paused to get a grip on her own feelings. "He got run over by a car on Kellogg Avenue."

"Oh no!" I burst into tears. "When? Where is he?"

"This afternoon. While you were at school. Daddy found him."

"But I went all over—Daddy said—"

"He couldn't bear to tell you. Cinnamon's up on the hill."

Grief flooded me. I was blind with it.

"Do you want to see him?" Mom asked. "Daddy dug a grave, but he waited—until you could decide."

I nodded my head. It was all I could do. Mom walked me to the top of the hill and over beyond the boats to a clearing. Jim came along. We were both crying.

Mom pointed to a little mound of freshly-dug dirt. Cinnamon lay in the small grave, whole, himself, but he was stiff. It was my first look at death. I screamed and wailed. Jim joined in. We keened, our voices flying out over the river. Mom let us go. We sobbed until we were breathless. Finally Mom said, "It's getting dark. You better let Daddy come up and bury him."

We trudged back to the boat, still crying. Every time I thought of Cinnamon, I broke down again. Mom tried to comfort us. "Life goes on," she said. "You think you'll never get over this, but you will."

At the second deck, I stood at the railing and looked back at the hill where Cinnamon would be buried. I saw Daddy, the tough one, walk up the hill with a shovel in his hand.

LAND AND water: one was becoming the other. Heavy rains forced the gangplank to inch up the hill. The river was running fast and was full of driftwood. Everything was changing.

The kids at school were more fixated than ever on who liked who. The girls gossiped all day; the minute one girl's back was turned, the others dug in. Penny, a plump redhead, became the center of all the boys' eyes as she bloomed, a pink-freckled Lolita. The rest of us envied her. At birthday parties, we played spin the bottle: a milk bottle was placed in the center of a circle of kids, and spun. The person it pointed to on stopping had to leave the room, choosing a member of the opposite sex to accompany him or her for a kiss.

It was hard to concentrate on the intricacies of proportional representation, the city's mode of electing council members, as we all sat blooming and blossoming and growing toward puberty.

My mother was changing. I noticed her growing heavier, but no one said anything. I thought she might be pregnant; I had seen the wife of one of Auntie's grandsons swell with a baby. But I wasn't quite sure of what happened to get her that way.

One day, Mom mentioned it, said she was going to have a baby, and I just said oh.

"Do you know what happens?"

"Oh yes," I assured her. I was afraid she might tell me.

Jim soon caught on; we weren't a bit happy and not at all interested. It seemed like a monstrous idea, a little bit obscene for one's mother to go having a baby. I had visions of having to take care of it. Several of my friends had baby brothers and sisters clinging to them, making them into little parents.

Mom's figure began to change more, but she still wore the same old clothes. It seemed the most heinous crime in the world to feel as I did, but I was miserably ashamed of my parents. I had seen *Alice Adams* and *Stella Dallas* at the movies, and the daughters were such monsters; further, my mother was always playing the sacrificial parent, saying she'd scrub floors for me to go to college, and I didn't want her to. What happened to "My life is over—you're all that matters now," one of her much-played refrains?

On the day of the school play, to which the parents were invited, I was frantic. I had written the script and was acting the starring role—it was about a Whig girl in a Tory foster home who would not give up her principles to please her benefactors. The whole morning, as we prepared the stage and got into costume, I could only think one thing: if my mother comes, I hope she doesn't wear that horrible white dress. It was a clinging knit and outlined her figure explicitly. That dress. I hated to see her in it. Even before she showed her pregnancy I disliked it—I wanted a mother like the one who presided in the falling-down frame house by the tracks: big and neuter and jolly and momlike—not a cute little number. Sweat poured all over me. Humiliation mixed with guilt. Why couldn't she look like the other mothers? Mary's mother was tall, wore demure housedresses, her gray hair in a bun, and sensible black Edna Jennick shoes, not toeless high heels.

I avoided the doorways to the auditorium where the guests would come in. I ran back and forth helping the actors dress and the stagehands move stage furniture. When the play began I still hadn't caught sight of Mom or the white dress. Then I began to worry. Supposing something had happened to her. I did love her, I did, and if something had happened, think how bad it was to have been thinking childish thoughts about how she would look. I prayed Mom would come, in her white dress or any other way.

If only I could see her. Oh come on, I prayed, wondering why nothing could ever be easy or free from worry.

After the play was over and we were putting the stage back together, I saw her. Chatting pleasantly with the teachers in the back of the room. She was wearing a navy dress with white collar and cuffs. At last, she had maternity clothes, and I felt once more I'd wronged her.

THE RIVER continued to grow wider. It nibbled away more and more of the ramp up the hill. But we had other worries besides rising water. Coming home from school one afternoon I found Mom sitting in a chair in her bathrobe. Her hair was uncombed. She stared vacantly into space.

"What's wrong?" I asked. She wouldn't answer.

"You fix dinner," she finally said. She turned her face toward the window. At dinner, she pushed her plate away and went to bed.

"What's wrong?" I asked Daddy.

"Leave her be," he said.

I figured she'd be all right by the next day; she'd be "up and at 'em" as she liked to say, trying to cheer us all up. But in the morning instead of bounding out of bed and rousing us and putting on the coffee, she ignored the alarm and left Daddy to fix breakfast. Jim and I went off to school, and when we came back for lunch she was still sitting in a chair in the blue fuzzy bathrobe. Daddy gave us money for hamburgers and sent us up to the White Lilly to eat.

When we came home for dinner, Daddy said Mom was in the restroom downstairs. "Don't ever get married."

I was to fix dinner again. Again Mom hardly ate.

The next day after school, I threw myself down by Mom's side. She was lying on the bed in a kind of doze.

"What's wrong?" I asked. "Don't you think you'd better be getting up?"

Mom just stared straight ahead and didn't answer for a long time.

"What *is* it, Mom?" I pleaded. I felt vaguely responsible, at fault. My mother had never turned away or refused to talk to me.

She finally looked at me.

"I just don't seem to care about anything," she said disgustedly. "Nothing. Phooey. Leave me alone."

"I can't. C'mon, Mom. Get dressed. Please."

"I don't *want* to," Mom snapped. "Go play."

I began to cry.

"What's the matter?" I insisted.

Mom was silent. She sighed deeply and stared away into space. She looked much older than she had before; her neck was thin and rough and she wore no makeup. Her hair was a mess of tangles and knots. Softly, almost to herself, she said, "Forgive them Father, they know not what they do."

I realized she had had another miscarriage. Another puzzle. It seemed that a baby was the last thing the family needed. We were poor, we were split—the parents both loudly proclaimed in anger that they only "kept on for the children's sake"—and still it dawned on me that Mom was terribly unhappy because she had lost the baby. What about the two kids she already had? We seemed like burden enough. Certainly we didn't need another. We—the big babies—didn't want another. I was mildly disappointed, wondering what a baby would have been like, but I remembered the awful infant upstairs at Harney Street with his sour spittle puddle on his stomach.

For about a week Mom guarded herself jealously, stared into space, wasted no words. She never changed her blue bathrobe or combed her hair. No pleading or exhortation roused her. She pulled away when we tried to talk to her. She wasn't interested in food. Her eyes, usually sparkling—tense, worried, but always eager as sparrows—were hard, flat, and full of hate. What had we done? She mumbled Jesus' words of forgiveness. Why was she blaming us for her suffering? We were hardly Pilate and his gang!

FINALLY ONE day when I got home from school, Mom was up and about. She'd combed her hair and put lipstick on. The house was at least partly clean.

"Are you feeling better?" I asked.

"A little," Mom said. She looked ashamed. "I won't be moping around any more. You'll understand some day. Things will happen in your life. . . ."

Oh dear, here came the dire predictions. When Mom wasn't painting my brilliant future as a great artist—she never just said artist, but always great artist—she was foretelling suffering and pain.

For the next week, Mom went through a real struggle. One day she was her old self, the next she was down again, wrestling with despair. She would stand in front of the dresser mirror and lecture herself: "Now Mildred, stop this foolishness. Millie, old girl, you better listen. Life goes on. It does."

Then she would sob in fits and starts, gasping, talking, and trying to reach her better self. Sometimes I cried along with her.

"But did you *want* a baby?" I asked.

"I thought I didn't. I prayed not to be pregnant when I found out. I wished it would die, and now . . . after four whole months, and all that . . ."

I said gee, or some such outstanding comment.

"Now I've got to accept it. . . . Thy Will be done."

I crept out to the porch and gazed into the swift water. Wherever I looked, mystery, and movement, blind movement. I tried to part the curtains and see into the future. I would grow, like Penny, like Mom. What would it mean? What would having a baby be like? Mom said it hurt, hurt worse than anything, but you loved them, all the more because they hurt so terribly. It made no sense to me.

I stood on the porch railing. A train across the water chugged away into the distance—oh, glorious symbol—escape of millions—it would take me away too, to a better, more beautiful life. The title page of the book I would someday write and the word "FINIS" appeared to me. I would dedicate it to my mother: "All I am or ever hope to be, I owe to my mother." No, too ironic—I hoped to be totally different, never to be a wife and mother, never to suffer. Maybe this: "To Bernard [or whoever the man in my future would be] with love."

Jim hailed me from the ladder to the second deck, his head appearing over the tarpaper, then the rest of him. "Hey, what are you doing up there?"

I jumped down from the railing.

"You sure look funny," he said.

"Oh you."

"You know what? Your neck is so thin, your head looks like a golf ball sitting on a tee."

I gasped for a rejoinder.

"Honest it does," Jim said, holding his sides. "Exactly."

When we went inside, the radio was mumbling away as usual. Mom was fixing dinner. Daddy was reading the paper and talking about a possible flood. We had missed the big one of 1937, the worst in the area's history.

The river took in more and more of our hill. Eventually the club boat and floats were tied off on the trees around the parking lot at the top of the hill. The river crept up over the field where we practiced kickball, then flooded Kellogg Avenue. It reached the railroad tracks. The Stegemyers' house was in water up to the second floor, and the gas station was under, while our home just floated up with the rise. We went to school in a rowboat: trees were now bushes, houses were now boats. For us, it was fun.

Out in the skiff, we poked about in the fascinating, newly aggressive waters. We found an old chest that we were sure contained treasure. It took us a long time to pry it open and discover a single bug that had survived the deluge in its tightly sealed home. Floating near the club boat was what we took to be a nice big kickball; we poked it with a stick and got a hollow humpf. It would be ours, we decided, until we turned it over and discovered the stiff little snout and four cloven feet of a drowned pig. The river coughed up sinkers and floaters in the way of dead bodies, and this was a floater, bloated on its own waste. We pushed it on down into the current.

The floodwaters lapped the schoolyard at McKinley and reached Eastern Avenue in places, but traffic still flowed and school stayed open. Compared to '37, this was minor, but it was our first and only flood. At last, people had to notice the river and see its power.

When the water gradually receded, it left a landscape like the moon. Mud from the river bank to the railroad tracks: gooey, slippery, brown mud. To walk on it to school was like struggling to move in a frustrating dream, where you try to walk and can't get anywhere.

Then the sun came out strong and baked the mud into a stiff land-scape of curling puck-sized pieces. The pattern of dried mud seemed to stretch forever; the dried hunks flipped up as you stepped on them, while beneath was still ooze.

Our floating home gently went back into place as the water returned to its ordinary width and depth. Daddy re-secured all the lines, urged the spar back into place, cleaned the ramp of mud. Land and water parted once again, became separate, opposites.

The East End people cleaned out their homes and rebuilt their sagging porches. Everything was the same, but different. Some families had a relative leave for higher ground; some lost animals and crops.

The river flowed on. Both beautiful and ugly, always full of strange creatures. In the morning, going to school, we might see a flock of birds lifting off the surface of the water in a lovely flutter of wings. There were gars, primitive fish with long snouts and scales like an alligator's; "junk" fish and predators, they were the ugliest creatures in the river. Wallowing in the mud were nests of salamanders or mud puppies, nasty little things with webbed toes and external gills that seemed more mud than animal. Doc Behymer once caught an eel, which Mom fried and which made me deathly sick. Daddy trapped a possum: he put it in a pen on the second deck and warned us away. Wanting to hug this new pet, we soon noticed its sharp teeth and nasty disposition. And there were numerous dogs and cats that people dumped along the banks, roaming around, searching for a home.

The flood brought one of these to us: a dog suddenly appeared at the boat, looking half-starved and acting as though he had been beaten. He was big, brown, and white, about the size of a German shepherd, but he had long fur and an abundant, friendly, wagging tail. When we petted him, he would crouch in fear, as though we might hit him. His eyes were a soft brown, and his expression wise and loving. We named him Drift, and he stayed with us until we left the river. Our greatest pleasure was letting him jump up on our cots and putting our arms around his muddy, burr-encrusted fur. We could feel his wonderful heart beating in his big chest.

OUR LAST year at the yacht club ended with the usual job of getting the boats out of the water and onto blocks. The restaurant was closed, but Mom was in the kitchen cooking beans and cornbread for us instead of cooking steaks and burgers for strangers. I can't recall what I could have been doing to help in this process, but I seem to have been necessary— maybe just as liaison between kitchen and work crew. It was anxious work, getting the clumsy boats out of the water and onto a launching platform. Daddy and Jim and a shanty boater turned the handle of the winch, winding the cable on the platform around the big spool and dragging a boat up tiny rails to the hilltop. Our cheeks were bright red from the wind, and there was much yelling and good-natured cursing. We felt good. The autumn sun was brilliant and the trees blazing. The wind blew our words away. Several boats were soon safely in the field, high up on concrete blocks and dripping river water into the weeds. Soon, the large club boat was a lone duck again, deprived of her offspring, alone with a line of empty stalls. The water was turning dark, and a flock of geese took off from its surface, ruffling wings and water.

DRY LAND

1942–1950

22

THE SAN CARLOS

FOR MANY YEARS when I awoke in the morning—even after I was married—I would have to review where I'd been and try to bring myself up to the present: Auntie's farm, *Valley Queen*, Del Mar, Harney Street, Council Bluffs, Manawa, West Main Street, Pop and Lulu's, Covington, Uncle Lester's, the yacht club. As I grew older and tried to recapture the past, I had to remember the buildings and houses, the rooms and how they were arranged. I had to remember the wallpaper, the furniture, the patterns in the linoleum—just as in childhood I had to remember the landmarks on the way to yet another school and how to find my way home.

The moves from place to place in Cincinnati were even more blurred than those longer ago in time. During my last year at McKinley, while Jim started at Withrow High, I went back to the East End on the street car every day to finish eighth grade: I was terrified of Withrow's junior high on the sprawling campus in Hyde Park. At one point we lived in a top-floor apartment in a frame Victorian near Peebles Corner and in several other places I could barely recall. The year I started high school, one or the other of my parents gave me a key and told me to go to an apartment building on Madison Road.

The San Carlos Apartments looked like a lot of other places with fancy names like the Alhambra or the Cadiz: tall, maroon-red brick, two buildings at angles to one another, a small lawn. I climbed the four flights of steps and let myself into the top floor left. The air was musty in the tiny dark hall. I saw that we had a good-sized living room, a large dining room, a tiny kitchen, and a solarium looking out on the street.

I went into the bathroom: a tub with a shower, a sink, a toilet, a door. I turned on the sink faucet, and water came pouring out. This plentiful flow still seemed miraculous after the tin can and dipper at the yacht club. I let the water run.

Because of my being a girl and presumably needing space to myself, I was given the solarium for my bedroom. Jim slept on the living room couch, and the parents had another Murphy In-a-Door bed that pulled down into the dining room.

Instead of the sound of boat motors and the trains on the Kentucky shore, at night we heard the streetcars on Madison; a loud *carom* as a car chugged up the hill and an occasional small electric *zap* as the wand holding the car to the overhead wires broke loose and the motorman had to stop and replace it.

My father was now the manager of a fruit-drink bar called "The California Orange Bar" in downtown Cincinnati. One of several in a chain, it was a small storefront operation with stools along the wall and a bar where people stood and drank orange, pineapple, and grape beverages. In the window was a machine squeezing oranges while a woman cut more and fed the machine, giving the impression that the product was genuine juice. In fact, the drinks were a mix of water, sugar, fruit flavorings, and some citrus juices. But as my mother always said—she was completely loyal to everything she touched!—"There's juice in it." The drinks were colorful, refreshing, and cheap; along with coffee, doughnuts, hot dogs, and rolls, they brought in a big breakfast, lunch, and theater trade.

In the forties, downtown Cincinnati was the place where everyone shopped and went for entertainment. There were five big movie theaters —one, the Albee, was a true cinema palace with oriental carpets, crystal chandeliers, a grand staircase, tapestries, and fake Louis XIV furnishings in the long halls. There was a small jewel box of a theater, the Cox; a large theater for big plays and musicals, the Schubert; and a third theater notorious for bad acoustics, the Taft.

Fountain Square, the center of town, was dominated by the famous Tyler-Davidson fountain with its green-patinaed female figure, the Genius of Waters, surrounded by boys on sea creatures, who appear to be urinating. Around the square were thriving buildings and shops: the

Gibson hotel, the Albee, Potter's Shoes, Planter's Peanuts, Maude Mueller candies. There were over half a dozen department stores: upscale Pogue's; Mabley-Carew with its big corner clock (the only reminder still there); Rollman's, a step down; Shillito's; Bond's; McAlpin's. There were several men's stores: Dunlap's and Burkhart's, and two ultra-stylish women's stores: Jenny's and Giddings.

The sidewalks around the square were crowded with shoppers. Mr. Peanut, a man dressed in a yellow peanut costume and wearing a monocle and a black top hat, mingled among them, giving out samples of Planter's nuts. People offering free cigarettes, two to a box, walked up and down, while Roy Ketz, well-known newspaper vendor and philosopher, talked to anyone who would listen.

The Orange Bar my father managed was just off the square next to the Keith theater and the Wheel Cafe, a big busy cafeteria catering largely to men. The drink bar was owned by a man named Fred Williams who was getting so rich he was moving on to grocery stores and oil wells. He had no sooner made a success of the California Orange Bars than he wanted to sell.

My parents at last saw an opportunity to get out of the financial hole they had been in for so many years. They approached Uncle Bud and a bank for loans so they could buy the Orange Bar. Bud became a silent partner, the bank came through, and my parents went into business. They worked around the clock. Mother would open up in the morning for the breakfast trade and come home around four in the afternoon. Daddy went down to work sometime while I was at school and stayed to close the place at midnight. They had taken on a large debt.

I seldom saw Daddy, and Mom would come home exhausted. They oversaw two shifts of porters and bar servers, who came and went from their employment with frustrating speed. The parents often had to mix the drinks, cook the food items, and serve the customers themselves. We did not have a single family meal together in the four years we lived on Madison Road.

On Saturdays it was my job to clean our apartment: I dusted and swept, and scrubbed the bathroom. Until the Orange Bar started bringing in money, we still had an icebox requiring a visit from the ice man. There was defrosting to do and the emptying of the overflowing pan of water. Until we acquired a vacuum sweeper, we used a broom to sweep the rugs. While I worked, I dreamed of love with someone like Maxim de Winter in *Rebecca*.

I WENT FROM McKinley, and an eighth-grade class of maybe twenty, to Withrow High School, a huge place with hundreds of students, a big football stadium, and a junior high. I was lost. At McKinley I knew everyone and was part of everything. Here I was nothing and nobody. The students in my large homeroom seemed to know each other. Many had gone to grade schools in Hyde Park, the affluent area Withrow served, and then junior high at Withrow. I didn't know a soul: McKinley students tended (as they still do) to drop out and go to work after seventh or eighth grade.

At Withrow the kids everyone looked up to wore silver fraternity or sorority pins on their sweaters. They belonged. No one else did. The girls among the elect wore cashmere sweaters and pearls, saddle shoes or loafers, white socks, pleated plaid or plain wool skirts. The boys wore corduroy or wool pegged pants, button-down cotton shirts in blue or white, cashmere V-necked sweaters, loafers or saddle shoes. To vary this style was to show yourself a drip, a jerk.

The kids from the best sororities and fraternities sat at special tables in the cafeteria at the head of the hot lunch line where everyone else could watch them flitting about, talking and laughing and looking totally self-assured.

I came home crying every day. I was confused by the crowded halls, the noise and clatter, the long lines at lunch, having to change rooms five or six times a day, the sleek-looking students. I felt muddy. As though I were crawling out of a social ooze more nightmarish than the real stuff left by the flood.

Mom found me sobbing in the bathtub one night and asked what was wrong. I said everything. I hated high school and would never fit in. I couldn't diagram a sentence and I didn't know how to attract boys. Mom rather unhelpfully looked at herself in the mirror and said, "I could always get any man I wanted."

Life at home was the usual crucible. My parents and my brother could be heard arguing in the kitchen late at night. Jim hated school, played hooky a lot, and hung about with a group of neighborhood boys my mother didn't approve of.

He was brought home one night by a policeman for throwing snowballs at a streetcar. Daddy and Mom were both waiting for him, bawling him out with the brio of a Verdi duet. Mom went into one of her dramatic tirades: "My son, a common criminal!" She twisted her hands. "My son, my son! I bore him in my womb, I nursed him at my breast."

"Oh, Mom, ugh."

I, the "good" child, could often see Jim heading for trouble and tried to warn him away: maybe he shouldn't set his model airplanes on fire and launch them out the apartment window. I dreaded the loud words that would follow his misdeeds. But Jim ignored my prissy advice. He snitched the parents' cigarettes and left the evidence in the ashtrays. He sipped their beer and never covered up his trail. At Withrow, he was infamous for insubordination. My homeroom teacher, on reading my name from the attendance sheet, gave me a suspicious once-over, then asked whether I was related in any way to Jim Coomer. When I admitted that I was, she said, "I thought so. I recognize that *look*." I had to be twice as goody-goody as ever, while my brother enjoyed his notoriety.

Jim was fascinated by car motors and spent a lot of time at the corner garage. Mom swore he was wasting his life, destroying his brain. "My son, the grease monkey!" she lamented. Still, when he got into trouble at school, she went to bat for him, charming Mr. Peoples, the principal. She had once worked in the Withrow cafeteria and conducted a mild flirtation over the steam tables with this soft-mannered, polite older man. I was fascinated watching her work.

"Your mother capitalizes on her experiences," Mr. Peoples once told me. "She's an amazing person."

Mom and Daddy argued about how to run the business. Daddy was no sooner making a success of their one store than he wanted to acquire another. Mom wanted to pay off the debt. They both began to complain about Uncle Bud, who was collecting a good return on his loan without stirring from his easy chair.

I was withdrawing from the family, at the same time resenting them for being absent so much. I yearned for a peaceful family group. I went back to a church I once briefly attended with a friend from Bevis Avenue, to a Sunday supper. But I felt totally left out. No one spoke to me all evening. I went to the youth group; everyone knew everyone else.

The war was still going on. It seemed as though it would never end. Every day the news was of men killed, towns destroyed.

Jim was determined to join the navy. Though he was underage throughout most of the war years, he ran away and tried to lie his way in so often that by the time he was seventeen, Daddy and Mom signed for him, and he left home. He served on a ship in the Pacific. If he wrote letters home, they were not shared with me. I didn't miss him—I was too busy making new adjustments.

MY LIFE at Withrow was saved by a girl named Janie. I had met her at the art museum in the young people's classes, and she began to call me regularly and stop in at our apartment. She was unattached like me, but much more confident. She was interested in music and art and books, just as I was. She was a striking brunette, not conventionally pretty, with flawless skin and coloring. Pretty soon, we were staying over at each other's houses every weekend and were together as much as possible at school. Since her streetcar came past the San Carlos, I would hang a white cloth out the window when I was home and wanted her to stop in. She was the first friend I ever had that I didn't leave behind after a year or two.

My parents both liked Janie and she seemed to like them. Compared to her home life, mine was pleasant during high school. Janie was a leftover from a divorce, and she and her mother waged constant war. Her stepfather and younger brother crowded her out at home. My parents tore only each other down. Me, they held up as the paragon, the family hope. Mom told me how good a brain I had, and Daddy said I was the only one in the family with a drop of common sense. They encouraged me to use my own judgment in everything.

Both Mom and Daddy welcomed guests to the apartment. Though Janie and I were sometimes awakened by their loud voices from the kitchen, on good nights they might invite Janie and me to share a midnight snack with them.

As I walked to Withrow beneath shade trees and observed the well-kept lawns and large houses of Hyde Park, I envied the lives of the girls who lived in them. But being right on the streetcar line proved to have advantages: I was free to go wherever I wanted in the city. Janie and I got volunteer jobs as ushers at the various theaters on weeknights, as well as weekends, and were permitted out of school to usher at the symphony on Friday afternoons. Other girls had to be driven everywhere, and until the war ended gas was rationed and cars were scarce. There were advantages to my parents being so busy, too; they weren't hovering over me. And the Orange Bar provided a spot downtown where I could duck in to get carfare or a doughnut.

I saw Jascha Heifetz and Yehudi Menuhin, the greatest violinists of the day, at the Taft. I saw Paul Robeson in *Othello*, Katherine Cornell in *Candide*, Frank Fay in *Harvey*, and Maurice Evans in *Julius Caesar*. The American Ballet Theater and the Ballet de Monte Carlo both came to town and performed for several weeks instead of the one or two days typical of today's runs. The symphony brought Artur Rubinstein and Leonard Bernstein (a hot young conductor little known to local audiences). In summer, Janie and I ushered at the Zoo Opera, a season of grand opera that lasted about six weeks and was performed in an old wooden pavilion in the heart of the Cincinnati Zoo. All the great stars of the day, Rise Stevens, Ezio Pinza, Gladys Swarthout, Jeanette Macdonald, Alexander Kipnis, and Richard Tuoker, sang at the zoo, backed by a motley chorus, the occasional roar of a lion, and the high-pitched cries of water birds on the lake. The audience and singers sweltered in the heat, but the seats were filled. Paper fans stirred in the dark.

Janie and I worshipped the singers and we joined the gang of young people who hung about backstage. All we asked for were autographs and to be chosen as "supers." Extra spear carriers were needed in *Aida*, soldiers in *Faust*, and peasants in most everything. But *Carmen* provided the big opportunity for those of us without height or clout with the stage manager. Escamillo's entourage of bull fighters, picadors, and hangers-on had to be large as he marched triumphantly to the bull ring. Thus, dressed in ages-old satin britches, boleros, and ballet slippers, our hair tucked into snoods and tri-cornered hats, we joined the parade, as unlikely a pair of picadors as ever piked a bull. We loved our brief moment on stage—and it was brief. We were on and off in seconds, as fast as you could hum the first few bars of the Toreador song.

We were not afraid going out at night. I had to transfer at Peebles Corner to catch the Zoo-Eden bus to the opera and walk six or eight blocks to and from the streetcar to Music Hall for the symphony. The streets were well-lit and amazingly free of crime. The only time I felt a little fear was after concerts, alone, on the dark block from the streetcar to the San Carlos. And I always ran up the four flights of steps, trying to outrace any mugger who might have slipped in the unlocked front door.

I thought nothing of my freedom and my art-filled world. Didn't everyone go to the theater or concerts several times a week? The part the Ohio River and my father played in my new life never occurred to me until long after his death: the way the steamboats made Cincinnati a city. The way they brought culture along with pigs and horses, so that within minutes of some of the tiniest, most out-of-the-way river towns like Rabbit Hash (then truly a one-horse town with a single general store) or Petersburg (where some of the people had never been off their porches), Cincinnati offered a sophisticated culture of music and theater in which little girls of fourteen and fifteen could participate.

While I was benefitting by these experiences, my parents were learning the hard ways of business. They learned to keep books, and they found their fellow restauranteurs were more interested in cutting in on their trade than in making friends. Soon after they started work, the building their first bar was in was slated to be torn down, and they had to move. There were painful issues. In the forties, restaurants, theaters, and hotels were strictly off limits for black people; even Duke Ellington and Ella Fitzgerald stayed at a hotel called the Manse in a segregated neighborhood. Food services throughout the city had a policy of serving black people carryout only. One day a customer threw a cup of orange drink in Mom's face. This incident upset my mother, but she was more upset at the discrimination. She had worked hard to promote racial understanding at the Community Chest camp and the Neighborhood House. Daddy paid no attention to the system: he grew up in a Whites-only world and had never known any African Americans except the stevedores on the river.

Every week at the Orange Bar seemed to bring some new stress. One night while Mom was on duty, a soldier on leave, having finished his drink, suddenly began to shout that the help had stolen his watch. He barred the door, refusing to let customers in or out. After a futile half hour of reasoning with him, Mom managed to contact the police, and he was hauled off. She felt terrible when she found out that the young man was on sick leave.

My parents were not real business people. Mom was too softhearted: she would have preferred to give things away. And she was so eager to please, she wore herself out ingratiating herself with the customers. Daddy was bored by bookkeeping; he seemed trapped in the small office overlooking the bar, counting and packaging pennies. He was impatient with the porters who lugged sloshing buckets of purple and orange liquid from the mixing vats in the basement to the fountains.

Daddy covered the walls of the office with a collage of magazine and calendar pictures. After he finally acquired a car, a big green Buick, he kept urging Mom to take a road trip to Alaska or Canada, but she would not go with him because of his fast, erratic driving. He piled up some two hundred parking tickets because he insisted on parking directly in front of his business in spite of clearly lettered "no parking" signs.

At the apartment there was always a bubbling pot of green beans on the stove and an argument brewing. Daddy and Mom disagreed about everything: he cooked the green beans into a mush flavored with heart-stopping amounts of ham and salt; she liked them less rich. He wanted salad vegetables cut in large pieces; she liked them chopped. She worried about what the neighbors would hear through the open windows that were just a few feet from ours; he didn't give a damn.

To walk down the street with them was an experience: she always crossed on the green light; he always crossed on the red. He simply held up his hand and flagged the cars to a stop. He took long, fast strides, while she tottered along on her high heels, making little click-click sounds on the sidewalk. She was constantly asking him to lower his voice, which boomed out in restaurants or on the street.

He wanted to travel; she wanted to go to the opera.

In the few hours she had at home, Mom began lolling on the couch, wearing her old blue bathrobe, sipping wine and reading. One night, she suddenly got up, swept through the dining room, and pushed everything on the buffet onto the floor. A set of glasses and a pitcher I had hand-painted for her birthday shattered all over the place. She looked shocked at herself, like a small guilty child (Anger is for beasts). She looked apologetically at me.

I was more astonished than upset at the destruction of my handiwork. I helped her sweep up the glass. I often felt like the mother of my mother, instead of the child. She was so tiny. And she was trying so hard.

Daddy took to sitting on the garbage cans on the fire escape outside the kitchen door. He would stare out at the sky through the grating and mutter over and over, "You're born, you get married, you die. You're born, you get married, you die."

Still, they kept on trying. To Daddy, a man's job was providing for and protecting his family. One of Mom's favorite guilt trips—and she was the Delta hub of departures—was to claim she was only hanging on for us children.

But when they went out to a restaurant for dinner, she would mascara each eyelash until her lashes looked like the fringe on an apple blossom. Her lips would be bright red and her dress low-cut. She and Daddy had lots of dinners with Uncle Bud and Marie, with Daddy teasing Marie about her cooking and he and Bud outdoing each other in drinking Carstairs 52, a cheap brand of bourbon.

One afternoon while I was making the beds, I lifted the Murphy-in-a-Door and proceeded to push it into its closet. Pinned to the underside of the mattress was a poem Mom wrote for Daddy: "Just a little smile from you, dear, would lighten every task. Just a little smile from you, dear, is all that I would ask."

She must have forgotten Daddy didn't make beds.

23

CHANGES

FRANKLIN DELANO Roosevelt was our president ever since I could remember, since I was three or four and we lived at the Del Mar Hotel and the men talked about him in the lobby. I couldn't imagine anyone else being the head of our country. We knew his reassuring smile, his tilted cigarette holder, the bags under his eyes, his pince-nez, his jaunty hat. When he died—I was a sophomore in high school—Mom and I, together with Janie, cried. It was as if God had died. We knew he was ill. Recent pictures showed him not so jaunty, the eye bags dark—yet we never believed he would die so soon. He had just been elected to a fourth term. We had to keep him in office. He was winning the war. The radio had blared, "Don't change horses in midstream."

Later that year, May 8th, 1945, Germany surrendered. On Fountain Square, people climbed on the bandstand and fountain and danced all around the Spirit of Waters. Boys in uniform kissed every girl they could catch. Beer and champagne foamed out of the fountain. A blizzard of confetti came out of the windows of the buildings. I wanted to be kissed like the bold girls who let themselves be grabbed and whirled around, but I hung back—just wishing for the warmth of the boys' arms, the feel of their uniforms.

We read about Hitler committing suicide in his bunker. We saw pictures in *Life* magazine of Mussolini and his mistress hanged upside down by his own people in the public square of Milan. In September, President Truman ordered the atomic bomb dropped on Japan. In those pre-TV days, the horror of the bomb was not brought home as it was later. We were just glad the war was over.

I BEGAN to catch on at Withrow. The girls at school talked me into buying some clothes and fixing my hair in a long pageboy in the "peek-a-boo" style of Veronica Lake, then the most popular glamour girl in movies. I wanted to look like everybody else, so though I couldn't afford cashmeres, I wore sweaters (enhanced by the obligatory pair of "falsies") and imitation pearls and traded in my clunky brown oxfords for penny loafers. I never mentioned McKinley School or the river. When my mother would say brightly to some visitor, "We used to live on a steamboat," I'd try to change the subject.

Withrow was all about football and popularity. Status was largely based on whether you had a date on Fridays and Saturdays. Nobody was asking me (I had no sorority pin). So when Tally-Ho rushed me, I joined. The blackballing and snobbishness bothered me, but I was flattered, and I grew to like my sisters. They were not all the smooth, perfectly poised girls I had seen from afar as a freshman. They just looked that way.

Getting to know them I found the same conflicts and problems Janie and I suffered: what did we want to do with our lives? Where would we find love? What kind of women did we want to be? Smart and brisk like Katharine Hepburn? Sweet like June Allyson? Teachers? Artists living in garrets? Housewives and mothers? Broadway stars?

If football was our high school's religion, sex was our obsession. Both were closely refereed. Nice girls didn't "go all the way." The scale of intimacy decreed that "necking," i.e. kissing and hugging, even a little soul kissing, were fine. Petting (necking and fondling of breasts) was "risqué" and thus taboo; intercourse was totally out. We were somewhat frustrated, some more than others, but the absolutely clear lines were rather comforting. We were no more unhappy than today's adolescents with their putative freedom. The word "sex" was seldom used, and "ass" was still "arse."

We were almost all white Protestants. Most Jews and African Americans went to Hughes or Walnut Hills and would not have been welcome at Withrow. One fraternity boy—with money and his own convertible—was rumored to be a Jew passing himself off as one of *us*. The few Asian students were, to the rest of us, as exotic as museum porcelains and as distant. No one ever spoke to them.

The African American kids were treated outrageously: forced to swim last bell on Friday, before the cleaning of the pool, because the others, according to the school, would not tolerate sharing the water with them. All the while, displays around the school announced Brotherhood Week.

Big events like war and issues such as prejudice only touched at the edges of our small world. We were going through puberty.

I MOVED BETWEEN the various school groups, never quite fitting into a niche. I read Dostoyevsky and represented my sorority in a beauty pageant. I attended a life class at the studio of a local artist and went to dances.

Everybody wanted to be in the Withrow Minstrels, the school's famous variety show held every spring—replete with end men in blackface (!), tap dancing, a girls' pony chorus, and solo singers and dancers. I got in junior year by writing a skit based on *Carmen*.

My parents would have been horrified if they had known what I was doing in those high school years. The group of friends I liked best ushered with Janie and me. The boys were mostly gay and the girls were fellow "intellectuals." These were the only friends I invited to my home, and I only dared invite them when my parents took a rare trip out of town. We did evil things like listen to records, sing, and drink a little wine.

I was dating a variety of fraternity boys, going to Lookout House and Beverly Hills, two "supper clubs" in notorious Northern Kentucky, then known for mob nightclubs, gambling, and prostitution. Until the fifties, Cincinnati could remain pompous and superior because it did all its sinning across the river. We kids drank plenty, using fake identification cards to convince willing waiters we were old enough. The driver of whatever car we were in was usually drunk.

One night, speeding along Kellogg Avenue, a group of us crashed into a tree. I went flying from the back seat to the front. I woke up in a little tavern in a small room; a cop was staring at me, muttering, "Concussion, concussion." I was examined by a doctor, who found I had a broken arm. My right eye turned black.

When I was back at home, my mother told me that when the phone call came that I'd been injured in an accident, Daddy turned white. I was surprised. I didn't think he cared much one way or the other.

That's how far the family had drifted. And Daddy never expressed feeling for any one in the family, except for a kind of mildly affectionate teasing. He never called any of us nicknames, except me: "Duchess" was based on my supposedly imperious will. Mother was always "Mildred" or "Millie," never "dear" or "honey." When Mom complained that Daddy never praised any of us, he said, half joking, "I give credit where credit is due." He called hugging "lollygaggin'" and discouraged it.

I went to the junior prom with a black eye and my arm in a sling.

A lot of good things came my way in our four years on Madison Road. At Withrow, I had excellent English teachers: Miss Moorman and a pair of old maids, Miss Atkins and Miss Meredith, who lived together at Miss Atkins's home. All three loved their subject, their work, and students with the intellect for Shakespeare and nineteenth-century novels. I won a number of literary prizes and wrote for the school paper. But with all my opportunities and activities, I still felt like an outsider. No matter how well I wore the protective coloration of the sorority girl, I felt I was dragging mud and river water behind me.

In junior year, Miss Moorman assigned us the task of writing an autobiography. Though I was a timid girl and always close to tears, I refused. I didn't want anyone to know I had been thrown out of a hotel, that I'd been poor and was a river rat. I wanted to be exactly like everyone else. But I had no hometown, no house with trees, no Dad at work and Mom at home in a nice crisp apron: it was all confusion, a whirl of places and people coming and going. Miss Moorman said she realized that I felt my life was none of her business, but she insisted that I give the assignment a shot anyway. I wrote a crude stream-of-consciousness piece, not knowing there was such a thing. I was amazed at the number of places, people, and events I had already experienced in sixteen years, but I knew none of these things fully: they were paragraphs in my life. Mom, Daddy, and Jim were the only constants.

My Withrow teachers, along with those I'd had since I started school, gave me tremendous support for my writing and art and even for my academic achievement, though I did most of my homework while walking to school, and got only modestly good grades. My high-school counselor, another old maid and probably a lesbian—she had a very affectionate live-in relationship with another counselor—was a tough, no-nonsense woman who sized up her charges with a cold and critical eye. She called me in to talk about college, with my French teacher in attendance. They didn't ask me where I wanted to go to college. I wouldn't have known anyway. Most of my classmates were going to Wooster in Ohio. The French teacher said, "Dottie's too big for Wooster." (Was I? I had only the vaguest idea of myself. I didn't even know my weight or my height. A fellow student said I wasn't even a Christian because I questioned Christ's divinity and had never been baptized. I guess I wasn't.)

My counselor agreed with my French teacher. "University of Chicago," she said. "We'll get her a scholarship."

Auntie and More-Pop, too, wanted to help. Sitting with me on their front porch one night, they shyly said that if I wanted to study art or go to college and needed money, they would be glad to contribute.

College applications came my way, and I casually filled them out in ink, never stopping to agonize over how I answered questions. I took a day-long written test at a local school to qualify for Chicago. The other applicants were from Walnut Hills, the competitive-entrance college-prep high school. I had been admitted there, but Mom had thrown the accept-ance postcard away because she thought I'd want to go to the school within walking distance. I didn't find this out until years later. In the meantime I assumed, feeling dumb, that I hadn't passed. I was willing to undergo everyone and anyone's tests—anything for acceptance, for confirmation.

Our family's last year at the San Carlos and my last year at Withrow, Jim came home from the navy. Typically, there was no big party or cele-bration for him, and the family never once sat down together and asked him about his navy adventures. He looked like the same old Jim: almost-white hair, big sheepish smile. He looked trim in his white uniform, and I wanted to take him to the drug store where I worked after school to show him off. But he was no longer interested in the company of his little sister.

Only gradually did we become pals again. He told me about finding a little dead boy in a phone booth in Shanghai, China. He played his Josh White records for me, and "The Lass with the Delicate Air" filled the apartment. He started listening to my opera records and fell in love with classical music. He made the mistake, though, of leaving the wax discs on the heat register and they turned into Dali's limp watches. Then they grew crisp and wavy like potato chips and we gleefully crumbled them into bits and threw them out the window, laughing hysterically. It was like old times.

Jim's voice soon joined Mom's and Daddy's, which I heard from my perch on the solarium. He was a veteran who had traveled all over the Pacific. He didn't want to be told what time to come home at night or how much beer to drink. Or to explain a black eye he got at a bar. I only once joined in one of these contretemps. After Jim had slammed out the door, I accused my father of driving him off and was told to mind my own business. I was always excluded. Mom and Daddy tried to throw me clear of the wreck, to protect me. But being left out kept me from ever talking back, something Daddy had always forbidden anyway. I had to be all right. If things got rough, Daddy would say, "You're OK, aren't you Duchess?" Of course, I'd nod my head yes. I didn't want my father to think I was a sissy, or anyone to see me in pain.

With Jim always taking the parents on, serving as advance troops, my activities went unnoticed. Daddy was mildly suspicious of the various boys who came to pick me up for dates, but was not around enough to supervise. I did my necking in cars, never on the living room couch. I didn't care about any of the boys I dated. They seemed so callow.

Then I met Sid. We were on a double date. He was with a sexy-looking older girl and I was with a fellow theater usher. Sid had just been discharged from the army, so he had a more worldly aura than the boys at Withrow. He had thick black hair, a big smile, and handsome features. He seemed really intelligent—and funny. He had a cool air about him, and I liked cool things. His only flaw was that he was wearing a suit at least two sizes too large, rimless glasses (definitely not sharp), and white socks (taboo). We dumped our dates after this first get-together. I invited him to my sorority dance.

My father took one look at Sid and declared him a communist. Sid was going to law school and working with the NAACP to integrate the movie theaters. He showed up at the apartment with a bloody nose administered by an usher. He was deeply interested in the Charter Party, a reform political group in Cincinnati that rid the city of crooked political bosses in the 1920s. He answered all my father's challenging questions politely but firmly. As he became a regular at the apartment, Daddy gradually accepted him, and eventually respected him highly. A man who was successful in his work and cared for his family was my father's ideal.

My mother was lukewarm toward Sid. He had a somewhat sardonic sense of humor, and she thought he was sneering at her. But she too eventually became a convert and thought him the most wonderful man in the world.

My family was still trying to be a family. Daddy set up several parties that included Janie and her boyfriend; me and Sid; Jim and whoever he was going with at the time; his friend Harold, who was working for the Orange Bars; and Mom. We went to the ice show at the Restaurant Continentale at the Netherland Plaza hotel and other fancy places. Of course Mom accused Daddy of showing off and wasting money. She worried about the debts. Daddy had gotten his way as usual, and they were acquiring several more stores. Mom always wanted to save, Daddy always wanted to spend.

To Daddy, money was something to have fun with, not something to pile up as the Beamers believed in doing. He complained that mother and the rest of us could live in a tent, that we didn't know how to enjoy life. Running into Janie and me at a downtown restaurant, he found that we had as usual, like Mom, ordered the cheapest thing on the menu: spaghetti. "Try the lobster," Pop demanded. We were fine with the cheaper fare. Finally, Daddy called the waiter over and ordered each of us girls a lobster dinner. He didn't know any other way, so he just forced us to have a good time.

Daddy did not fit in in the city. He talked to everyone—on the bus, in elevators. His accent and his small-town friendliness were considered peculiar. He was not a businessman, he just wanted to see what it was like to have money. He was not acquisitive, he just had to see what it felt like to wear a diamond ring. He liked good clothes and bought himself expensive double-breasted suits and fine silk ties. With decent outfits, he was once again a handsome man, except for his teeth. He frequently bragged that he had never once been to a dentist, and had a smile full of chipped, brownish incisors to show for it.

When the acceptance to the University of Chicago came, I jumped around and yelled. I could escape. School. Family. Cincinnati and all its meanings. Here was something I'd accomplished. I felt vindicated: Miss

Moorman, who loved my writing, had nevertheless predicted that I would never get anywhere in life because I was so "lackadaisical." Yet here I was, accepted by a big college with the largest scholarship awarded to a Withrow student that year.

Daddy muttered against the place: Robert Hutchins, the Chancellor, was at that time defending the school against charges of being a communist hotbed. Mother didn't read the newspaper about issues like that. She just knew it was a good opportunity for me. Daddy tried to throw his weight around, exercising his usual tactic for getting his way—outshouting everyone. But Mom said, "She's going. Period."

24

STRANGERS

I STILL have the first possession I ever bought myself: a Modern Library edition of *Les Miserables*. Buying it, holding it, felt strange and new. Possessions had to be packed up—just more stuff to be lugged around. But at the San Carlos, I felt somewhat settled; after all, I'd been there longer than I'd ever lived anywhere. So I bought the book, the first one I read that was not from the public library. Then, with the allowance Mom gave me for taking care of the apartment, I bought records, and by the time the Chicago scholarship came through, I had a good collection.

I still like 78 records best: round black wax disks with the Victor or

Decca label clearly readable. You lifted the arm of the player, checked the needle at the end for lint. Carefully, you placed the needle in the first groove of the record, and gorgeous, if less than faithful, sound filled the room. Yes, you had to turn the record over if it was a long piece or replace it if a multi-record symphony. But there was something fun about participating—you couldn't walk away and forget about it.

We bought our records at Willis's Music Store downtown. Janie and I would go after school or on Saturdays. We took endless albums into the small glass listening booths where customers played their records before buying. We could be seen through the glass by the clerks, and we could see into adjoining booths where other listeners were moving to other rhythms.

At the San Carlos I had acquired many friends, a new boyfriend, an interesting life—a cat. I would miss all these if I went away to college.

I had airy plans for my future. Of course I'd marry and have several children. I felt I should go into the orange drink business because it was thriving and a way of earning a living, but I wanted to be a writer and an artist too. I told Sid I would manage one or more of the Orange Bars, instituting new practices and policies for the women employees like better restrooms and classes in reading and art; I would then start a newspaper carrying real news and uplifting editorials instead of the conservative stuff of the Cincinnati *Enquirer* and of course write books and paint.

"Whatever happened to that poor rag you married back there?" Sid asked.

I saw his point. Maybe I should narrow down. But I had no idea which of my many ambitions would have to be pitched overboard.

Graduation at Withrow was wonderful: we wore long robes and mortarboards and marched around the stadium to "Pomp and Circumstance." I felt I'd really accomplished something. None of my family came to the ceremony, though Mom had made me a formal to wear to my sorority's dance. My parents played a kind of Stella Dallas role in my life, pushing me out on the stage and hiding behind the curtain. I never knew whether they were uninterested, bored, too busy, or afraid I'd be ashamed of them.

As fall of 1947 approached, I knew I would be going to Chicago. I had a second scholarship, for art, at Rockford College in Illinois, but the

Chicago offer was larger—four hundred dollars for a full year's tuition—and Chicago sounded more exciting than Rockford. I hadn't the slightest idea what I was getting into. I was ahead of my classmates in poetry, fiction, and art, but my grip on geography was weak—I found it boring, with its drab green textbooks full of uninspiring facts, ugly relief maps, and lists of "raw materials" shipped among countries (with America ahead in everything). I thought I was going east to college.

I got cold feet one evening when the time to leave was near, but Sid assured me I would be fine. I wanted him to come along, but he was racing through law school on the G. I. Bill of Rights, a government program offering college tuition to veterans. He had been on his way to the front, wedged into a "40 and 8" boxcar (forty men or eight horses), when the war in Europe was declared won. Happy his adventure was over, he was eager to graduate and be on his own. I was amazed at how he went about his work. While I was sloppy, dreamy, and disorganized, he was totally in charge. The night before exams he would take me out to a restaurant or for a drive, scorning last minute cramming. He had the subject mastered, the necessary studying done, and fully expected the usual A.

September came: I got my small wardrobe together—a few sweaters and skirts, a pair of jeans. I ironed a blouse. As usual I was the only one home. This wasn't like the college send-offs I'd seen in the movies.

Mom did not take a single hour off work. She had become even more afraid of wasting time or anything else, including affection, than ever. I did find a white suitcase with "D. E. C." engraved on it, which Daddy had bought me, waiting in the hall. I read the letters as the abbreviation for December, but that didn't make sense, so I asked what D. E. C. stood for. Daddy said, rather impatiently, "Dorothy Elizabeth Coomer."

"But Pop, my middle name is Louise," I said. I was named after Auntie.

Daddy looked really puzzled.

"I thought it was Elizabeth."

The morning I was to leave, I was picked up by Pop Beamer, whom Mom had asked to drive me to Union Terminal to catch the train. I told the empty apartment goodbye. Only Janie came along—she was going to stay in Cincinnati and study nursing. Pop and Janie walked me to the gate. They shyly wished me well and left. I watched another girl I knew was on her way to the university hugging and kissing a line of relatives at the train gate. I felt jealous and a little sad.

I found my seat on the train, my hair still wrapped in pin curls and a red bandanna. I had awakened late—I was always late for everything—and had skipped breakfast and all but the essential grooming. This was my first trip on a train. I got hungrier and hungrier as I watched Cincinnati recede into the background, replaced by miles of dreary suburbs and then flat, endless fields. I knew there was a dining car on the James Whitcomb Riley, but how to get there? The car I was in was separate from the others, just like the freight cars I used to crawl under in the East End. How would I hop to the next car? Finally, I asked someone for help and was shown the doors and platforms over the couplings.

At the breakfast tables I met some other students heading for the university. They were all from Walnut Hills High School, very earnest and no doubt very brainy since they were heading for Chicago (it never occurred to me that I might share this trait since I was going in the same direction).

THE CAMPUS took in many blocks; the buildings were mostly gray stone, medieval looking, and were set among the shady residential streets of Hyde Park. My dorm, Kelly Hall, was on the Midway, a great stretch of trees and grass separating the university from the neighborhood to the south. I parked my suitcase in the tiny room assigned to me—two desks and a bunk bed—and, being an early arrival, took off for Sixty-Third Street where there were shops with an elevated train, or "L," overhead. I almost danced along the street, whispering "Free, free!"

LIKE WITHROW, Chicago was frighteningly big. We were registered among masses of students in long lines, then sent to large halls to sweat over the placement tests that would determine how many courses we would have to take to acquire a Bachelor of Arts. If we did well on a test, we were excused from taking that subject. We were free to attend class or not, read the assignments or not, but at the end of the year, we had to take a six-hour exam in each subject, which was all that counted. The Bachelor of Arts requirements were rigorous, but we were encouraged to complete them as quickly as possible and move on to graduate school. Those with four years of high school were expected to complete the courses for a B.A. in two years. We read only original works by influential thinkers of Western civilization: no textbooks watering down their words.

I had to take quite a few courses, especially compared to the fabled George Steiner who had to take only one. At Withrow I was special. Now I was just one of many. Everyone was smart, and they had read things besides novels and poetry. My assigned courses were in subjects I'd never been interested in, heavy on science, social science, history, and mathematics. The only courses I would be good in and enjoy were humanities and philosophy.

I became obsessed with getting through the undergraduate program in two years. That was what was expected of me and that's what I would do. I had a downright self-destructive desire to please everyone, whether for my achievements or my personal traits. As to the latter, people seemed to feel quite free to criticize. My posture was poor: Mom. My voice was too high: everyone. My record player was too loud: neighbors. My neck was too thin: Jim. When someone at the San Carlos had asked why I never smiled, I went around smiling, whether I was happy or not. So it was not inconsistent that I would insist on doing the difficult thing instead of stretching my B.A. out over the few extra semesters that it would take to earn it without killing myself.

Still, after a few weeks of terror and confusion, I began to have a social life. I acquired two boyfriends: one was the football player I had wished for during high school (because everyone wanted a football player). He was dark-haired, handsome, and very nice. But he wasn't the brightest guy around. I spent more time with my other friend, Paddy, who was an excellent student and a thoughtful, sensitive person. Along with a group, we went to the Indiana Dunes for beach picnics, the midway for ice skating, and Lake Michigan for long walks at night. Jackson Park, the lakefront, and Hyde Park were safe then.

On nights out, we mostly hung around the university, venturing downtown to the loop mainly to see foreign movies at a theater on Michigan Avenue: *Open City, The Bicycle Thief, Children of Paradise.* And we went to plays: *The Wild Duck* and *A Streetcar Named Desire* with Anthony Quinn.

The atmosphere at the University of Chicago was serious. Many of us were the first in our families to attend college, and most of the people I knew were on scholarship. It was exciting to be taught by professors who had translated Aristotle and Plato. Walking around Hyde Park, we passed houses by Frank Lloyd Wright and the labs of the atomic scientists. We were thrilled to be reading Chekhov and Ibsen, going to campus productions of Aeschylus and Sophocles.

I felt guilty about my parents working so hard while I had no idea where I was going and was actually enjoying so many things they had to pay for. While the big cost of college, tuition, was earned by me, the parents had to pay for my room and board, books, and travel. Mom sent me cash every once in a while and even sent toothpaste and hairpins and other little sundries.

When I went home at Christmas, I felt even guiltier. When I was doing a language assignment at the Orange Bar, Mom said proudly to one of the porters, "She's reading French." He was lifting heavy buckets of grape drink, and earning a living at it. I was ashamed of my vaunted accomplishments—as it happened, I wasn't even very good at French. Mom was running a business, with lots of loud criticism from her husband and little social life.

Jim had joined Daddy and Mom at the Orange Bars. He was unhappy there and accused me of being a parasite and not caring about the family, but only about art and music. I *was* very withdrawn around the family, a watcher rather than a participant.

I went out with Sid, feeling guilty toward him, too, about my dates at school; but I was living in two separate worlds, and he and I had no formal commitment to each other. I felt superior to everyone in Cincinnati. And like the lowest of the low.

BACK AT school, the students were talking about the dearth of blacks in the medical school and at Billings, the hospital of our supposedly liberal university. A movement for change swept the campus. Someone put a piece of chalk in my hand, and I was soon running around to as many classrooms as I could reach, scribbling "Strike!" on the blackboards. We emptied the school buildings, a big rally was held, and the discriminatory practices were stopped. Mom, alone among the Coomers and Beamers, would have been proud of me. But we didn't discuss much of what I was doing at school.

Women students took our rights for granted. When we read of "mankind" or "man," we assumed we were included. We mildly resented the fact that the male students had better dorms and more menu choices and were served coffee in their big living rooms after dinner. It seemed strange, too, and somewhat unfair that they packed their dirty laundry in light valises that they sent home to their mothers to wash and iron. We washed our own clothes in the basement sink and dried them in huge closet-sized gas dryers.

I BEGAN to form pictures of my future life. Paddy showed me a photograph of his family: his father, a magazine editor in New York; his mother, a well-educated homemaker; and his five brothers and sisters. They were holding hands and running together toward the camera, smiling. This was the kind of family I wanted. Mine never touched. Seldom smiled.

When we went to the art movie on Michigan Avenue, we wandered into a room in the building where a new art gallery was opening. Beautiful-looking men and women stood about drinking wine and talking animatedly, as though they were really interested in what was being said. I overheard a woman say, "John was in the bottom of the boat reading Maritain." This comment told me so much about what I wanted.

In spring, Mom and Daddy came to Chicago. They stayed in a downtown hotel. Mom came to the campus to look around, but Daddy remained in town. He had stopped carping about the university, but why didn't he visit? Of course, I didn't ask. Would he have felt out of place? What did he imagine the university would be like? With all his well-tailored clothes and spiffy hat, my world must have seemed beyond him, with no overlap between the things he knew and the things I was learning. Cattle and men and boats were what he knew from the past. Cash registers and buckets of juice were his present. They had little in common with books and lecture halls and professors.

Mom, powdered and mascaraed and wearing her little hat and an enormous diamond ring Daddy had bought her, looked no happier than ever. Her eyes were sad when she wasn't smiling or trying to look bright for someone else's approval.

Mom and Daddy and I had dinner in a restaurant in the loop, three strangers.

25

THE BRIDAL PARTY

I HAD left my family, but they hadn't left me. I felt guilty about their paying for the room and board at Kelly Hall. I wanted to be as independent as possible. Fall of 1948 I moved across the quad to a dorm that provided room only and was less expensive than Kelly. Instead of all the young students, there were older women returning for post-graduate work.

We residents bought our own groceries and cooked for ourselves in a drab basement kitchen; we labeled our food and stored it in a huge communal refrigerator. I shared the cost of groceries and cooked with four other girls. We hung about my room and the one adjoining which was occupied by another member of the group. Because of our tight friendship and—I suppose—our raucous laughter, we became known in the dorm as The Unholy Five.

A letter from Mom told me that we had moved again: Daddy had taken a suite at the Terrace Plaza, a new hotel in the center of downtown Cincinnati near the Orange Bars. The Terrace Plaza was the most up-to-date building the city had ever seen. It was red brick, "modernistic," with no windows on the lower floors and a straight, unadorned shape that looked sleek and strange among the ornate old buildings of the city. It was the most expensive place in town. With his usual skewed logic, Daddy had justified the move on the grounds of saving all the cab fare he and Mom were spending to get back and forth between the San Carlos and downtown.

When I tried to comprehend our moving from our small, dowdy flat to the most costly hotel in Cincinnati, I burst into tears. I had caught

Mom's fears about money and her distrust of display. We were being pretentious and foolish. Further, was I a girl who needed a scholarship or not? Should I be accepting support? I felt on even more insubstantial ground.

All this worry ate away at me as I joined in the excitement over the presidential election. President Truman, going for his first elected term, was supposedly in trouble from Thomas Dewey, the popular New York governor. I ushered at a rally for Henry Wallace, the Progressive Party candidate: he seemed like a nice man, and Paul Robeson (Othello) was for him. Now Daddy would have some grounds for his fear of the communist influence at Chicago, though I knew nothing, really, of Wallace's connections.

The campus was jubilant when the *Chicago Tribune,* having published the headline "Dewey Wins" on election night, had to retract it the next day. I shared the general glee. By election night, Sid's letters had pretty well convinced me that Wallace had no chance and Truman was the right choice. But I had little time for or interest in politics. I was too busy trying to keep up with the reading for courses in the physical sciences (I never understood a word), linguistics (the same), history, humanities, and philosophy.

AT CHRISTMAS break, I found Daddy and Mom ensconced in their suite on the top floor of the Terrace Plaza. Everything was brand new. Big picture windows provided a wide view of the city and even a glimpse of the river as it took a sweeping turn to the west. The main room, a large living room where I slept on a pullout bed, was full of free-form furniture; there was a mural on the wall over the bed that looked like a pair of fried eggs. My parents had a large bedroom and bath—the first time in our lives they had a private space of their own—and there was a powder room and a tiny kitchen.

The first seven floors of the Terrace Plaza were windowless offices, while the hotel lobby was on the eighth floor. The hotel was decorated with *modern art*—something new to conservative Cincinnati. There was a Steinberg mural in the Skyline dining room and a Joan Miro mural in the Gourmet Room, a revolving restaurant atop the whole place. In the lobby foyer hung six red disks that moved: this was the strangest piece of all to us—an Alexander Calder mobile. We had never seen anything like it.

The room clerks and bellboys and the hotel manager greeted us and kowtowed to us as we went to the reception desk to pick up mail or make a restaurant reservation.

MY BROTHER, I soon found, had a new girl friend. Her name was Terry, and she was voluptuous and pretty. Jim had brought a few girls around whom he'd met on his service-related travels, but Terry was different. Her smile was broad, and she seemed much older than her seventeen years. She had surfaced as a waitress at one of the Orange Bars, and though Daddy seemed to have big reservations about Jim dating her, he said she was the best worker he'd ever had.

Mother did not seem fond of Terry. She was too vivacious. Mom liked people with poise and control. Terry's charged high-pitched laugh and happy moments were too liable to be followed by lows, missed days at work. Terry was like a bright, shiny Christmas ornament, lightly attached to her branch.

Jim was working with the parents in the Orange Bars, but he yearned for adventure and poetry in his life. He was still dreamy and impractical, no businessman. Daddy frequently bawled Jim out in the office that overlooked the bar in the Walnut Street establishment, so that everyone below could hear. Mom was in the background, reminding Daddy, "Your family are not a bunch of stevedores!"

Jim and Terry eloped in March; they went to Lawrenceburg, Indiana, then a well-known "marriage mill," where you didn't have to wait three days after getting a license as you did in Cincinnati. When I went home for spring break, I found Mom busily planning a big party for them. She might not approve of the match, but she would not let her son go without a proper send-off. The party was to be held in the Skyline Room at the hotel and would be costly, but Mom still had her little ways of economizing. She and I got very hungry one evening and ordered from room service: one dinner to split. I had to hide in the bedroom so the bellboy wouldn't know there were two of us.

Another evening, I found Mom crying in the office at the Vine Street

Orange Bar. On her desk were piles of nickels and quarters and pennies which she had been stuffing into packets. I pulled up a chair and stacked a few pennies into a pile.

"What's wrong?" I said. I was used to Mom's periodic tears, but never unmoved by them. She looked so lonely and lost.

"It's that girl," she said.

"Terry?"

She nodded. Tried to continue her work.

"You don't like her?"

Mom looked vague. She was holding something back.

"She's trouble," Mom said. She was biting her lip. But she couldn't let go.

"What do you mean?"

"Nothing." Mom pushed away the change she was trying to count. She pulled a handkerchief out of her purse and mopped at the mascara that was running down her cheeks, mixing with tears.

"What is it?"

"Your father likes her, too."

"What do you mean?"

"Too much."

BACK IN Chicago, while studying in the theological library, I heard laughter and people talking in the garden. I couldn't concentrate on Thucydides and walked out into the cloister. From its shadow, I watched a bride, all in white, her friends and family fluttering about taking pictures and posing. The white azaleas and tulips were gauzy as the bride's gown. A black-vested waiter with a dazzling white shirt was serving champagne. I began to cry.

I went back to the dormitory, where I wept so hard my eyes were swollen.

Other days, too, I would suddenly begin to cry, in the women's rest room of the Harper Library or in the shower. Mom's empty eyes haunted me. I was physically low, skipping breakfast and eating poorly. I worried about how I could have the things I wanted—love, sex, marriage, children —without losing my ambitions and becoming a "house frau." The teachers and social workers who shared the dormitory kitchen with us, single women returning for graduate credits, looked rather forlorn and drab and sexless. The only girls I knew that were having sex were the campus slut, who had a different live-in lover every quarter and who had dropped out of school; a particularly bold girl who had gotten a diaphragm; and a sort of hanger-on being taken advantage of by the men in the math department.

Sid was miles away. He visited me just once at school, and we met once in Indianapolis. We wrote regularly, but almost never talked on the phone (long distance cost money). My Chicago friend Paddy had gone down south to work in a hospital. I was lonely. And I was working too hard. The heavy load of courses I was taking and the nature of it left no room for enjoyment. No drawing or writing. I needed something beyond what the University of Chicago thought I should have: though I felt I was learning a lot, my education was more like a cure than an opportunity to develop my particular talents.

When I saw a notice for a poetry seminar with Alan Tate, the Southern Agrarian poet, I submitted some poems, even though the class was for graduate students only. I was excited to be accepted. At last I could do something I really enjoyed. I looked forward to the class for days, and felt really let down when my undergraduate status was discovered and I was kicked out. One of the poems I had submitted, "To Sid," said, "Flying blind I could count on you."

SPRING OF 1949 I moved out of the dorm and got a room-and-board job. A friend was leaving the post and recommended me as her replacement. I lived with a family of two doctors and their son and daughter, who were in grade school. My chores consisted of helping with dinner, washing the dinner dishes, and baby-sitting. In return I was given a room and bath on the third floor of their house and my meals, which I ate separately in the kitchen.

The house was on the street facing the I. C. The trains rumbled past and screeched as they pulled into the stop. The front porch of the house, probably one of the few charming features of the old frame building, had been removed. The wall between the dining and living room had been replaced by a kind of glass panel that would have looked more appropriate in an office.

Once again, as I observed a home and family, I failed to find a model for my own life. Both husband and wife were pleasant, polite, and distant. No one in the house ever laughed. The bland, health-conscious cooking was totally foreign to me. I was raised on fried pork chops, corn bread, slaw, and ribs—when we could afford these things—and at Auntie's I learned to love fried chicken, cake, pie, and homemade bread. I had difficulty facing boiled celery, gray roasts, and sea-foam whip. However, I felt good about being more independent and not having to ask my parents for extra money.

I was cut off from my friends in the dorm. Several of them got room-and-board jobs too, and we were scattered around Hyde Park. I missed them. I was so obsessed with getting through the undergraduate program that I had not taken on any extra activities or groups. On Sunday nights, my night off, I often went alone to a little Greek restaurant near McArthur Boulevard, a fast-moving thoroughfare. Sitting on a bench after dinner, watching the traffic whiz by, made me feel even more lost. When I looked around for something to hang on to, there was nothing there. My Jewish friends among our group in the dorm had such defined backgrounds, such a sense of belonging. I couldn't even remember my birthplace. Where was I from? To what or whom did Jim and I belong? We had never known our father's family and didn't feel part of the Beamers. Jim had once said, "They're the salt of the earth, good German Burghers, as like us as men from Mars."

WHEN SID wrote that he was going on a trip to Florida, I wanted to drop school and go along. For once to just chuck everything and do something fun. But he wouldn't let me go with him. I should finish my degree. I stayed put, passed my final comps, and was offered a graduate-school scholarship for the next year. Instead of taking it, I made plans to return to Cincinnati.

I wanted to marry Sid.

I wanted to paint.

All of The Unholy Five graduated in absentia. We never wanted to do anything conventional.

THAT SUMMER, I worked at the Walnut Street Orange Bar as a server, between classes at the Cincinnati Art Academy. We wore orange uniforms and caps with a net snood—no hair was allowed near food and drink. We would sing-song to the customer: "Orange, pineapple, or grape?" Fill a glass from the appropriate foaming spigot, provide a napkin and anything else ordered, hot dog or doughnut. The work was routine, easy, boring, except for the occasional unusual customer: a man who barked like a dog, one who shook constantly, and an old lady who came in every day and sat on the same stool in the corner. If some unknowing person took her place, she would shoo them away loudly.

On the afternoon shift, I was in the office counting change with Daddy when a young woman came up the steps. She was pale, and puffing from the heat. Her clothes, clean but without style, looked as if she might have gotten them at a country-church rummage sale. Daddy told her to sit down.

"What can I do for you, little lady?" he said. His voice was kinder than I had ever heard it.

"Job," she said. She was definitely from the country. Her accent sounded somewhat like Daddy's. She pulled a newspaper ad from her pocketbook.

Daddy asked her what work experience she had. It wasn't much: a short stint in a dime store, baby-sitting.

"Well, that doesn't matter if you can put in a good day's work," Daddy said. He hired her, and she looked as if he had just saved her life. Maybe he had. I was surprised at this gentle side of my father, but realized that this job-hunting was something he had a lot of experience with.

This was the father who lay down beside me when I was crying from excitement and nerves after a birthday party Mom gave for me at Lulu's where I didn't know any of the guests. This was the man who had protected me from the wind and waves of the river.

But Daddy was bored managing the bars. And angrier than ever. He had the usual stack of parking tickets. When a policeman came into the place and ordered him to move his car from a no-parking zone, Daddy told him to get lost and got into a scuffle with him. His accountant-lawyer, an owlish fellow with the worst wig ever made from an old fur coat, had to bail him out of jail.

Like Mom, Daddy could shift from his genial, humorous self to a person I barely knew. One midnight, he and Jim and I were closing the store. As we went to the front door to lock up and leave for home, a man who was camped on the doorstep of the bar refused to move.

"Go on, go home," Daddy ordered.

The man was very drunk and could barely stand up.

"Hell wi' you," he said.

Jim tried to ease him out the door and had almost convinced him to move on when Daddy grabbed the man and proceeded to beat him. Jim and I begged him to stop, but he kept on until the man collapsed on the sidewalk.

His clothes smelled of vomit and his head was lying in a puddle of spilled orange drink.

"Trash," Daddy said.

He pushed us toward the car, grabbed the parking ticket off the windshield, and tore it up.

26

FLYING BLIND

TO MOM, home meant a garden, a picket fence, and a little house. She loved trees and growing things. My father always said there were three reasons never to own a house: the yard, the basement, and the attic. Our next move, inevitably, was to another hotel. In fall Daddy moved himself, Mom, and me into the Vernon Manor, a staid, old-fashioned place in a residential neighborhood. It was a red-brick fortress with turrets, a lawn and trees, and a doorman.

Daddy negotiated with the manager over the rent while Mom cringed in embarrassment. She was always cowed by any person in a position of authority, anyone she felt she needed to please. Her hands shook when she paid bills or made arrangements to buy things on the installment plan.

The suite we moved into at the Vernon Manor wrapped around a corner of the lower floor of the hotel and looked out on a small area of grass and trees. There was an attractive frame house across the street. I had a bedroom and bath all to myself and was separated from my parents' bedroom and bath by a living room and dining room. It was furnished in an unremarkable traditional style. We still had no real furniture of our own.

Mom at this period was still in her mid-forties. She looked young and stylish. She dressed up in an emerald green dress with fur pom-poms at the neck, her bristly salt-and-pepper hair styled in a "poodle" cut. But instead of being proud of her, I looked down on her interest in her appearance. I was enrolled in the art academy full time, cared only about art, and wore only blue jeans and tee shirts. Also, I still wanted a traditional Mom like those of my friends, most of whom were overweight and frumpy. I had caught Daddy's disapproval of working women—that is, mothers. He had always wanted Mom at home in Woman's Rightful Place, and I had missed her when she was working. Our various apartments were dusty and empty without her touch.

During the Vernon Manor period, she was usually her cheerful everyday self; but sometimes it was as though a hidden woman parted the curtains of her house and stood crying at the window. I had not yet learned the impossibility of making anyone else happy, and I still wished I could do something to end her periods of depression. Mom and I had been alone together so much, with I as her only friend, and she as the mainstay of my life, that I could not bear seeing her in pain.

One morning as I was packing my bag of supplies for school, I heard her crying. I found her in her bathroom, sitting on the edge of the tub.

"What's wrong?"—Me.

"Daddy wants me to quit the Orange Bars. He wants me out."

She sobbed out how much she'd devoted to the business and how little else she had in life. "I've had so little happiness," she said. Now she was feeling the discomforts and insomnia of menopause. "I've had seven miscarriages. Seven. Some of which I brought on myself." I didn't want to hear these revelations. She repeated how painful childbirth was, but how a woman loved her children all the more for the suffering they caused. I didn't know what to say. She was so hard on herself: she was a failure, stupid, misguided. Daddy was the cause of most of her pain, that is, "your father." She had bequeathed him to me.

I had heard many of these things before, whenever Mom was feeling down. If I turned away or failed to be sympathetic, she predicted similar pain for me. I would learn what it was like to suffer.

I helped Mom wipe her face and get on her feet and then left for school. She didn't quit working, but continued in the business for some ten years.

THE ART academy was built of stone and marble and was connected to the art museum in Eden Park. I felt at home in the messy studios, in the halls lined by lockers with racks for paintings. I liked the smell of oil paint that hung in the air and the earthy odor of clay coming from the sculpture studio.

The museum, with its high-ceilinged marble entrance hall, and twin staircases sweeping to the second floor, was the same as in my childhood days when I attended Saturday classes. The Winged Victory and the other old plaster casts of Greek gods and goddesses were gone, but the vast chamber still echoed with footsteps and whispering voices. The carved sacred figures and serene, painted faces took me back to the Joselyn Memorial where I had loved the mosaic room and the fountain.

I spent a pleasant summer at the academy studying drawing. On weekends I went on dates with Sid, or we spent time in his car or the apartment kissing and making out. During the week, he was busy at law school, and we had almost separate lives. We barely noticed that we had such diverse interests. He knew almost nothing about art, and I was naive about law and politics (though luckily the university had made us read

Learned Hand's opinions about free speech). We had the same sense of humor and always liked the same music—Beethoven, Mozart, and Bach.

SOMETIME DURING the winter term, Daddy moved us once again, to a suburban apartment building on Ledgewood Drive. It was a brand new Art Deco, with lots of glass bricks. Daddy seemed very impressed with it. Mom had to go out and buy good furniture for the first time in her life. There were two bedrooms and two baths again, large living and dining rooms, and a good-sized up-to-date kitchen. Mom installed wall-to-wall carpeting and, goaded on by Daddy, filled the china cabinet and buffet with Noritake china and crystal glasses, a silver cocktail shaker and goblets, silver trays, and Gorham flatware in a fancy pattern.

Jim and Terry moved into a smaller apartment on a lower floor. Their baby had arrived, a girl they named Terry Susan. The baby was adorable, but the tension between the parents was so obvious, and I was so involved with Sid and my art classes, that I saw them very little.

Once the full-time faculty was back from vacation and the art academy was in full swing, I found that it was like a small family—a dysfunctional one. Gossip flew around constantly. When a visiting instructor came to teach a quarter of painting, the permanent faculty, usually fighting among themselves, turned on him as one. We students were caught in the middle.

For the first time in my life I experienced real male chauvinism at school. Always the friend and competitor of my brother, I expected men to treat me as an equal. But the all-male faculty—the ones who spoke to each other—hung together as pals in a way that I'd never noticed before in men. The dean of the academy often reminded us women students that we were "females" and therefore, no matter how good we were as painters, not likely to succeed in the arts. Our sculpture instructor constantly and contemptuously referred to painting as a "feminine" art.

One instructor praised my work highly and offered helpful critiques, all the while chanting into my ear "Küche, Kirche, und Kinder" (Kitchen, church, and children—good old Kaiser Wilhelm II's prescription for women). In spite of their clubbiness, the academy faculty awarded me the biggest painting scholarship available, for a second year's work.

I was confused. No one seemed to know what they expected of me or what my possibilities were. And I certainly didn't. The negatives stuck in my craw, and the good things were stowed away someplace. My mother's low opinion of herself was passed on. It's inherited, something mothers hand down to daughters like their wedding gowns and little seed-pearl caps.

My father added to the confusion. He had always said I should be a schoolteacher and live with another woman, like Miss Hall and her companion (had he realized what he was suggesting he would have been horrified). Now he sent other messages. On Ledgewood Drive, I found a basket at the door of my room containing a green wool suit, a good brown leather purse, and a pair of matching high-heeled shoes. The outfit actually fit, amazingly, as I was a size four, but rather big in the hips. And how did Daddy, who couldn't remember my middle name or my age, know my shoe size? Another time, he left me a similar present: a burgundy suit with a peplum, a red leather bag, and red pumps. Were these comments on my blue jeans? They clearly encouraged femininity. On the other hand, he bought me a compact with my sign (Scorpio—he got it right!) and the words "The Artist" on the lid. Still, when I brought home artwork, he often repeated, "Try to buy a hamburger with it."

As I sometimes scribbled away at poetry, Daddy recommended that I travel the Ohio River Valley and write about what I found there. This, of course, I scoffed at. ART was Paris, London, Rome. If it existed in America at all, it was in New York.

Daddy hinted at the stories he could tell of his early life on the river, but they were something he could not express. Perhaps he needed better listeners. He gave us only scraps and bits.

He bought a tape machine and tried to make a record of his memories on a trip to Alaska—without Mom, who hated the thought of car trips and had even given up her attempts to learn to drive (Daddy had ridiculed her all along, saying she was so cautious and slow a truck laying blacktop could pass her). His tape came back full of comments such as, "Now I am leaving Ohio and am in Indiana. I stopped for gas at a Texaco station and got a full tank." There wasn't a single story or recollection. The car and Daddy came back worn out; he had destroyed all four tires and three fan belts and turned the car over on loose gravel. It had to be pried out of a ditch by local Indians.

The night I received my painting award, none of my family was present. My parents expected me to achieve things and did not give either praise for success or blame for failure. I can't say I felt bad about my parents not being there; I didn't expect them. What I needed more than praise was someone to put my various achievements in perspective, for no matter what I accomplished, I felt it was not enough. I turned my gold medals into dross.

Janie came to the awards ceremony. She and her fiancé planned to marry in August. Sid and I had set a date in September: by then he would be graduated from law school and (we hoped) have a job.

IN EARLY June, 1950, I was at home alone. The phone rang. It was Terry's mother—a woman I had met just once, at Jim and Terry's engagement party. She was crying, and said simply, "Terry died." I lost my breath. What was she talking about?

Terry had swallowed a toxic medicine and had been rushed to the hospital. Her veins had collapsed.

The news came like a plane crashing into the house. Though Jim and Terry did not get along, I had no idea she was on the verge of suicide.

I muttered something to Terry's mother and sat down heavily in a leather chair by the phone. It was buzzing and I put the receiver back into its cradle. The leather of the chair seat stuck to my legs.

What would happen to Jim? And to Susan, who was only a year old?

For Terry I felt dismay and horror. I had never really known her. Though it wasn't her fault, Daddy's attraction to her had caused Mom too much pain for me to want to be close to her. I felt very sorry for her mother.

I called Mom and told her about the phone call. For her, there was no time to cry. She came home and she and Jim spent hours alone in his apartment. The rest of us were left out. Jim was so distraught Mom had to make the funeral arrangements. Daddy, of course, locked up whatever he was feeling. I was left on my own to cope with the reality of suicide. The newspaper account of Terry's death was unsparing, and I had virtual strangers in the apartment building ask me what had been the reason for my sister-in-law's act.

The Presbyterian minister who spoke at Terry's funeral refused to allow Terry to be buried in his church's cemetery because she had committed an act against Biblical teaching. At the visitation at the Mack Johnson Funeral Home on Woodburn Avenue, Mom and I were like hostesses at a macabre party. Terry's father and two brothers were suspicious of Jim; they had hinted at murder, and they hung about the funeral home like a lynch mob. Daddy refused to enter the place, but paced in the street. We could see him through the picture window in front, walking up and down past the entrance, up and down.

Following Mom's example, I tried to put on a brave front. The Beamers had only one way of coping with death, and that was a stoic refusal to give in to one's feelings. There were relatives and friends to greet and condolences to be accepted. Gail, an art school friend, and Janie came to the funeral home and stayed with us until the day was over. At about four o'clock in the afternoon, I suddenly felt weak and began to shake. Sid saw my distress and took me out into the foyer for a rest. I could trust him, as my poem said, "flying blind."

After that day, Jim took off across the country on his motorcycle. He could not face the apartment or the child left behind. Mom took Susan in, just as her grandmother had done when her mother died. No one in the family ever spoke again of Terry's death.

I WAS twenty years old. My life so far had been a blur: one month here, a year there, constant uprooting, moving on. With the guilt that suicide spreads to everyone near, like run-off polluting the water, it's no wonder that I was nervous about my upcoming marriage. That summer I dropped from my normal 105 to ninety pounds. Going to look at apartments took me back to the past, to the endless searches for decent housing Mom had taken us on.

Most of the apartments Sid and I could afford were small and dreary. I wasn't ready to relive the past. Mom saved Sid and me from at least one bad choice. My mother-in-law finally picked out our first apartment. I was as afraid of marriage as I was compelled to take it on.

ON THE heels of a funeral, Mom had to plan a wedding. Sid and I were determined to do nothing in the conventional way; to do so would signify that we would have a conventional marriage, and we had vowed that we would both have careers. Sid was the top student in his class and had been sent to interview for the best job available. We talked that evening on the phone.

Me: "How did your interview go"?

Sid: "They offered me the job."

Me: "Great. What's the salary?"

Sid: "A hundred and fifty."

Me: "That's good. We can live on a hundred and fifty a week, can't we?"

Sid: "It's a hundred and fifty a month."

Me: "Oh." (Our rent alone was eighty dollars a month.)

Because Sid's salary would not provide enough money to buy food, gas, car maintenance, clothes, and other necessities, Sid's father offered us a wedding present of a hundred dollars a month for our first year.

"Of course we can't accept it!" I said. (The Coomer code of self-reliance kicked in.)

"Sure we will." I was glad Sid wasn't as crazy as I.

We requested good music at our wedding, and Mom hired players from the Conservatory of Music instead of the usual soprano singing "Oh, Promise Me." We had asked for the sprightly Wedding March from *The Marriage of Figaro* instead of the traditional, staid *Lohengrin*. We got both. I had refused to wear white because it was too conventional, and Mom helped me find an ice-blue satin short dress and cap at Jenny's. Mom did everything the way we asked her to; she was at her best—and her worst. She had always promised me that I could come to her with any question or problem, especially having to do with sex. I asked her to go with me to a doctor to get fitted with a diaphragm. She shook her head abruptly. "I want grandchildren," she snapped. I was too scared to go alone.

Neither family objected to our unorthodox plans. Sid was a mongrel just as I was. His mother was a Teutonic German, the daughter of Chris and Ida Ackerman. Like Mom, she had lost her mother and sisters young. Sid's father was from a large Jewish family, all of whom but he remained within their religion. He and his brothers and sisters were first-generation Americans, the parents having come from Alsace-Loraine. Sid thought of the Weils as German, but the French influence had touched them as well. He remembered his grandmother as an old lady who would ask him to play the Marseilles for her on his trumpet and would weep as she listened.

Sid's parents dealt with their mixed background by pretending it didn't exist. The only Jewish touch in their home was a Passover meal Mr. Weil enjoyed: sponge cake, matzo ball soup, and matzo crackers with lots of butter. Just as I had been sent to the nearest Protestant Sunday School, Sid had been sent to the local Presbyterian church. Neither emerged a believer.

Mr. and Mrs. Weil (I never called Sid's parents anything but Mr. and Mrs. Weil) were as quiet as my family was noisy and feisty. Mrs. Weil was a homemaker, a tall woman with pretty features and snow-white hair. She was completely deaf, and we had to talk to her by enunciating our words very carefully; the difficulty she had with communication added to her somewhat remote air.

Like my father, Mr. Weil—who with his brother Leo owned a fish market and restaurant in Louisville—tried to be all business. A portly gentleman, he hid behind his newspaper when we visited his small suburban house. Sid occasionally kissed his father, something I had never seen any male do; Mr. Weil would put his arm around his wife when we said goodbye, but he liked to sing a little song: "I'll get by as long as I have *me*."

The Ohio River had affected the Weils' lives by destroying Mr. Weil's wholesale fish house in Cincinnati during the 1937 flood. The cleanup in the cold water of the warehouse worsened his asthma, and he had suffered terrible attacks ever since. The sounds of coughing and a man trying to catch his breath were the sounds of Sid's childhood.

The wedding was held on September ninth in a neutral venue: the Julep room at the Netherland Plaza hotel. It had little cocktail glasses in the carpet design. Sid's extended family attended. Uncle Leo was a bundle of energy who would start a new sentence before he had finished the previous one—like a chain smoker starting one cigarette from another. He loved the fish business: in Louisville his raspy voice could be heard in the street in front of Leo's Hideaway, the Weil brothers' funky fish eatery opposite the old open-air farmer's market. Leo's wife, Miriam, was a proper matron with social ambitions who was horribly shocked when Leo insisted on hanging one of the nudes I'd painted in art school in his office. Uncle Manny was the sick brother, whom I first encountered at the fishery, eating baby food out of a mason jar (he outlived all the others). Uncle Ted was the family intellectual (he worked for the Louisville *Courier-Journal*), and Aunt Helen was a housewife. "Aunt" Nan was a wild Gypsyish near relation who loved whiskey and poker and had red-purple hair and lipstick to match.

Daddy's sisters Edna and Alma and their husbands came to the wedding from Burnside. We still did not meet the brothers. Jewel, who had moved to Oklahoma, appeared; she was a handsome, dignified woman, and we all liked her and wished we might know her better than the brief visit allowed. Pop Beamer and Lulu, Mary and Chuck, Ray and Marcella —all the family from Bevis Avenue came. The great aunts, Ethel, Dessie, and Ninnie Esther, came. Auntie and More-Pop were there. It was quite a mix.

My father raced me down the aisle and to the altar the hotel had set up. True to form, he joked that he was in a hurry to get rid of me. My own legs shook as I took the marriage vows (without the "obey" oath of course). The ceremony was conducted by the minister of the Presbyterian church where Sid had been sent to Sunday School as a child.

And so there we were, another multicultural couple, and off we flew into matrimony with shiny new hopes of leaving our parents and all their generation's problems and sorrows and traditions behind, eager to make our own "free choices" of what and who we would become.

Jim at seventeen, off to the
Pacific, World War II, 1945.

Sid and Dot, first date, 1947.

One of Daddy's get-togethers at the Netherland Plaza hotel. Left to right: Mom, two friends, the author, Sid, a friend, Janie and boyfriend, Jim and girlfriend, Daddy. Christmas, 1947.

Author in Cincinnati Art Academy sculpture studio, 1950.

Author as student at Cincinnati Art Academy, 1950. *(Photograph by Raymond Harris.)*

Mildred, ca. 1950.

The author and Sid at a
political fund-raiser, 1957.

The author in her political
wife period, ca. 1960.

Daddy on the *Belle of Louisville*, 1962.

Dot, Daddy, and Sid in
Burnside, ca 1979.

The *Delta Queen*, ca. 1982.

Adventure Galley II, the flatboat built by Jim and his students at the Inland Waterways Vocational School, 1982.

Jim watering the roof of the flatboat. In the old days the animals grazed on the sod.

The flatboat crew bathing.

Cozy cabin of Jim's flatboat.

Jim in his mid-sixties, ca. 1990.

FALLING APART

1950–1956

27

A HOME IN THE FIFTIES

SID AND I moved into our small one-bedroom apartment. It was too cramped to share with paints or paintings. While Sid began his career as low man at a law firm, I continued at the art academy on my scholarship. I was pregnant a month after our wedding. I was both happy and scared: I wanted a family, but a baby put a crimp in my ambitions. However, my career plans weren't very well thought out, and with an aplomb that I often drew on, I assumed I'd spend a few years totally involved in raising my baby, and then get back to my painting. I'd have the best of two worlds. At school, as I grew bigger, leaning into the clay pit in the sculpture studio was awkward, but I enjoyed my classes. Every afternoon I raced home, pulled out *Joy of Cooking,* and tried out a new recipe until I had worked my way through the better part of "About Beef."

Pregnancy was easy at the age of twenty: I was completely innocent of its dangers and problems, and suffered none. I did dread the actual birth after all the tales of horrible pain my mother and all the popular novels of the day described. But in the hospital I came awake from the heavy anesthetic given in those days, to hear a nurse saying I had produced a healthy boy. I hadn't the slightest pain and I thought, good, I wouldn't know how to raise a girl, and thanked my lucky stars that I had escaped my mother's dire predictions.

At one point during the five days of recuperation, I overheard several nurses talking about me and my young roommate: "Just kids having kids," they agreed. I began to worry about my lack of preparation to be a mother, and when Rex (a strong, proud name—one for a king, or a movie star like Rex Harrison) was brought in to feed, I cracked to the nurse carrying him, "Don't you feel sorry for this poor kid?" "No," she replied, "I think he's going to have a lot of fun." She showed me a diagram of a uterus and recommended waiting a while for the next child, then tossed a copy of Dr. Spock at me: "Just do what he says."

With two adults and a baby sharing one small bedroom, our apartment seemed even more cramped than ever, and Sid and I looked about for a house with a yard. When I wasn't following a real estate man into dreary-and-still-out-of-our-price-range houses, I typed Sid's notes for a class he was teaching at the University of Cincinnati's law school, prepared formula, and worried that if I read a book while feeding our son he might be forever scarred by maternal inattention.

Our first little house was a cracker box in a subdivision outside the city limits of Cincinnati: there wasn't a tree in the whole place. It was miles from a bus line, and our one car (like the house, being slowly paid off) went to work with Sid every day. I was stuck. Miles from the art museum, a library, stores. I had a sweet child whom I adored, but the afternoons were long.

IN 1950, I could not afford to continue at the art academy, nor did I want to. My last year there had been marred by an all-out war among the faculty over who would replace the retiring dean. My best friends from the school moved out of town. I had to start all over again as I had too many times before, with no links to the past. School had been my only continuity, my only community. The thing I missed most in my new life was my report card.

Marriage did not solve all the problems of the past or bring unalloyed bliss. Sid and I didn't realize until after we were married that we were near strangers, Jack Sprat and his wife in the flesh. We had conducted much of our courtship long distance, I in Chicago and he in Cincinnati. Sid's background, except for being culturally mixed like mine, was very different. He had lived all his life in one house, and his parents had only a single brief period of being slightly hard up in the Depression. (His weekly allowance shrank to a quarter. A quarter!) He was raised somewhat like Topsy by an absent father and a mother who could not hear, a little surprise born nine years after his one sister. He was loved in a sort of distant manner, indulged in ways I found wonderfully strange, like being allowed to roller-skate in the dining room because, as his mother said, it was raining outside. The Weils were shy, kindly, polite. Where I was used to people shouting their feelings at top volume, they were masters of denial and control.

My life had been filled with people—at the Del Mar, at the yacht club, at the Beamers. Sid had had little contact with either outsiders or his parents' families. As a child he only occasionally saw his paternal grandparents and, because of the religious mix of his parents, did not really fit in among the Weil cousins. His mother's father, Christopher Ackerman, lived with Sid's family, and was a taciturn, dour old German —a retired lumber-mill employee who justified his dependence on the younger people by doing the yard work and repair jobs around the house. His hard-headed character was impressed upon Sid when he replied to his grandson's announcement that the Japanese had attacked Pearl Harbor with the comment "I don't think so."

Sid's family was fanatically punctual and somewhat fearful of anything new. I had always been encouraged to try everything—new places, new foods, new people. I was physically adventurous, liked to take risks, always wanted to go to the end of road, the outermost island. Sid was time-conscious, practical. I lived through my senses; he lived in his head. He was so unaware of matters like clothes that he once came home from work in someone else's overcoat; he hadn't noticed it was a few sizes too large.

I thought I was marrying the opposite of my father, but Sid, though without the anger, had a similar sardonic sense of humor and was totally involved in his work. He was trying to succeed in law, a very competitive and difficult profession, especially for a Democrat in solid Republican Cincinnati. He had gone into the party side of politics and was away many evenings at meetings. As election day came around in fall, he almost disappeared from home. I was stuck alone, in a kind of repeat of my mother's early life. I thought that was the way it had to be.

Art had always been my savior, colors and words my way of putting order into the world—and into myself. I rigged up a small studio in our attic, but when I was painting, I felt I should be baking a cake, and when I baked a cake, I felt I should be painting.

Sid and I were both excellent students—at school. In life, we seemed to lack sense. We didn't have to choose such an out-of-the-way house, but we were terrified of debt even though we were healthy, young, and ambitious, and our prospects were good. Still, I had the specter of the Depression behind me, and Sid's family was as fiscally conservative as Cincinnati gets. His father kept his money in five different building and loan companies in case any of them went out of business.

Sid and I had just as many issues of disagreement as my parents had, though we were more "civilized" about addressing them. We both refused to argue. Sid had no practice in fighting outside a courtroom, and I was determined not to challenge his role as provider and head of the house. I blamed my mother for a lot of the tension in my family. Though she talked peace and compromise, she fought just as hard for what she wanted as Daddy did.

I tried to be like Donna Reed, a perfect fifties Mom. My dreams were stored away, gathering mildew. I thought it was bad to have ambitions. The perfect woman should sew, bake, be self-effacing, a credit to her husband and children. I could not have worked outside the home, even if there had been opportunities. I had too many unpleasant memories of empty rooms and skimpy meals, unmade beds and dirty dishes in the sink. I would not allow Sid to wash a single dish. I sliced and removed the seeds from grapes for salad because he did not like grapes with seeds. I arranged his clothes in dresser drawers, shirts ironed, socks mated. A true daughter of the "scrubby Dutch," I cleaned the house with the same religious fervor my mother had in our little flats in Omaha and on the river.

I read hundreds of books on psychology and joined a child study group, where I made friends with other young mothers. I spent many hours with Rex, just the two of us, reading and drawing at the tiny dining room table — just as my mother had done with me. We colored eggs and made an Easter-egg tree and Christmas cards.

Sid and I had many happy moments in the four-and-a-half years we spent in our treeless subdivision. We played badminton with our friends in the good-sized backyard. We had our Christmases, always our favorite holiday. We had a boy with a sweet disposition who wore his heart on his sleeve, laughing as he ran around the yard — making friends with other kids. We had snowball fights.

As Rex grew close to school I knew I should be thinking about how to go back to my writing and painting, but I had no examples of feminine achievement in my family. My mother's desire to work hadn't inspired me to copy her. My other women relatives had never gone beyond their roles as homemakers and mothers; when children and husbands left them, they got old and died. Even Auntie. After More-Pop died, she became querulous and pitiful, sharing an apartment with another woman, wrinkling like an Albright portrait, her heft confining her to a chair. The symbol of the women's lives was the inevitable set of false teeth with bright pink plastic gums floating in a fizzy-stale glass of water.

My life seemed to be over as an individual.

The expectations for women in popular culture fortified the reluctance I had about moving on, becoming a real person. Everything we read and saw told us that we should be "fulfilled" if we had children and a husband. That to be "unfulfilled" was as sinful as adultery in Puritan times: the scarlet "U" would burn through our blouses no matter how hard we tried to hide it.

For a long time social life for our little family consisted mainly of Sunday dinners at Sid's parents' house: a feast that left the diners fit for only one activity, an afternoon nap. It followed a pleasant but rigid pattern. Mrs. Weil had everything ready on the stroke of noon when we walked in the door. She filled us with pot roast or lamb, fried chicken, and German-style hot slaw. Everything was perfect and delicious, from the grated cheese and mayonnaise appetizers to the caramel pie or chocolate-ice-cream-and-meringue tarts. Cleanup was accomplished with Teutonic efficiency. Wiping the dishes, I marveled at the Weils' ability to sit in a room together and never engage in a single significant exchange. Every Sunday, Mrs. Weil would offer one comment on the dinner: "We eat too fast."

We had frequent cookouts or picnics with my brother and his family. After working at a lab (he could not stand the animal experiments) and driving a soft drink truck (he hated the mundaneness of it), Jim had gone back to the river to begin his career in towboating. He had remarried. His new wife, Alice, was a nice woman who was a very good mother to Susan. Jim and Alice had three other children in fairly rapid order and lived on the opposite side of town from Sid and me. We seemed to have very different aims, and after Jim went on the long-haul boats, we drifted temporarily out of each other's lives.

Sid's sister Ruth and her husband and two daughters moved to Staten Island soon after Sid's and my wedding, and we saw little of them until the late fifties when they returned to Cincinnati.

MOM AND DADDY came to visit Sid and me now and then, never together: Mom would come sweeping into our small house wearing stiletto heels and a mink stole with big shoulder pads; Daddy would sit down and, with a serious man-to-man expression, offer Rex a cigarette. Rex was quite fond of "Habaw," and of my mother.

My parents moved again, to the Phelps, a downtown apartment building on a lovely little park where a huge statue of Abraham Lincoln welcomes visitors to benches, flower gardens, and the Taft Museum of Art.

The old Konjola Man had become Cincinnati's "Orange Juice King." When he and Mom opened a fourth store, my father was so dubbed by a newspaper reporter. Daddy gave the new bar some of the touches of a fancy restaurant. Mom was supposedly the dreamer, but she kept her imagination out of the business. He indulged his fantasy and playfulness in this new outlet: he had fancy sauce trays holding three or four dishes of condiments to put on the hot dogs, cruets of vinegar and oil for the newly introduced salads. He hung some of my paintings on the walls. He told the newspaper, "There's an urge to beautify and your mind gets to drifting. You wonder what you can do with an old store front and pretty soon the thing starts shaping up. Of course you can't worry about spending money, but then I'm not interested in getting rich anyway." Of my art works, he said, "We have so many of 'em around, we might as well put 'em up where people can see them."

Many nights Mom went to the opera, alone.

Occasionally she and Daddy invited us to the Phelps for dinner. One evening, I went early to help Mom prepare the food. The kitchen was neat as a laboratory, except for one unwashed knife lying beside the sink. Mom picked it up and scrubbed the hardened jam from it, complaining that Daddy was always messing up the kitchen (Cleanliness is next to godliness). While I set the table, she stirred and boiled at the stove, cut up salad vegetables, and worried about whether I was arranging the knives correctly.

Daddy came home. Peace was instantly shattered by the radio, which he played loudly while whistling and pitching change on the buffet. He came into the kitchen and lifted the lids of various pots on the stove, a habit that infuriated Mom. She stood patiently until he was out of the way.

Daddy had a bad cough, and soon retreated to the bedroom. He blamed the cough and the aching legs he had developed on a fall he took in the icy river at the yacht club. Mom looked skeptical as he disappeared; she considered these aches and pains psychosomatic (It's all in the mind). She hinted that their sex life, the one thing that had often held them together, was over. She said, "What good is he to me?"

After dinner, Daddy whispered to me that Mom was a little dotty with "the change." His proof? She put the salt in the refrigerator a time or two. Before the evening was over, she threw a bag of potatoes at him.

CRASH

THE ONE feature of our subdivision that Sid and I liked was a woods just beyond the backyard fence. When the newspaper announced that a shopping center was taking over that property, Sid declared that we should move. I was glad. We found a new house a few blocks away, but within the city. This place had trees, even an apple tree, and a large "wood-burning fireplace," a feature young families like us dreamed of. We wanted a hearth that would enhance "togetherness." I was pregnant again, and we pictured an ideal home. In spite of my desire to be an artist, I wanted equally to have a happy family, one that held hands like the one in the photo my Chicago friend showed me.

We had hope of becoming such a family. Sid and I loved each other. We adored our son. While we had all those temperamental differences and sometimes conflicting desires, we had in common a love of children, nature, animals, movies, and music. Best of all, we had the same sense of humor and laughed a lot. Though we both went along with the prevailing idea that the male's career came first and Mom should be at home—and this Mom (at least one side of her) wanted to be at home— Sid did what he could to give me time to myself. On Saturdays he and Rex played baseball together so I could paint. And in spite of my frustrations, we both cared deeply about the political scene. The local Democrats were not just pariahs, they were invisible, little more than cronies of the Republicans, accepting a few favors instead of trying to win elections. Sid soon joined a group of young men bent on throwing out these old-style bosses.

MOVING STIRRED up bad memories, invisible but harmful, like dust mites. I went about the move in a frenzy, packing and, as I worked, remembering the boxes my mother used to lug around and the day we were kicked out of the Del Mar hotel. I organized all our possessions, even putting labels saying "dining room" on the table and chairs and breakfront, as though the movers could not figure out where to put them. I was getting bigger and bigger with the second baby, feeling a little winded as he crowded my lungs. I waked frequently in the night, and Sid would play gin rummy with me until I could get back to sleep.

This was a planned baby. What was I so afraid of? Getting deeper into my mother's trap. Not being perfect. I had a low opinion of women in general and of myself when I could not live up to my ideals. To be loyal to my mother was to be disloyal to my father. I had two parents. Since they spent so much time tearing each other down, I felt at least half of me was rotten. I was divided about everything, off-kilter like a print in which the colors don't register.

Time was moving fast: the baby was near due. I speeded up my moving activities. The new house needed a lot of work. The living room wall-paper, a sad, dirty blue, was sagging and needed to be steamed off. All the woodwork needed painting. Everything needed to be cleaned and scrubbed: windows, bathroom, everything.

Mom came to the new house to look it over. I was surrounded by buckets and mops, pictures to hang, boxes to unpack.

"I'm suing your father for divorce," Mom said.

I was not totally surprised by her announcement, but still shocked. She had been threatening divorce ever since I could remember, but always came back "for the children."

"I hope it won't upset you." She glanced at my bulging abdomen.

"Of course not," I said. I could hardly condemn my mother to any more years of living with a man she could no longer stand.

We moved into the new house on a hot July night in 1956. I felt fine. We had been to a picnic at our best friends' house. I read for a while, en-joying the insect sounds in the trees just outside our new bedroom win-dow. The baby was not due for a week or so. But before I fell asleep, the bed was covered with water, and we left for the hospital. Rex, now five years old, was taken back to our friends' house.

By the next morning I had a new baby, a picture-book boy we named Bruce. I was groggy from the heavy dose of anesthetics they gave me even though I had requested a lighter dose.

When I was able to stand up, I got out of the hospital bed and took a shower, then got back under the covers, feeling groggy and done in. I wanted Mom, but she didn't show up. On the second day of my hospital stay, several visitors came and went, none of whom seemed to really see me. One endlessly described her own labors. Then Daddy came to visit.

He barely said hello. He did not ask about the baby. He complained about Mom and her divorce plans. His voice grew louder and louder, rougher and rougher as he raged. "I won't sign anything that says I was cruel. I was never cruel!" I knew that the charge of "mental cruelty" had been explained to him as a mere formality. There had to be legally ac-ceptable grounds for divorce. "She's the one who's running around. Do you know who he is?" I didn't, though Mom had told me about a man she was seeing. Daddy paced the floor, retreating to the window and then coming close to the bed, where I felt more and more helpless and trapped. He kept on railing against Mom. I smelled old sweat, felt heat coming from his clothes. I could not say a word. His fury filled the room.

Finally he left. I was in a kind of daze, like something left in the road. I began to see faces on the white sheet of the hospital bed. . . .

Then the nurse arrived with the baby, followed by the hospital photographer come to take pictures of the happy mom and her new child. "Look this way," "Do this," "Do that." I'd had enough orders and enough being invisible. The faces on the sheet wouldn't go away.

When the nurse, baby, and photographer left, I began to scream and I couldn't stop. A second nurse came running into the room with a large hypodermic needle in her hand. I shouted no, get away. I wanted to be treated like a human being, not to be stuck with that thing that would shut me up, make me invisible again and tuck the outrage I felt beneath a smile. But the woman was stronger than I and managed to plunge the thing into my arm. I rolled around and around, trying to fight off the drug, calling for Sid and my mother. . . .

I was sent home with the assurance of my obstetrician that I'd feel better there with a little rest.

"We from happy families don't understand these upsets," he told Sid.

At home, I could not settle down. I got up in the middle of the night and sat by the window feeling like an alien. The moon made my arms and legs look transparent. The rooms of the new house seemed too large, and nothing was where it should be. I was still seeing disturbing images.

My father had been banned from the house until I felt better. I could not even look at a photograph of him.

My mother arrived with a strange man. They came into the bedroom where I was resting. The man was tall, sandy-haired, obviously younger than Mother. She introduced him as "Gene." Mom was dressed in a swingy cotton sundress, her hair pulled back in a pony tail. She seemed to have turned into a teenager. She and the new man stared at me like something under a microscope. They glanced into the room where my baby was sleeping in his crib. Mom was more interested in her new mate than in either of us. When they left, I flew apart like the pieces of a jigsaw puzzle swept to the floor.

I couldn't make contact with reality. I ran across the living room and crashed into a swinging door to the kitchen, breaking its hinges. Sid tried to get me to lie down until he could call a doctor; I felt as though I were flying away. He lay down on top of me gently, holding me, it seemed, to earth. Then I heard him talking on the phone. When he came back into the room, I was in a kind of trance. I could not see or hear much of anything around me. Sid's family doctor, a man who was deeply interested in psychology, arrived after a while. I knew who he was, and I could see the worried faces of Sid and my mother behind him. He sat next to me on the bed and looked me over.

"She's scared stiff," he said. He spoke with a Hungarian accent. He asked me some questions, but I could not talk. His voice was soothing, and though I could not answer his questions, I did not want him to leave. I was wearing white socks, and I put my foot on his hand to indicate that he should not leave. The white sock on the broad hand was like a blown-up detail from a painting.

He gave me some sleeping pills, strong ones. I did not want to take them. "Afraid of a little pill?" he said. I *was* afraid. Of dependence on anything or anyone. I believed in courage, in character, in moral strength.

Before the doctor left, he held my face in his hands and kissed me on both cheeks. I was surprised, moved to tears. How could he touch my unworthy stinking flesh? I who was never touched by my family, and who had proved imperfect, ugly and raging like the fairytale girl who opened her mouth and belched out frogs.

The doctor came back every day for what seemed like a long time — probably a week or ten days. When I was finally able to tell him what had happened in the hospital, he said, "At last this makes sense." But he told me my progress would not be all upward, that I would have bad times.

I was surprised by the physical pain I was in. I felt as though I were being tortured. My arms and legs, my whole body worked at an excruciating nervous pitch. I broke out in a red, bumpy rash from a medicine I was taking: sunlight did not combine with the medication and my arms and legs looked like inflamed tongues.

Sid and my mother tried to calm me down at some point, and I screamed at them and threw a hairbrush across the room.

"Stop trying to control me!" I shouted. I felt hedged in.

"You're scared of your anger," the doctor said. I knew he was right.

It had built up and up: all the years of being good so as not to upset Mom or start Daddy off. Being dragged around the country, constantly uprooted. Never being allowed to be anything but a good little stoic, a good little sport.

Daddy saying, "You're all right, aren't you, Duchess?" Mom, with her sad little face, saying "I'm the one who will suffer" if we did anything childish or wrong.

One night I thought a prescription I was given had been sent to poison me. I knew this was paranoid. My inner recorder that was always on duty took note of my own craziness.

I felt lost, as though my body and mind had gone in two different directions. I felt the meaning of "losing your senses."

When I was able to take over completely the housekeeping and childcare, the doctor began coming several times a week. We talked about everything that bothered me, from work to religion. He drowned out my mother's "Not every woman can have children and a career" with "This one can." About our lack of a church he said, "It's all right to say you don't know." He assured me that my confusion would not last forever and that I would be better for the breakdown, but that it would be a long time before I felt all the way normal.

I had to believe the doctor that I would someday be myself again, but it seemed impossible. How long would it be? Maybe a year. Maybe two. I tried to see into the future. I clung to the skirts of time.

The most helpful things were human touch and love. Sid built fires in our fireplace and read *Bleak House* to me when I couldn't sleep. My baby needed me, and I could communicate with him without words or being rational; I rocked him and myself endlessly. Rex helped with the baby, clowned for him, brought diapers to me, and fed him with the bottle.

My doctor had advised me to get some help with the household and children — not just sitters for an occasional night out. I accepted a helper who came in one afternoon a week. In my free time, Rex and I took walks. I had developed a fear of large dogs, and one afternoon a mean-looking brown Rottweiler came rushing out of his yard toward us. He was barking angrily and gnashing his teeth. I stiffened all over and walked almost on tiptoe. I was trembling, but determined not to flinch. I repeated to myself, "I must not show fear in front of my child."

As the dog came nearer, Rex held out a hand and said, "Hi Boy!"

The dog jumped on my son, wagging his tail and pawing him all over. Rex petted him, and they wrestled around, playing happily, free of fear and full of the joy of being alive.

"Maybe," I thought, "I will feel better some day."

Several months after his visit to the hospital, my father, who had been asked not to come to the house, was allowed back. He said he was taking off on a trip and wanted to say goodbye. We had a stiff, polite, distant chat. I didn't expect him to say anything about what happened in the hospital.

When he was about to leave, he said, "What caused ye to take on this nervous spell?"

The family soon after scattered in all directions like the pieces of Chaos.

RIVER JOURNEYS

1981-1988

29

TURNING BACK

THE SUN cast a soft rose light on the darkening water, on the red brick of the True Way Pentecostal Church on River Road. Its steeple was bright against the green Cincinnati hills. I stood on the top deck of a harbor boat in Kentucky, waiting to be picked up by the *Eastern*, a towboat pushing a full load of coal.

The sunset, the river smell, the clutter of the harbor's work boats were all familiar. The nearly forty years I'd been off the river didn't matter. The sounds brought me back: a saw whining, a hammer ringing in syncopation with its own pounding, a load of coal being dumped into an empty barge.

The sky and the water of the Ohio River were black when the harbor dispatcher told me the *Eastern* was getting near. I went into the office and heard a radio voice, cool and easy: "Motor vessel *Eastern* to Southern Harbor. We'll be stickin' our nose around the bend in a minute. What've we got there?" The harbor pilot decided how to go about the exchange of barges he would make, and the radio voice said, "We'll take our guest on while you rework the tow." I was the guest, on a long postponed adventure, with some vague idea of writing about rivers.

A deckhand appeared and whisked me and my suitcase down to a harbor tug waiting to take me to the *Eastern*. He steered me to the end of the float, and we jumped over the dark crevice between it and the tug. She was small, top-heavy, almost as tall as she was long and with the same pushing "townknees" as the big towboat. Slightly lopsided from my bag, I followed my guide around the lurching deck. There was no guard rail, and the water was inches from our feet.

The giant *Eastern*, with a load of fifteen barges, idled in the middle of the river. Its great black hills of coal and long flotilla of barges were lit only by three small lights on the head of the tow. Its outlines were blurred as the past.

The harbor tug pulled up alongside her, and, with the help of the *Eastern*'s crew, I jumped onto her deck. A deckhand carried my bag and steered me to the small room where I would sleep. I was to share a bathroom with the only other woman on board, the cook. Then I was escorted to the pilothouse. I did not know what to expect. The pilothouses of my past were on steamboats and were sacred turf; permission to enter was granted to only a few, and the men running the boats were authoritative and, except for Captain Doss, formal.

The man at the towboat's steering levers greeted me with a friendly "howdy" and an offer of coffee. He was dressed in dungarees and a tee shirt and was missing several of his front teeth.

"Pardon me not puttin' in m' teeth, but them store-bought fangs was hurtin' bad," he said.

His name was Jim, just like my father and brother. I liked that.

In the dark, the other men in the room were just white shirts and glowing cigarette tips. They greeted me warmly, the mate and engineer. I had trouble following their West Virginia accents and cadences. The boat itself, though diesel-powered and carrying thousands of tons of cargo instead of passengers on their way to Coney Island, seemed right. It moved slow, letting me enjoy the night river, the tree-lined banks, and, once I got used to its noisy engines, the echoes crossing the water from the hills.

I stayed in the pilothouse until after midnight. My brother Jim, who had spent most of his life as captain and pilot of towboats like the *Eastern*, had advised me to get around the boat and talk to everyone, but I didn't need to leave—the deckhands on watch came to check me out, and Annie, the cook, came up and told me there was cake and coffee in the galley. Annie's face was soft and puckered like the skin on cream; she was round as a doughnut and friendly as the others.

The pilot, who came on at twelve and took the levers from Captain Jim, was a typical-looking blue-jeaned country boy. His name was J. B., and he was from a small town in Kentucky. As he and I hoved slowly upriver, just the two of us in the middle of the night, I asked myself what on earth I was doing out here on this towboat.

I was fifty-two years old. My children were grown and gone from home. I had returned to school and gotten a Ph.D. in English. I had published a book about an early American woman writer and a comic novel about going back to school in mid-life. I was depressed as hell—

Without my saying a word, J. B. seemed to know what I wanted of him: his life story. His parents were divorced and he lived alone. He was on the river because he couldn't stand the rat race on shore. "Two things I can't tolerate," he said. "Census takers and door-to-door salesmen." One time, a vacuum-cleaner rep came to his door. J. B. disposed of him fast. "Showed him my rifle. I pointed it into the air and pulled the trigger. When two blackbirds fell at the guy's feet, he took off in a hurry. Never had any more trouble from vacuum-cleaner salesmen."

I vowed that the next time I came to the pilothouse, I'd bring my tape recorder.

I went to bed excited. Though the boat shuddered and shook and the engines seemed to be made of boulders turning over and over in a metal vat, they lulled me to sleep. When I awoke for five-thirty breakfast, we were miles upriver. Mist was rising from the water like the steam from Mom's teapot at the yacht club. We were beyond the bridges and river-front industries of Cincinnati, moving past tree-lined shores and to-bacco farms. I walked down to the galley, prepared to eat my usual bowl of cereal, but the galley smelled so sweet and looked so cozy, I tucked into pancakes, bacon, butter and syrup, and lots of black coffee as if I'd been toting ratchets and securing lines like the deckhands.

I stayed on the *Eastern* four days. The crew, ten men and Annie, treated me like royalty, so glad were they to have an outsider to break the monotony of being confined to each other's company for a thirty-day stretch. They were so much more interested in my books than anyone at the colleges where I had taught.

Sitting at the galley table in the hours between lockages and barge exchanges, I became the resident psychiatrist and mother confessor. Annie told me how she missed friends on shore. "Can't even get to their funerals." She was from the South, like my father, but was a farm girl. She had been cooking since the age of seven. Her son had died in a truck accident. Her father was "eat up with cancer."

J. B. talked more about his life. "Look at 'em," he'd say of the cars whizzing along the banks toward the factories and towns. He liked the slowness of the boat. Had a retirement house all picked out, where he'd get himself a chain-link fence and "a couple of bitin' dogs" to keep strangers out.

I played poker late at night with the resident storyteller, who swore he'd seen "Big Foot" one misty morning, and a biker with a death's head tattooed on his arm. I was presented with poems the various crew members had written, songs they had composed, and even origami created in the dull stretches of their work. I learned a recipe for moonshine with maraschino cherries in it and how to make a sea gull explode (feed it Alka-Seltzer; sea gulls can't belch).

WHEN I GOT home from being on the *Eastern* I felt lost. It was mid-afternoon and the house was deadly quiet. The family warmth I had felt on the boat was gone. This must be what shore days were like for the crew. Suddenly empty. One deckhand told me that during time off, he put a pair of overalls, the kind with metal snaps, in the dryer to recreate the sound of the towboat engines.

I wandered around my house. Sid's and my fourth. It was the house of my dreams. Earlier dreams when I had children to raise. Now Bruce was an administrator at Cincinnati's Association for the Blind. Rex was a lawyer in Washington, D.C. With Sid working harder than ever, my days were my own. And suddenly hard to face. My work was stalled. I needed to find a new path. The small college where I had been teaching, Edge-cliff, had gone under and was being taken over by a school of mortuary science. I had taken a chance on writing as a career and had lost a contract to do an important book, a loss that made me feel like the kid whose crayons were yanked away when she wanted so badly to color. Writing and selling articles was something like being a salesman (like Daddy), out there on a smile and a shoeshine.

I looked around the living room. It was furnished with an inexpensive couch and chairs from our last house; there was a library table from Sid's mother, two pretty cut-glass vases Auntie had given me. Through the large windows I could see our lush garden and the many old trees around the house. The foliage and light patterns on the cathedral ceiling were beautiful, recalling the shimmer of the Ohio's water I had just left.

I decided to go back to the river as soon as possible. It seemed as though it had found me, had been patiently waiting for me to turn back to it. I did not relate my feeling to the fact that my father had died the year before.

I did know that the limbo I was in was a place I had been in earlier in my life: the years following my parents' divorce and my breakdown, when each member of the family went about the task of picking up the pieces.

I REMEMBERED the day of the court proceedings. Mom was upset by all the anger and arguments over the grounds for divorce, but was disappointed that she did not get to tell her story in court. The judge simply instructed the clerk to read the names of the participants and banged his gavel: marriage over, twenty-nine years canceled.

The "Orange Juice King" announced his retirement several months later. The newspaper that had so dubbed my father quoted him: "I haven't seen my shadow in forty years. When I was young the long rays of the sun cast a shadow before me when I walked. I can't see it in the city because the bright lights cancel out the sunset." He planned a trip to Mexico, but didn't take it.

The Orange Bars were sold. The more aggressive businesspeople in downtown Cincinnati could not wait to get hold of them when they saw weakness in the owners. Neither of my parents got much money from the sales—just enough to live modestly. Daddy walked away with none of the plunder he and Mom had acquired. Mom had the presence of mind and the Beamer practicality to hang onto the furniture, the silver, and the china.

Daddy drifted about, living in one or another third-rate hotel catering to older men, the kind with the rates painted on the outside wall of the building. We'd see his fellow guests in the halls and lobby, looking lost and disappointed.

On visits to us, which resumed when I was feeling better, he would pace around, have trouble sitting down. Something was on his mind.

He was standing in my dining room one evening, in the little house with the big fireplace. I had just given him dinner. Suddenly, he grew quite red in the face and blurted out, "Does your mother come here with him? If you have your mother and her boyfriend here, you can forget about me. I won't come here."

I had never once, in all the years of his bullying, ever cracked back. I was too afraid of his anger. But this order of his sent me into a fury of my own.

"Don't tell me what to do!" I screamed. "This is my house and I'll invite anybody I want here. If you don't like it, you can get the hell out and don't come back!" I couldn't stop. I shocked myself. "How dare you! Just get out if you want! I don't care!"

To my surprise, Daddy backed down immediately, obviously scared by his conforming and ladylike daughter telling him off in the tones of a packet-boat mate.

FREE OF MARRIAGE and business, Mom claimed to be happier than she'd ever been. Her friend Gene was good-looking and younger than she, and "a college graduate." They went fishing and camping, and did all the outdoor activities Mom claimed she had always wanted to try. On vacations they went to Canada, lived among the Indians, and hunted. Mom shot deer and even tracked moose. She offered me venison and squirrel to cook, but I was not fond of wild meat, and as for squirrel, I would sooner eat a rat.

Sid and I and the children got to know Gene and liked him. He worked on dangerous construction jobs: tunnels and bridges and skyscrapers. He had interesting stories to tell and was always pleasant, if somewhat mysterious.

Mother continued to live at the Phelps for several years; then she moved to an apartment in a clone of the San Carlos. She was employed for a while in a downtown restaurant as a cashier. She quit working while still in her early fifties, "sick to death of serving the public." She returned to her interest in art: she learned photography and took beautiful nature shots. She wrote a series of sketches about her outdoor adventures.

FOR ME, PUTTING myself back together after breaking down, gradually resuming my old activities, was like trying to learn how to walk. For more than a year I fought off confusion and panic. I remember calling Sid from a downtown store to ask him where I was.

I clung to my role as mom. By the time Bruce was a year old, the boys and I would sit at the picnic table on our small patio and model with clay and do finger-painting. We picked apples from our tree; I tried to bake them into pies like Auntie's, but my crusts were more the consistency of damp clay than of Auntie's perfect pastries. We enjoyed them anyway. When Sid came home we built fires in a half-ruined outdoor oven at the back of our lot. Everything said home. We wanted to build on higher ground where nothing could wash us away.

Trying to paint was hard. I felt old—I was pushing thirty. My hand shook when I held a brush. It was worse than the first time I ever tried to draw: then I was a child and never thought of success or failure. Now I hesitated, full of fear.

My space was a dark basement room. Working there made me feel even more cut off from the world outside. A Mom covered with paint and smelling of turpentine was not my ideal picture. I turned to my other passion, writing.

By the time Bruce was old enough for nursery school, I decided to take some courses at the University of Cincinnati. A friend told me the English department was "death on women," that no woman had ever been granted an advanced degree there. These welcoming words added to the cold, clammy feeling I experienced as I approached the campus and the dean of Arts and Sciences. He was a pale, controlled, buglike little man who listened with obviously strained patience to my request to become a part-time student. He rubbed his feelers together and glanced over my Chicago transcript.

"The university actually has no need of part-time students," he said.

I wanted to ask whether, as a city-funded institution, it needed tax-payers. But Mom had schooled me in considering the source, not answering back, being patient.

I sat demurely, hands in lap. Finally, having finished perusing my credits and answering phone calls, Mr. Dean handed me instructions for enrolling and said I could go ahead and try getting back to school.

"What about the children?" he asked as I left.

THAT YEAR, BRUCE went to his class and I went to mine. I had signed up for just one course, World Drama, about all I could handle along with two children, a house, and an ambitious husband.

If the dean was skeptical about my return to school, I was sure it would be a disaster. I found it difficult to get all the reading done for the course: some thirty plays, plus two or three papers to write and class talks to give. I had not written a term paper for over ten years.

Sid was the only person who encouraged me. A friend's husband asked why I didn't just tie my child to a tree instead of taking him to nursery school. Another described the feminine desire to do work outside the home as a disease of women.

None of my friends or the other mothers in my children's schools were doing what I was. They were serving as PTA officers and Brownie Troop leaders. They were driving car pools and gardening and doing all sorts of things. But not things I was interested in.

My course was taught by the head of the department, a tall, formal New Englander, a rigid but good teacher. He passed my papers among his graduate students as models of how to write. His praise helped keep me from giving up.

There were very few adult students on campus. In my early thirties, I felt old. I could always recognize a fellow matron: they wore skirts instead of blue jeans.

SID WAS DEEPER into politics than ever. We embarked on a constant round of banquets, rallies, cocktail parties, poll work, and election night wakes or celebrations. We met Jack and Jacqueline Kennedy when he was still a senator, but with an eye on the presidency. In his London-tailored suits Jack was hardly the boyish charmer the press described. She had the air of not knowing or caring what town she was in. By the time we met again, in his 1960 campaign for president, he had the allure of a movie star.

I HAD MOVED far away from the world my brother lived in. I never knew how the parents' divorce affected him. He spent his life on the river. I got as far away from it and everyone connected with it as I could.

IN 1962 I RECEIVED a phone call from the Cincinnati Veterans' Hospital: my father had suffered a stroke. Sid and I rushed over to him.

Daddy was in a white gown, his scant hair plastered to his head. He could barely talk and he could not move his left side. His nurse told us what had happened: he had been standing on a downtown street corner when his left arm grew numb, and he felt dizzy. He knew something bad was happening to him; he grabbed a cab and got himself to the hospital. He looked so weak and white we were sure he was dying. Jim, the riverboat captain, was in tears.

When I returned home, I was shaking, and I sat down on the living room couch. I closed my eyes. I felt happy. My reaction seemed strange. Shouldn't I be sad? I chalked up my euphoria to confusion and fear.

Daddy's left side remained paralyzed and his speech remained slurred. We pictured him becoming like old Mr. Joseph Kennedy, the president's father, blanketed and lolling like a vegetable in his wheel chair.

Then, on his third or fourth week in the hospital, we found Pop sitting up in bed. He gabbed away in a kind of baby talk and waved his bad arm about, demonstrating his growing prowess. The nurses clustered around him. "He's such a doll," one said.

I felt a fresh wave of happiness, one that made sense. I recalled my odd reaction when we first knew Daddy was seriously ill—that lifting of normal sensations. It was, I realized, relief. I didn't have to weigh my father's humor and strength against his temper and his bullying. I could forget the wrong-headed things he had done and remember the good. I loved my father, period.

30

THE MISSISSIPPI

I HOPPED another towboat as soon as I could after my first trip. I boarded a boat out of St. Paul, Minnesota, downbound on the Mississippi. The Ohio, the Missouri, the Mississippi: I was struck by how much they all seemed like home and by how much alike the boat crews were—with the captain as father, the cook as mother, the engineer as a fat old granddad, and the deck crew as sons. The differences were in how well these roles were played.

The trees along the Mississippi were the same as those on the other rivers, the water was the same—even though the demure Ohio's sister was swollen in the middle like a python that's swallowed a goat, and got so big in places you couldn't see across it. Like the one on the *Eastern*, the boat crew was a family, but this was an unhappy one. We had a troubled captain.

Lonnie was self-indulgent and whiny, and everything else went sour. The cook was flirtatious and oversexed, always bragging about her effect on men, even her brothers. The stronger, better-looking deckhands tormented the one boy, Wayne, who was weak and fat. Still, I felt better out here on the water than I had at home. I saw a family of beavers building their own dam right near a set of locks, swimming with sticks in their mouths and piling up brush into a sturdy barricade. I waved at Mennonite families, the men in black, the girls and women in aprons and sheer white caps. Along with other people from the many small towns on the water, they lined the lock platforms, watching our huge tow raised and lowered. I watched with envy small boats full of fishermen among the sloughs along the river.

Wayne was given the job of driving me from a lock above St. Louis, where I left the boat, to the city. We had to drop off another deckhand in Illinois, and Wayne wanted to stop at his parents' house. The trip over the bridge, which was in bad condition, combined with Wayne's driving, was hair-raising. Even the other young man kept urging him to slow down.

It was late afternoon as Wayne and I sped along narrow roads in the Illinois countryside. This kid's idea of fun was racing other boys around the rural hills. He showed me the scar from the last time he had totaled a pickup. It looked like a necklace. I asked myself again: what in the hell was I was doing here?

My doubts rested somewhat as we left the main road and traveled a long trail back to the Mississippi. The sun was setting on a magical little house on the water's edge. Here I met Wayne's parents, who made their living fishing. The father went out in a skiff every morning by the first light to make his catch; the mother iced and packed the fish in a small outbuilding. They were quiet, hardworking people. As I listened to them talk about their lives, Wayne practiced whirling some sort of metal weapon about in the yard.

The isolation of the family reminded me of our best days at the yacht club—how contented people could be, living close to the water and in contact with nature and the weather. I felt sorry for Wayne and his parents, sorry that something had come between them.

I hoped Wayne, and Lonnie too, could find a way back home. I knew how it felt to be lost. With all my years of homemaking, I still felt rootless. I had lived most of my life married to one man, in one town. Yet I had done a lot of moving.

AFTER DADDY'S STROKE in 1962, I was still trying to find the right place for myself in life. With the boys both in school, I was restless as Daddy. I dropped my classes at the university. I had begun work on a novel set in Puritan days, the strict morality of which intrigued me. We moved to a newer, bigger house, a ranch style: I had more windows to wash and more yard to take care of.

In 1968, Sid was elected co-chairman of the Hamilton County Democratic Party, a job that brought more campaigns, more banquets, more election nights. I was almost as passionate about politics as my husband: how could I not be when my earliest memories included the velvety voice of President Franklin Roosevelt on the radio, the Del Mar lobby discussions of his efforts to help the underdog, and a father who bought a car because it had a likeness of FDR on it?

But though I was interested in the issues, especially civil rights, I was not involved in real political work—my abilities were artistic and literary. I got the role of a sort of a small-town Jackie. Dressed demurely in suits, hats, and little white gloves, I accompanied Sid on his rounds of ward clubs to encourage support for candidates. Typical of my activities was a visit to a suburban picnic: the women who had written the invitations, put up the posters, set the tables, decorated the grounds, and cooked the food thanked me profusely just for putting in an appearance. Something was skewed here.

The new house was pretty. But on Monday mornings, with the children in school and Sid at work, I could hear the sound of the dog's nails clitter-clitter on the rubber tile of the kitchen floor. Looking out on the quiet, empty suburban street, I often thought I might as well be living on the moon.

I WORKED ON my novel and completed it after several years of research and hard work. It didn't get published, though I had landed a well-known New York agent. I felt stranded. My doodles were of women and tombs covered with drapery. I had a good life, and there were wonderful things in it: my husband; my kids, whom I was glad I had been at home to take care of; travel; four cats; and a dog who produced six puppies. But there was a slow leak somewhere. I felt anonymous, ambivalent. A non-person. Dependent on my husband for my livelihood as well as my identity. I was just the girl in his act.

I WENT BACK to school again at thirty-eight. I thought I was ancient. Everything in the culture around me agreed. This time I was determined to get an advanced degree and teach.

When I approached the English department chairman—the same New Englander who had encouraged me earlier—he advised me that there was no place for women in higher education. A diploma would look good on my wall—his daughter's did.

I ignored his discouragement (too bad it wasn't ten years later when

I could have taken him to court). But if I thought I would be accepted on my own, I was wrong. Sid had become even more prominent in the political life of Cincinnati. Having a successful husband was at times a drawback. At the university my instructors and advisers habitually asked me what my husband thought about various issues; they assumed everything I did was connected to his interests. I had the familiar feeling of being out of place, the wrong type, the wrong age.

Eventually, in the seventies, more older faces began to appear on campus, and in the five years I worked to earn a master's degree and a Ph.D., I made some good friends. One of them, Anne, traveled with me to Cambridge, Massachusetts, to research the women writers we had picked as subjects for our dissertations. It was the first time either of us had ever gone anywhere without our husbands.

My friends and I worked hard in graduate school, teaching sections of freshman English while taking two or three courses and studying for language exams. The campus was full of change, as were others all over the country. The Vietnam protests continued: we had occasional student strikes, chairs tossed out windows, scuffles between factions. Women's Liberation was a hot topic.

There was a wonderful ferment among the women: I found versions of myself coming from very different backgrounds going after the same thing: lives of our own, as opposed to standing in the wings and rooting for children and husbands. Few of the men were supportive. Though Sid was behind my work and helped in every way he could, he maintained standards of perfection in the running of the household that precluded a single dish unwashed or an item of clothing out of place (even if he had to take care of it himself). Other men were completely unhelpful. The general atmosphere was hostile. When I admitted to a local judge that I was in favor of Women's Liberation, he reacted as if I were a member of the Black Panthers.

Several of my friends' marriages fell apart. There were tensions in Sid's and my marriage, too. I had a temper and could be mean when frustrated. Sid was evasive; the cool quality I had so admired when we met was often the quality I found most infuriating after many years of living together. One thing never wavered: our complete trust in one another.

DURING MY YEARS of study and teaching, Mom was also moving on. She lived for some time with Gene, then eventually broke up with him and moved to Hialeah, Florida. Uncle Bud had died, and Mom signed on to take care of Marie—the aunt who first introduced her to Daddy on the *Island Queen.* As a widow, Marie was more helpless than ever.

Typical of Mom's relatives, Marie and Bud and Aunt Esther and her husband had formed a little Beamer enclave in Florida, with adjacent matching houses very much like the ones they'd had in Cincinnati. Mom became a good grandmother—to the kids next door in Hialeah. She had some enjoyable days there with her neighbors, fishing and boating. She tended to her avocado and lemon trees. She chased a burglar away with her rifle. She lived through a hurricane.

JIM AND I continued to drift in and out of one another's lives. We seemed to have very different dreams. I wanted security and normalcy for my children, and my goal was to find a sinecure in a college and live happily ever after. I kept my wilder side hidden. As always, Jim did whatever came into his head.

Between jobs in towboating, he built a houseboat atop Mt. Adams, a bohemian enclave crowned by a monastery and a Catholic church, the two structures that give Cincinnati its fairytale skyline. He opened a metal shop in Mt. Adams and sold medieval weapons, iron swords and shields that he created himself. He took off on a year-long trip down the river in a fourteen-foot hand-built boat. He taught for a while at the Inland Waterways vocational high school. Riding around on a motorcycle or in the car he created—a Volkswagen covered with homemade Maltese crosses and a giant metal fish—he was a true original.

While Jim confronted surly deckhands and crooked wharf agents, I had to confront misogynistic male professors and literary agents. Jim navigated tricky waterways and once almost drowned when a boat sank. I ventured into academia and publishing, trying to keep my head above university politics and tough market currents.

No matter how far our paths diverged, I always knew my brother was around. One afternoon when I was in graduate school, the stress of being a student, a mother, and a political wife made me feel like running away.

I drove down to the river to see Jim. During one of his occasional respites from towboating—and marriage—Jim was working as a harbor man at a marina. Just as his father had at the yacht club, he watched over a string of pleasure boats. He was living like a hermit in a little house about as big as our old yacht-club cabin.

As I came down the hill on Collins Avenue and got my first close-up glimpse of the water in years, I felt better: there it was, the same old stream moving slowly along, sparkling in the sunshine. I parked in a grove of trees above the floats, and there was Jim—a little thinner on top, but with his familiar sheepish grin. He had a set of tools slung around his middle, and was working on a boat hull. He said hi like I'd been tagging along without a break since the sixth or seventh grade. He didn't ask a single question about why I had come or what was the matter. He just said, "Let's take the skiff out." We got in the boat, and Jim rowed out past the harbor's floats and into the sunlit current. I dipped my hand into the bottle-green water and watched the clear droplets cascade from the ends of the oars. We could have been ten years old and back in the days when I wanted to dress the way he did and try everything he thought up.

Back at the marina, I thanked Jim for the boat ride. I was ready to go back to work. My brother and I went our separate ways again.

NO MATTER WHEN I returned to the water, I gained something. My trip on the Mississippi gave me a new dream: portraying the beauty of the river and the lives of river people in pictures as well as words. With excellent timing, Jane, a fellow teacher from Edgecliff, asked me to write a script for a TV production company she had formed. I said yes. We worked together on several pieces, then, in 1982, we began the first of a series about the Ohio River, covering the history of the working boats from rafts to towboats, from flatboats to steamboats.

During the research and shooting, I got to know more river people, my father and brother among them.

31

STEAMBOAT STORIES

I COULD HEAR the deep whistle of the *Delta Queen* from the Cincinnati suburb where I lived. I was quite excited to think I would soon be boarding this fabled steamboat.

I met her at the old cobblestone landing, where once a line-up of packets took on freight and passengers. This was where the *Island Queen* had docked, and where we had boarded when Daddy was mate. The *Delta Queen* was just four years younger than our old boat, which had caught fire and blown up in 1947. Built near the end of the line for working steamboats, in 1929, the *Delta Queen* was almost put out of business in the seventies because of the possible danger of her wooden hull. But she had been saved by a special act of Congress, and was one of only two tourist boats taking guests for cruises.

She was beautiful, her twin smokestacks sending out white puffs like a contented pipe smoker. Walking up her gangplank and then up the mahogany stairway took me back to the steamboats of my childhood. Her green carpets and crystal chandeliers made her fancier than the *Island Queen*, which had been built only for day trips, but the layout was similar: lower deck for work, second for salon and socializing. The calliope's raspy tunes linked past and present.

SITTING ON THE open deck of the *Delta Queen* on a summer afternoon, far upriver from Cincinnati, was lovely and peaceful. The banks were bright green tobacco fields. The only sound as we moved slowly along was the huff-puff of the boat's steam echoing among the green hills and over the blue-green water. I didn't want to stir—ever—but I had been given passage by the *Delta Queen* company to gather stories.

I spent hours in the pilot house, chatting with Harry Louden, the pilot. Harry was in his seventies, trim and spry, dressed in neat slacks, black string tie, and carpet slippers. I'd interviewed him once at his house in Sayler Park just outside Cincinnati. Back then, he denied knowing any stories: "Just because I'm a river man, people think I can turn everything into a yarn." Out here on the water, he underwent a radical change, telling stories non-stop: tales of a four-hundred-pound catfish, its weight made up of rusty fish hooks; a Civil War lantern still burning on the muddy river bottom. Harry's missing finger joint was the result of chasing a catfish into a sunken automobile: when he reached into the car to grab it, the fish rolled up the window on him. There is something about the river that makes people like to tell stories.

THROUGH THE *Delta Queen* I met people who had known my father when he briefly served on her as second mate. It was in 1959, during a period when he turned back to the river after the divorce. Captain Clarke "Doc" Hawley remembered Daddy as "a good boat man, very hail fellow well met." But Daddy was sixty-five then and had not grown in patience. The old river, when he was cock of the walk surrounded by girls, was gone. There was talk of a woman pilot. Dealing with modern passengers was difficult for my father. He did not feel too well, and left the boat after less than a year.

He took just one more try at making his mark on the river. He and the steamer *Idlewild*, two old-timers, went way back. The *Idlewild* was built in 1914, and Daddy and his brother Joe had worked on her together when she was a packet plying the Mississippi. Since Daddy and Joe's days, the *Idlewild* had been converted from a packet to an excursion boat: the staterooms had been removed and replaced by a dance floor—just like the *Valley Queen*. Renamed the *Avalon*, she had put in fourteen years taking passengers for short cruises.

In 1962 she was down on her luck, sitting on the river front at Louisville, bankrupt and in need of some fifty thousand dollars' worth of repairs. There were many ideas floating around about what would become of her. Some in Cincinnati wanted to keep her; there was talk of making her into a floating department store. Daddy tried to get a group together to buy the *Avalon*, but the effort did not succeed. She ended up in Louisville, having been bought by the Jefferson County Fiscal Court at auction and renamed the *Belle of Louisville*.

Daddy went down to see her and was photographed in front of the pilot house. He told a local reporter, "A boatload of money could be made with the *Belle*, but a steamboat can never make a penny tied to the river-bank."

At the time of Daddy's statement, there were only two or three real steamboats operating, and because of a combination of floods and pollution, many towns that had been created by the river had turned their backs on the water. Daddy saw a return: "From Pittsburgh to New Orleans, the people in river towns are hungry for excursion boats. This boat could be fitted out and put into operation by May 15 and could wildcat (make stops) from Louisville to Pittsburgh and back. Next season she could go from Louisville to St. Paul, with a good captain and crew, good concessions, and a good booking agent. Finish the season in Memphis. The *Belle of Louisville* is a fine boat. With a few repairs she could come out with steam up!"

Could he have been thinking about himself?

WHEN I BEGAN my river journeys, I reached out to my brother for help. Jim seemed happy that I had finally come around to the river as a worthy subject of interest. He could be big brother again. He set up trips for me, gave me advice on towboat etiquette, and steered me to river veterans who might have good stories. On the night I left on my first towboat ride, he dropped in at my house to see how I was holding up and laughed at my evident nerves (I was devouring a chocolate sundae, something I do only under stress).

One of the old-timers Jim guided me to was Bob McCann, a former purser on the *Delta Queen*. I found Bob in a hotel in downtown Cincinnati like the ones Daddy had lived in—full of old men lonely as dry-docked houseboats beached among the weeds.

Bob could remember back to a time in his childhood when he had sat on the roof of his house in Parkersburg, West Virginia, and had seen

President William Howard Taft greet the townspeople from a steamboat. His career as a purser spanned the first sixty years of the century. He knew everything there was to know about steamboats.

He took me to a meeting of the Sons and Daughters of Pioneer River Men, an organization of river buffs who meet every year in Marietta, Ohio. Bob insisted on going by way of the Muskingum River so he could show me the old hand-operated wooden locks. He was a big man who walked with two canes, and I feared for his life as he clambered onto the lock walls to explain each of the ten systems.

He told me he remembered Daddy, not only from the *Delta Queen*, but from packet boat days.

"He never overloaded the boat like some," Bob said. "And I can recall the *Liberty* being so weighed down with cargo, the water was sloshing over her decks." He told me about the mate's job of constructing seines to corral pigs.

"My father never told us any of this," I said.

"You never asked him."

The Sons and Daughters meeting was, as always, held in the Lafayette hotel, right on the water where the Muskingum and the Ohio flow together. The whole building is decorated in honor of steamboating: the restaurant is designed to look like a boat deck, with fancy white wooden trim, a bell, and life preservers, and there are little wheel images woven into the vast rooms of wall-to-wall carpeting. The bar and most of the guest rooms look out over the water.

Captain Fred Way, patriarch of the Ohio River and onetime owner of the steamboat *Betsy Anne*, was still alive when I visited Marietta with Bob. Ninety years old, totally bald, still slim and sharp as the pilot he once was, he was a living link to the steamboat era. Captain Way was still editing the club's monthly journal, the *Reflector*, which runs stories about steamers long sunk, or blown to bits, or saved from decay and turned into restaurants. He held court at the meetings, and people crowded around him to talk or get copies of his books autographed, as he and his wife "Lady Grace" strolled into the banquets and parties.

I met old-time pilots and captains, engineers, pursers, steamboat artists and model builders, and river buffs from all over the world. One graybeard, dressed like a salty tar in a striped tee, blue jacket, and captain's hat, had never lived or worked on the water at all. He just liked steamboats.

Between meetings, I strolled the grounds of the Ohio River Museum near the hotel. On a grassy lawn sits the pilothouse of an ancient packet, the *Tell City*, a small, simple box, a head with no body. I boarded the *W. P. Snyder*, a fully functioning steam towboat docked on the Muskingum. The Sons and Daughters help support these reminders of the past. They know the names of every steamboat ever made, even their distinctive whistles. A recording of the whistles, with a detailed discussion by Captain Way, is a big seller among the Sons and Daughters. Photographs, drawings, little bits of river information flow steadily into the office of the *Reflector*. The museum collects every life preserver, bell, uniform, name board, paddlewheel, and rudder that can be saved from the wear of water and time.

ONCE AGAIN JIM and I became pals, collaborators as in the days when we were a debate team at Horace Mann school. Jim appeared on camera as narrator in our documentary about the working boats of the Ohio. I never had to explain my ideas to him: he grasped them intuitively, just as when we had tried mental telepathy as kids. He was very photogenic and seemed to enjoy appearing at various river sites, delivering the lines I'd written for him—occasionally changing them to a more pungent style. As always, Jim and I picked up where we had left off.

He was another storyteller. He was working on a series of sketches about his life in towboating. It would be another ten years before he put them together as a book, but he finally did, and we worked together on it. I served as typist, grammarian, editor, and agent. We had long sessions on my porch, haggling over rewrites, fighting out the importance of proper punctuation as well as poetry.

During the video shoot, Jim led me to Captain Russell Lucas, a retired steamboat pilot and bank president in Manchester, Ohio. "Chick" was a tall, well-built man in his seventies, with white hair and strong features that somehow suggested that you not mess with him. He lived in a snug Spanish-style house in town, with his wife Doris, a plump, pretty woman who had served as cook on Chick's boats. The couple's more fitting home was their cottage right on the banks of the Ohio. In the cozy kitchen, Doris fed pie and coffee to our video crew; then we sat on the lawn overlooking the water while Captain Lucas told us about old times.

He remembered Daddy from packet boat days, describing him as "a fightin' trick."

"One day," Captain Lucas said, "I saw Harv jump over six feet of open water from a boat that was moving out—to catch some man that said something he didn't like. He let him have it when he did catch him."

Captain Lucas pushed back in his lawn chair. He could not keep his eyes from the river.

"You don't want to sass them Cumberland River boys," he said. "They'll work on ye."

These glimpses of my father kept bobbing up as I worked on river themes.

Listening to Captain Lucas reminisce, I could see the steamboat mate and roustabouts working in the mud, trudging through the night corralling hogs and cattle. The roughness of their world had touched me through my father's voice, his brusqueness, his braggadocio. Just as the coolness and compassion of my mother's grandmother and the meanness of the lumberyard hand had come through Mom's touch.

The river was bringing my family back.

The stories I heard were life preservers, taking me from past to present, present to past, like the detritus, wheels, bells, name boards, and bits of wood the Sons and Daughters collected.

32

THE MISSOURI

THE LAST river I returned to was the Missouri. I boarded the towboat that would be my home for a week at the dock where the *Valley Queen* had moored. The river looked so small. As we moved north, there were so many twists and turns the sun hopped back and forth across the banks. Dykes and sandbars allowed only a narrow channel. We had a good captain, Bill, whom everyone respected and liked. He had such an air of competence and sense.

He was in his late fifties, like me. When I went up to the pilothouse to meet him, I was hoping he wouldn't be anything like the captain on the Mississippi. He wasn't: while Lonnie was plump, which emphasized his babyish quality, Bill was slim. His face was round and honest. He was much friendlier.

"Hope I'm not bothering you," I said, entering his turf.

"C'mon in," he greeted me. "Jim here and me are just sittin' around tellin' a few lies."

He introduced me to his mate, yet another river Jim. The mate was tall, with a lion's mane of hair and features that looked frozen into a grimace by the wind and cold that he battled out on the barges in winter.

Like most people, Jim couldn't pronounce my name.

"Dorothy Weel, right?"

"Wild," Bill said.

I shook my head. "'Weil.' Rhymes with 'Nile.'"

"Gosh, I'm sorry," Bill said. "Weil. So, Miss Dorothy, is there anything we can do to make you comfortable? Bunk O.K.?"

"It's fine."

"They tell me you're a doctor," Bill said.

"Not a real one. A Ph.D.," I confessed.

"You're an authoress, too, right?"

I felt embarrassed at the admiration in his eyes. Teaching parttime was the most I'd done with my degree. Though my TV production work was successful, it wasn't the work of an "authoress."

"Penny for your thoughts," Bill said.

"Not worth it."

As usual, when conversation came close to the personal, I changed the subject. I asked Bill how the radar operated.

MOLLY, THE COOK, greeted me in the hallway outside the suite we would share. She was about my age. Wearing a gray housedress and covered with flour, she was dowdy as a moth. She and I soon began taking chairs out on the open deck to enjoy the November sun. She told me about her mother and father. They had lived all their lives in Omaha. They were going on a cruise in January.

Both my parents were gone now. Mom had died that July, 1988. I told Molly about my mother, how she had saved my cat when we lived on the *Valley Queen*.

DURING ONE OF Molly's and my conversations, Bill came by where we were sitting. He plopped down in an empty deck chair.

"Hi ladies."

Normally I wouldn't let anyone refer to me as a lady (feminism forbade it). But Bill was too genuine and good-hearted to pick on. I liked him.

"Print near dinner time, I guess," Molly said.

She had laid out a big lamb roast and had rubbed it with rosemary and bread crumbs and olive oil. I'd seen it in the galley.

She rose from her seat. She was as big as Auntie, and took the canvas seat with her when she stood up. She fought her way free of it and waved.

"See you later."

The sun hopped across the water, darkening it and giving us a little shade from the pilothouse. I'd been far away, ignoring Bill. I needed to say something. But I couldn't think of anything. I hoped he didn't think I was rude.

"What kind of camera is that?" he asked.

"Canon." I handed him my camera and he looked it over.

"I've got an old Olympus."

He had a sweet smile. One that drifted across his face like wind ruffling water. His talk was slow as the boat.

"I take a lot of pictures. Nature stuff. I'm fascinated by the Monarch butterflies. They flutter all over the boat in season and then they migrate down south."

"I'd like to see them." I told him about my mother's photographs, and about her hunting and fishing.

"I love to fish, but I'm not much on hunting. I've got a little boat I putter around in."

Puttering around in a small boat: my idea of heaven.

Bill got up. "Gotta go to work. Don't wanta, but I gotta."

He climbed the outer steps to the pilothouse. I watched him go. He had a certain grace in the way he moved.

There was still light, so I took some pictures of the shore. I'd been up since five-thirty, running from the galley to the pilothouse to the head of the tow—some fifteen hundred feet—recording the stories I got. I'd spent two hours with Don, the chief engineer. Like all the "Chiefs" I'd met on boats, Don amply filled the chair he sat in at the door to his kingdom. His breed tends to be sedentary, solitary, and more comfortable with their machines than with people. They like to control their kingdoms without interference. Trying to pry a story out of Don was hard work, especially over the noise of his underworld rudders and engines.

About seven o'clock, when the river was almost dark, I went up to the pilothouse, where I usually spent the forward watch. My legs were starting to shake. This was the time of day at home when we might be relaxing and having a drink.

"I'd give my right arm for a gin and tonic," I muttered to Bill.

I was joking. I knew alcohol and drugs were forbidden on towboats.

"I've got a bottle in my room," Bill said. "I could make you one."

"Oh thanks, I'm just kidding."

Soon the river was black. We passed Kansas City, lit up like a carnival on a dark country road. I had once lived in that town, in the days when Daddy was selling Konjola—Mom had told me.

The radio exchanging barge information and river conditions muttered away in the background, a constant low accompaniment to the murmuring of the men in the room.

I couldn't sleep that night. I put on my clothes and went wandering around the deck. We rode so close to shore I could hear the tree toads and frogs in the willows. I loved the metal beneath my feet, the dangerous water below, the long flotilla of barges out front of the boat, the shore lights and the hazy moon.

There is someone awake on a boat at all times of day and night, someone to talk to, at four in the afternoon or four in the morning. The galley is always open, coffee going, cake and cookies laid out for the crews exchanging watch or for the person who can't sleep. I walked down to the equipment room and found a couple of deckhands squatting among the lines and safety gear. They gave me a brotherly howdy.

I went up to the galley. It was midnight. I decided to eat a piece of pie. I laughed at myself. "Do I dare to eat a peach?" I recited T. S. Eliot. "I shall wear the bottoms of my trousers rolled."

THE GALLEY WAS lit, the coffee pot bubbling on its little stand. Someone else had the same idea. It was Bill, stirring sugar into his cup. He had just come off watch and was preparing to go to bed.

"How can you drink coffee before going to sleep?" I said.

He shrugged. "Used to it, I guess. Anyway, I like to have a little time when I'm not at those sticks. Gets monotonous pushing those barges up and down."

I poured myself a cup of coffee and picked up a few crumbs of coffee cake from the edge of a platter.

"Been meanin' to ask you something. I'm not a big reader. I like to read. But I'm slow. What would you consider is a good book? I mean something you've read lately that you think is really good."

I couldn't think of anything. Just Faulkner. Mark Twain. Melville. All old-timers.

"Gosh, I don't know," I said. "Have you read Captain Fred Way's books?"

But maybe he wanted something that didn't have to do with the river.

"Ha, a captive audience," I said. "I'll send you a copy of my novel." I had plenty of copies in my basement.

"You've done a lot for a woman," Bill said.

"Excuse me?"

"You know what I mean."

"I did start out before women's lib," I said. That had required some grit; I could give myself credit for that.

Bill took off his glasses and rubbed his eyes. I saw how pale the skin around the sockets was, where the sun hadn't hit. He folded the glasses neatly and gently and placed them in his breast pocket. I had noticed before how careful and deliberate his actions were.

"I guess that caffeine has done me in," he said. "'Night."

"'Night." He left.

I devoured a piece of coffee cake.

WE HAD TURNED back toward Omaha, and I would be getting off the boat in about twelve hours. You never know exactly when anything will happen on the river. The home office might send orders to exchange loads with another boat and you might find yourself traveling in the opposite direction. A harbor might send out a tug to take barges out of the tow, and that would slow you down. However, I packed my suitcase, my tape recorder, and my camera equipment and made ready to go when I was told.

I went up to the pilothouse after dinner as usual. Jim was sitting on the lazy bench. His lion's mane was backlit and his kindly but ferocious features were more pronounced than ever.

"So we're gettin' ole Daddy Jaws," he said to Bill.

"'Pears like it."

"Daddy Jaws?" I said. "Who's he?"

"Captain comin' on duty. Never shuts up," Jim said. "He's the opposite of ole Bill here. Though I do declare Cap's talked more this trip than I ever heard him do."

"Guess you better go see how that paintin' in the engine room is goin'," Bill said. "Chief's been on my case about it."

Jim got up and swung down the stairs.

Bill spoke quietly into his radio mike. The boat made a sound like the steam from a dry-cleaning shop.

"Guess you figured, I'm gettin' off at Omaha too."

"You live there?" I said.

"Nope. Out in the country."

I told Bill about the *Valley Queen*.

"We're gonna be passing over that spot where she went down some-time durin' the night," he said.

I stood beside Bill and looked out the window. The giant river of my childhood looked about as wide as a creek. But it did have a fast current. I could feel Bill's breath on my cheek.

"I'm gonna be in town a few days," Bill said. He took one of his long pauses.

I had a feeling about what he was going to say next.

"Maybe we could get together."

I had noticed him watching me as closely as I watched him.

"Let me think," I said.

"Sure."

I wanted to run out of the room. Like the time the lady upstairs and her husband started to fight. I could hear myself saying, "I think I hear my mother calling me."

In a little bit, I did leave. I walked lightly on the warm deck. I felt somewhat high.

Seeing the town with Bill would be fun. He had nice skin. He smelled good. We had the river in common. I loved my husband. I loved his calm and strength, his eyes and nose, his laugh, his white shirts and pinstriped lawyer suits. But I was restless, angry at my Mom for dying—and Sid and I were still sometimes as clumsy as partners in a three-legged race. He liked our life exactly as it was. I was a city girl who loved the country, a bookworm who felt trapped in libraries, a homebody with an itchy foot, a lover of routine who craved adventure. The last thing on earth Sid would enjoy would be puttering about in a leaky skiff or rumbling down the Missouri River on a noisy towboat.

I didn't fall asleep easily that night. A fling with Bill would tear a big hole in my marriage. But wasn't I from a family of movers? We got restless and moved on. Pulled everything apart and started over. My brother had been married three times and always lived like a bachelor. He'd had numerous affairs. When he wanted to take off on a trip down the river, leaving young children at home, he did. He made fun of me for being such a square.

I was tired of being the good child.

I TOSSED AROUND on the hard bunk, looked out at the moonlit shore, so dark and noisy with summer insects. I thought of Daddy and Mom and how they had wandered around. They weren't happy poor, and they weren't happy rich. They weren't happy together, and they weren't happy apart.

AFTER HIS LAST venture on the river and her sojourn in Florida, Daddy and Mom retreated to the places they had come from. He went to his side of the river, and she went to hers.

Daddy moved back to Burnside when he had recovered enough from his stroke to leave the hospital and take care of himself. In the years we were a family he had expressed little affection for this starting place; only once do I remember him saying, when in the midst of business problems, that we ought to get a little cabin up in the hills.

His hometown had changed. In the fifties, the hills had been dynamited and the valley flooded to create Wolf Creek Dam and Lake Cumberland. The highway through Burnside and the old town were under water. The new town was built on higher ground. The old wooden Seven Gables hotel had been torn down long ago, but there was a modern Seven Gables motel. There was a marina on the lake, quiet streets, a few churches. Daddy spent a lot of time with his sister Edna and his nephew Jim Ed, who had worked in the Orange Bars briefly and was back in Burnside. Daddy claimed the town would be dead as a doornail without him.

He didn't completely give up trying to make his mark. He and his older sister, Alma, now on her fourth husband, opened a restaurant—in Matty's new store. Full of plans, Daddy went to Somerset, the county seat, and brought back a load of pots and pans and dishes. The venture lasted only a few weeks. The reason was, as Jim Ed said, "Two Coomers trying to work together."

Daddy took long walks, occasionally went to church meetings or to his sister Sarah's house, where he sometimes spent an afternoon talking over old times with Sarah, Edna, and Alma—and his brothers, with whom he had finally gotten together. Jim Ed said Daddy was the one who "got them going—the others were more sober." But for the most part, Daddy was still the loner.

He lived in a dreary motel. His room was filled with half-packed suitcases and piles of scrapbooks, photos, cards from the family, newspaper clippings. He ate his lunch at a local diner, always the same: coffee and a hamburger with one pickle slice. He would sit long over his coffee and kid the waitresses.

He who had never expressed a single soft emotion for his children took to sending me sentimental birthday and mother's day cards. When Sid and I visited him, Daddy would pat my hand or shoulder. A friend we took along on one occasion said, "I just love that old man." With his shaggy beard and snapping black eyes, he was appealing. But he could still be devilish.

When he came to visit in Cincinnati—never on the day he specified nor at the time agreed on—he would take Sid and me to a good restaurant and then tell us we ate too much. He would complain loudly about the service or the food until I was in tears.

He was always dressed nicely in a suit and tie and a fedora hat. He complained that the people and the manikins in the department stores looked so much alike he couldn't tell them apart. He brought me small presents, a deer's foot or a box of gourds.

I cried aloud when I heard he was falling down on his walks and had been taken to a nursing home. He had become a danger to himself, strolling along the highway. I blamed my mother for abandoning him. For not letting us get to know him.

In the nursing home they cut his clothes off him and tied him to his chair with soft bands of cloth to keep him from wandering away. When we visited, he always gave us a big loopy smile and a glad hello, and as usual patted my hand. His shaggy beard was invariably decorated with little bits of celery or gravy from lunch. He would ask us for money. We would give him twenty dollars or so, and he would happily put it in his breast pocket. He always returned it before we left.

I pictured Daddy, before they tied him down, studying the waters of the lake and wondering where his river had gone. He would see the old town down below the surface: the jail, the poultry house, and the old steamboat landing. He would remember the day his father came home, his collar red with blood.

IN FLORIDA, MOM had missed the river and hills of her hometown. She missed the change of seasons. In the late seventies, she returned to Cincinnati, where she moved back and forth between her stepsister Mary's house and mine. I finally found her an apartment near Sid and me. Like Daddy, who had never arrived for a visit on the day he said he would, Mom did not have a real grip on time. She decided it would be fun to take Rex and Bruce on trips to the zoo and the Flower House, but by then Rex was in law school and Bruce was away at college.

As she aged, Mom stopped reading. She gave up her writing and photography and spent a lot of time embroidering. She let her mind go.

She never lost her compassion for others, her good heart. One of her best friends was a severely handicapped man she had gotten to know during her work at the Orange Bars. Harold, who sold newspapers on the corner near the business, got around on a square platform on wheels. He was about two feet in height; his unformed legs just fit on his board; his arms, with which he propelled himself, were short; and some of the fingers of his hands were missing. Here was the man who had no feet.

With typical Mom practicality-mixed-with-craziness, she claimed that on visits to her apartment Harold was a great help to her in the kitchen because her developing arthritis made it hard for her to bend over, and it was so easy for Harold to reach the lower shelves.

Mom was inordinately proud, as ever, of my accomplishments. At the bookstore near our house, the clerk assured me that *Continuing Education*, the novel I published in 1979, was selling briskly: "A little old lady comes in here and buys six copies at a time."

She always had a man. Herman was her last. He was a big man with white hair and a ruddy face, about sixty-five to Mom's seventy-something. They seemed to get along well, and I would occasionally drive Mom to his apartment. She always carried a small overnight bag.

"We just play cards," she would assure me.

"Fine," I would say.

"We don't do anything. Just play cards and have a few drinks."

"Mom. You can do anything you want," I'd say. "But hey—if he's only sixty-five, aren't you robbing the cradle?"

Mom: "I always do."

As she got close to eighty, my mother, who had always been physically daring and fearless, began keeping her hunting rifle next to her front door. We tried to talk her out of it: "You're going to shoot one of us some time when we come over."

"Call first," she said.

Cigarettes, chocolate, and her rifle were the last things my mother gave up. The building Mom lived in circulated a memo saying that anyone found with firearms would be evicted. Since she had such a good deal on rent, she allowed my brother to disarm her.

Her arthritis ultimately turned her stiff and knobby as a winter rosebush, and she lived her last years in a wheelchair. She who had cared so much about our futures, who lectured and harassed us and goaded us into achievement, would look at us as though she had known us someplace, but couldn't remember where. She had the sad tiny face of the child nobody wanted.

WAY OUT HERE on the Missouri, I found warm tears trickling into my hair. In July we had arranged a memorial service for Mom. Jim had scattered her ashes on the Ohio River.

But we had no tradition for dealing with grief.

I could not let my parents go. Nor could I bury my resentment or regret. I continued sifting through the past, trying to separate the wheat from the chaff.

I remembered what my Aunt Edna said at my father's funeral, "Harv thought you was the prettiest and smartest little thing ever was." You could have fooled me. The wall around him had never come down. I still hadn't seen the affection our formidable father was trying to express in his various little presents; I had forgotten his patting us children to sleep.

There were still so many unanswered questions. So many unasked: why did Daddy move us to Manawa then back to the city. Why did he leave a good job on the *Island Queen* not once but twice? There was too much unsaid: I hadn't told my mother how much I loved and admired her, nor how mad I was at her for using me, confiding in me when I was too young to cope with her unhappiness.

But my feelings were not just a matter of "unfinished business." And the idea that the death of parents simply reminds us of our own demise I found shallow. I had pounded my fist on the kitchen counter more than once. "I don't want my father dead!" "I don't want my mother dead!"

I GOT OUT of bed and wandered the decks again. A warm breeze was blowing. The collar of my shirt tickled the back of my neck. A square of light, solid as a sheet of gold foil, rode the waves beside the open door to the engine room. I decided to go down and try the chief one more time.

He was sitting as usual propped in his chair near the doorway. The big engines in his clean, well-marked lair rumbled loudly.

"Hi there, Miz Doahthy," he said.

He didn't ask why I wasn't asleep. People often can't sleep on the river. They have time for reflection, for worry about what the wife or child back home is doing, for mulling over mistakes and misdeeds.

I tried a tack that sometimes works in interviews: come up with a general question. I asked Don if he'd seen any of the ghosts the river people talked about. The time of night seemed to bring his thoughts to the surface.

"I can tell you some strange things happen on this river," he said.

"Like?"

"Well, one time, when my wife was in the hospital—she had cancer —me and a friend were remodeling a cabin I had on the water. I was real worried about my wife. Her and I were close."

I could tell by Don's expression when he spoke of his wife that he had loved her.

"Well, this friend and me, we heard a boat whistle. We looked out over the water, and up and down the river, but there wasn't a boat in sight. Then the next day, I was a little ways up in the woods, and I heard this same whistle blow. This time it was one long blast and a short. Somethin' like my wife and I used to hear when we would ride the excursion steamboats—oh like the *Island Queen* or the *Avalon*—back when they used whistles to signal each other."

Don looked over at the dark shore we were slowly passing.

"Somethin' told me to go back to the cabin," he said. "Sure enough, the doctor was calling. He said my wife had just died—exactly when I heard that whistle blow. I got to thinkin', and I called the captain of a boat we rode on a lot. I asked him what was the meaning of one long blast and one short."

Don paused for effect.

"And?" I said.

"He told me, 'Departing or leaving a dock.'"

I PULLED THE heavy window curtain aside in my room: it was light out. We were almost at Omaha. I looked at my watch. Six-thirty. I was late for breakfast. I tore down to the galley. I didn't want to keep Molly from cleaning up. I knew she'd wait at the stove until the last person requesting pancakes had been served. Jim was nursing a cup of coffee, but Bill was not there. I poured myself a cup of coffee and filled a bowl with cereal and fruit. Time to go back on shore rations.

"Sure you don't want to stay on another week or so?" Jim said.

Was he prying? Insinuating something?

"Can't," I said.

"Well, you're better off, I guess. Since Bill won't be with us."

I gulped down my coffee and carried my dishes to the sink.

"'Bye, Molly," I said. I hugged her. She smelled like butter and syrup.

"Wish you could stay on," she said.

"Me too."

I taped a message on the fridge telling the off-duty crew so long, and went around the boat to say goodbye to the others. I found two of the deckhands in the TV room and then went down to the engine room to hug Don. As I passed Bill's room, I noticed his suitcase on the deck outside his open door. He wasn't in his room.

We were tying off at the dock now, and I carried my suitcase and camera equipment down to the lower level. A deckhand appeared beside me to help me get it across to the wharf, a small step over open water. I waved away his offer to help me make the jump. He put my stuff on the dock and disappeared with "Have a good trip home." I looked up at the pilothouse.

I checked my watch.

Just when I thought I might be leaving without him, Bill appeared, rounding the corner from the equipment room. He came over to me and stood beside me. His question was clear in his expression.

"So long, Bill," I said.

He looked at my stuff piled on the dock.

"I had a great time."

He looked disappointed.

He said, "Don't forget to send me that book."

"I won't."

"I want it inscribed."

Bill shifted from foot to foot, pushed his hat back on his head.

"At least let me give you a ride to your hotel."

"I'm fine. I'll get a cab."

Bill held out his hand for me. I took it and hopped over the water. I turned around and waved goodbye.

He waved back and smiled. Shook his head.

As I picked up my gear and started up the ladder to the road, he called out, "So long, Weil-d lady."

DRIVING THROUGH OMAHA to the airport, I asked my cab driver to go through the neighborhood I had known as a child. I wondered whether the things I remembered had actually been there. They seemed unreal, like something from a story. It took a while to recognize the area. Blocks were leveled. Like most cities, Omaha was changing, being fixed up. The funeral home on the corner, which I passed every day on the way to school, was gone. The beauty parlor where Mom got her hair marcelled was gone. The small store where we bought candy was gone.

The cabbie turned the corner to the street where we'd lived after the *Valley Queen* went down. The Muse theater and everything around it was gone. But there on its deserted block, as though stranded on a vast plain of time, the Del Mar hotel was still standing, like a persistent memory.

ON THE PLANE home, I looked down at the Missouri River. A towboat negotiating the tight curves was the size of a toy. I ordered a drink and passed the flight staring out my window at the arctic waste of white clouds. I mulled over the story Don told me about his wife and the ghostly whistle signaling her departure. Only as the broad bends of the Ohio came in sight did I figure out its meaning: it was Don's way of mourning.

My river journeys were mine.

Epilogue

HANSEL AND GRETEL

2000

WHEN JIM started to school a year ahead of me, I was dying to go also, but worried whether I could do the work. I begged him to tell me what school was like.

"It's easy," he said. "All but arithmetic."

School *was* easy. And I have never been good at numbers.

As in childhood, when my brother led the way and I followed, our last river journey together, in 1982, was one Jim thought up: a trip on an old-time flatboat. This small wooden ark had a cabin, an open deck area, and a large oar at the stern. It was just like the ones the pioneers used to navigate the river before the steamboats took over. The kids, dogs, goats, chickens, and all the household goods were crammed aboard, and the boats went over the falls at Louisville and through the rapids without the help of locks and dams. Jim's flatboat, called *Adventure Galley II*, was traveling down the Ohio and Mississippi from Pittsburgh to New Orleans.

The crew members were two teenaged boys, students at the Inland Waterways Vocational School where Jim was teaching. Classes were held in a former elementary school next to the river on Eastern Avenue. Inland Waterways was an alternate public-school program for kids who were not good at academics and wanted careers on the river. Jim taught the rules of the road and demonstrated practical skills such as lassoing timber heads and lashing barges together, on the school's own towboat, the *Marilyn McFarland*. He and his students had built the flatboat in a nearby field, adding only an engine to the traditional design.

I joined Jim and his crew at Maysville, Kentucky. My brother was standing on the roof of the cabin, watering the grass where the animals were supposed to be grazing. The two boys, Kenny and Rob, were wearing jeans, no shirts, and no shoes. They jumped to the task of tying off the boat and helped me over the tiny gangplank enthusiastically. They were grinning happily, obviously enjoying every move they made in the bright sunshine. The wetter they got, the happier they seemed.

"This trip has improved their luck with the girls considerably," Jim said.

Down the river we went, living the Huck Finn life, idle and happy. While one of the boys manned the big oar, Jim and I and the other boy swam off the side of the boat. It was my first immersion in the Ohio's waters since I was twelve and had dived off the side of the yacht club. The water was cleaner: mossy turds were a thing of the past and industrial waste was policed by the EPA. The current was tamed by the modern dams. But it felt like the same old river, pleasantly warm—every once in a while, a cold spot. The feathery willows at the water's edge dipped their heads into the stream. We passed a group of black cows quietly wading, a family of ducks, a group of church people holding a baptism.

While we moved along, I sunbathed on deck. Rob brought lemonade on a handmade tray, serving it with a flourish, like a butler. He and Kenny took baths by soaping themselves from head to toe with soap and then plunging into the water. They shaped their hair into elfin points.

At each landing we made, people came on board to look the *Adventure Galley* over: children, old men, motorcycle gangs. Some of the towns staged river pageants or festivals: the folks dressed up in pioneer and Indian costumes, and bands played everywhere. Local housewives brought us blueberry and peach pies, and we ate on deck, juice rolling down our chins.

JIM'S WORLD in the new century is a small room bounded by a window with an air-conditioner and a curtain between him and another patient. It is over a hundred years since our father was born, almost a century since his father was killed. I sit in a folding chair, wedged between a small metal chest and a sort of Barcalounger on wheels. Alice, Jim's former wife, and his two children who live nearby, Melissa and Jimmy, have decorated the room. The chest is crowded with photos: the

Valley Queen as she lists and collapses on the Missouri sand bar; the *Vulcan*, a boat Jim built and almost went down with in the harbor at New Orleans; the *Idlewild*, still going as the *Belle of Louisville*. There's a copy of Jim's book of stories about his life on towboats.

Jim is propped among pillows, wearing a backless blue-flowered gown. Beneath the bed hang plastic bags for urine and waste, like great udders. His hands are clenched in "spastic grip." He has become so thin there are dark gullies beneath his collar bones. His elbows are torn by great purple bedsores the color of rotten plums. Among white pillows and sheets, he seems to be drifting slowly away, like the time he floated off on the ice around the *Valley Queen*.

He tells me he gets up every morning and shaves and dresses and goes to the river. He becomes angry if anyone suggests he needs help in getting into his chair. In fact, he is lifted and lowered into it by means of a canvas sling, like cargo being loaded onto a ship.

"Why does everyone insist I have to be 'taken' anyplace?" he demands. His voice is whispery, his sentences hard to follow even though we have rigged up a microphone and a boom box to amplify his speech.

When he is angry, he looks like his father: the same expression, nose wrinkled, mouth twisted. He can still describe how to make an exchange of barges or lash together a tow, things he did so many times in his thirty years on the river. He is usually cheerful, smiles when Sid and I come to see him.

We knew this moment would come: Jim had previously suffered a stroke that paralyzed his left side. He retained his speech and brain power, and after several surgeries and hospital stays was able to walk with a cane. He worked out in therapy, even invented and patented a piece of equipment. He designed a system by which he could drive a car, and for years went to work at the Travelers' Aide Library five days a week. He resumed a hot romance with a woman friend, a lovely lawyer named Kate.

But then came this massive stroke. There was blood seeping into the brain. Jim could not even swallow. The doctor at the hospital gave Jim two days to two weeks to live. Jim was a member of the Hemlock Society and had a living will that forbade the use of a feeding tube or any other life-prolonging procedure. The doctors and the family went along with these instructions.

The body and brain did not. In the hospice, Jim regained some movement in his neck, and his speech became clearer. Here at the nursing home, where he's been for many months, he's one of the staff's favorite patients. He has something to give: a big smile and a laugh at a funny remark. When the younger women staff members come into his room, he perks up and flirts. He enjoys watching videos of his favorite operas.

Today I've brought my dog along, a five-pound Papillon who climbs onto the bed and licks Jim's hands. I sing a theme song from the old radio program we listened to long ago:

> Who's a little chatterbox?
> That little girl with curly locks.
> Who can it be? It's little Orphan Annie.
> Arf, goes Sandy.

I read aloud for a while from Jim's book. We recall the work we did on it, our arguments. I had accused him of preferring real surgery to the cutting of a word. He had originally dedicated the book to Mom and Daddy, whom he had described as "the two most wonderful parents in the world."

I had asked him, "Is that the way you really see them?"

He thought. "Don't you?"

"I remember some pretty rough days. Daddy had me in tears sometimes."

"He tried to convince me I couldn't pour piss out of a boot," Jim said.

"They were both good people."

"When Mom was young she was really something."

"Remember when she tried to drown us?"

We both laughed at the melodrama of the story, as well as the lingering pain.

The patterns of people's lives are so complex, I thought, though some—looked at in the context of the past—emerge as starkly as *Citizen Kane's* "Rosebud": kicked out of the Del Mar, my father moved into the fanciest hotel he could find; I drive a red convertible and my closets bulge with clothes; Jim proved himself among the toughest men on the river. If only all the connections in life were so plain to see.

I READ a little more, then put Jim's book on his bedside table.

"I still think you should have let me put the glossary in the front," Jim says.

"Wouldn't work," I say.

Jim seems to have a comeback ready, but we both sense that we might be on the verge of one of our old "did not"/"did too" arguments, and we let the topic drop.

Pretty soon, Jim drifts off to sleep. I wonder where he goes.

MY THOUGHTS go back to the flatboat trip. As we passed old Coney Island and the deserted landing where the *Island Queen* docked, I noticed that the lighthouse, through which people entered the park, was still in place. It is yet. The dying fall of the roller coaster is no longer heard. Rowboats and water rides operate on the lake, the big Sunlite Pool is full of bathers, but the once-great mall is crowded with rides for small children. The big thrills are way out in King's Island in the suburbs.

Downriver a few miles, we passed the spot where the Cincinnati Yacht Club, once throbbing with music and the sound of motorboats, had long since been displaced by industry. All I could see were big oil tanks instead of willows along the shore, and all I could hear was the noise of cars whizzing by on Kellogg Avenue. The shanty boaters, except for "Shanty Dan," had left the riverbank years ago. Pig Iron had "caught steel" in a knife fight.

Gigantic marinas had replaced the small ones like the yacht club, and hundreds of pleasure craft buzzed all over the river, paying little attention to the monster towboats that moved quietly among them like elephants among pygmies. Like time sneaking past the living.

Occasionally the old boats come to town: we see the *Delta Queen*, a music box lit up at night, the *Belle of Louisville* steaming into the Cincinnati landing for the Tall Stacks celebration, a big blow-out of steamboat-days romance and nostalgia.

I PLACE Jim's book on the metal table and prepare to leave. I wonder how long my brother can hold out. His arms and legs are terribly thin.

Soon after he arrived at Community Care, he said, "I think I'm on the upside of this thing."

"That's a good outlook"—Me.

"Of course, I may die tomorrow."

"Are you afraid?"

"No, but no one wants to die."

On Jim's seventy-second birthday, Sid and I took him a chocolate cake with one candle on it. I blew it out for him. We fed him a piece of cake mashed up in milk. His birthday wish was to live to be a hundred. I reminded him of his grandfather the marshal, who survived for six weeks after being shot in the neck. "You can't kill the Coomers," I told him.

But he grows farther and farther away from reality. He says he's been locked in the basement, or asks for a lift downtown to pick up his car. Other times he is the poet who wrote a good river book.

"I'm letting my lines go one at a time."

"Is it hard?" I ask.

He shakes his head.

"Easy. All but . . ." He loses track of his thought.

"Arithmetic," I whisper.

JIM'S FLATBOAT made it to New Orleans, where it was put on display. Then, like all no-longer-useful vessels, it went from place to place. It sat in the water at a marina, a strange sight for the pleasure boaters come down to the river for dinner and fun and a fast ride. It spent some time as an outdoor exhibit at a museum, its timbers rotting and its metal corroding. Then it sank into oblivion. One more victim of water and time.

When dark fell on the flatboat, I remember, the kerosene lamps on the deck were lighted, tiny glowworms in the great black valley. Inside the cabin, candles in homemade holders gave off a sleepy half-light. Jim had thought of everything: the windows were held shut with wood pegs dangling from leather loops. There were wooden tables with storage underneath and a pulldown desk. The beds were built-in, with rope mattresses that felt like cheese slicers when you lay down on them. But the room was warm and snug. Where had I been in just such a cozy home?

Maybe my brother and I do go to the same place in our dreams.

I LEAVE Jim in his small room. He's snoring.

As I fall asleep myself that night, I go back to the river and the hills of our childhood. The landscape I see is the one my father and mother came from, the scene of their romance, and of our family's life together. I see my father, the wind making his cheeks glow as he hauls the yacht-club boats from the river. I see my mother in her perch high above the current, watching the towboats go by and dreaming of finer things. I see Jim and me on the water, frolicking in the sunshine like otters.

Twilight blurs the valley, and I float through the trees to the water's edge. The sky is turning into tarnished silver, bright metal with streaks of purple.

My brother is on the opposite shore, moving toward the darkening river and the iced-in boat.

Other Works by Dorothy Weil

BOOKS

In Defense of Women: Susanna Rowson (1762–1824)

Continuing Education

Nightside

TELEVISION DOCUMENTARIES

River Calling: Flatboat to Towboat

Fire on the Water: Ohio River Steamboats

Beautiful River: Rediscovering the Ohio

We Listen to the Water: Ohio River Voices

Dream Big: the Over-the-Rhine Steel Drum Band

Mountain Shadow: Four Appalachian Artists

Keeping Community: East End Voices